**Anatomy
of the
Ship**

—THE CUNARD LINER—
QUEEN MARY

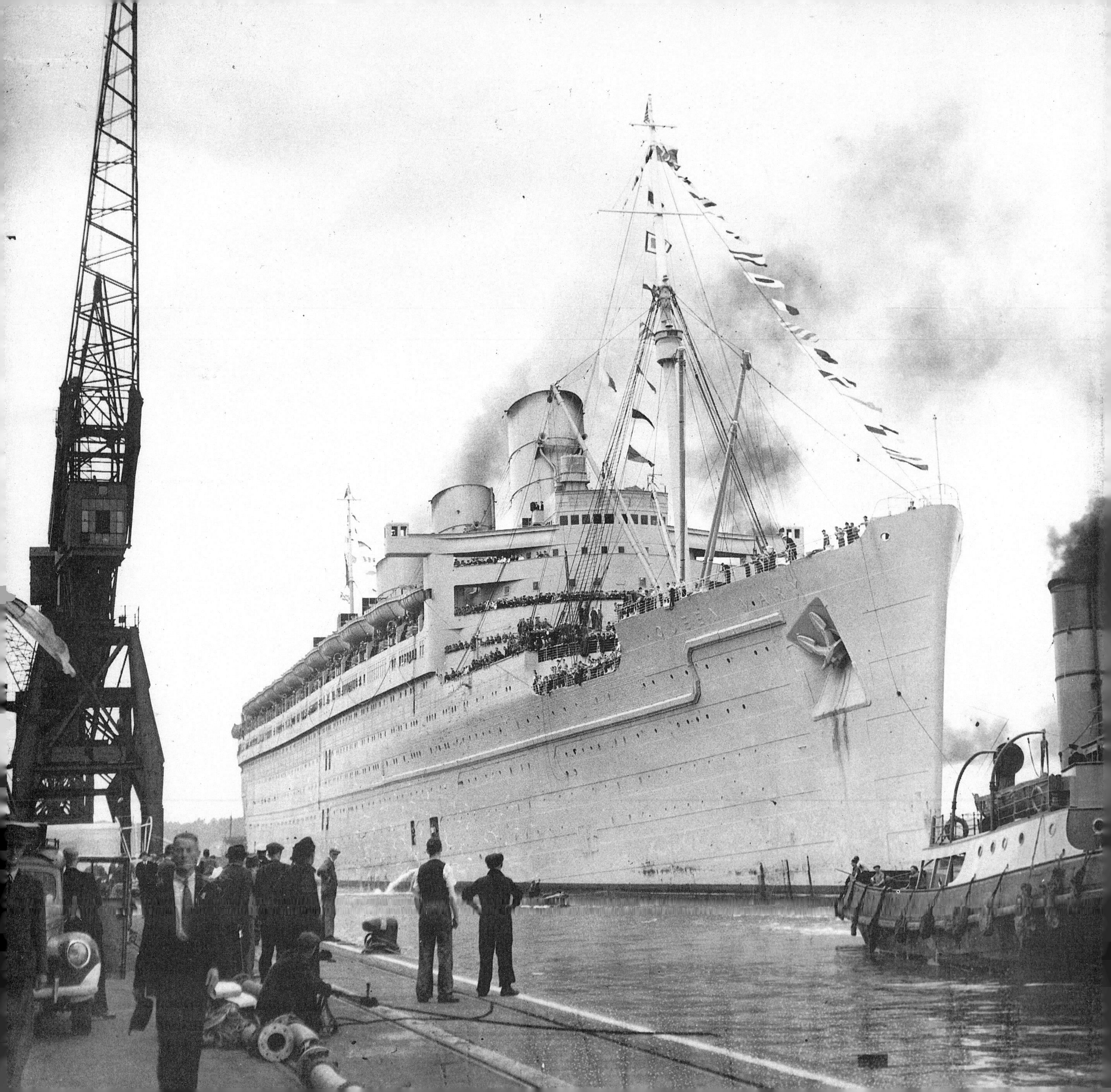

Anatomy of the Ship

—THE CUNARD LINER—

· QUEEN MARY ·

— ROSS WATTON —

CONWAY MARITIME PRESS

ACKNOWLEDGEMENTS

Most of the drawings in this book were redrawn from plans held by Glasgow University Archives. Mrs Alma Topen, manager of the Business Records Collection, has been of great help in providing copies of the material.

Across the Atlantic, Mr William M Winberg, Exhibits and Archives Supervisor on the *Queen Mary*, and his assistant, Ellene Mahoney, have been immensely helpful with additional information. I especially wish to thank Bill Winberg for graciously agreeing to write the foreword to this book.

Last but not least, my thanks are due to Mrs Dianne Cook and Mrs Deborah Cook, for typing from my original manuscript in record time — no mean feat.

Ross Watton

Frontispiece

1. The *Queen Mary* in grey war livery, arriving at Southampton on 11 August 1945, for her first visit since 1939. The anti-magnetic mine degaussing coil is clearly visible around the hull. *Popperfoto*

© Ross Watton 1989

First published in Great Britain 1989 by
Conway Maritime Press Limited
24 Bride Lane, Fleet Street
London EC4Y 8DR

British Library Cataloguing in Publication Data
Watton, Ross
　　The Cunard liner Queen Mary. – (Anatomy of the ship).
　　1. Passenger transport. Shipping. Steam liners: Queen Mary, (ship), history
　　I. Title II. Series
　　007.2'432

ISBN 0–85177–529–2

All rights reserved. Unauthorised duplication contravenes applicable laws.

Designed by Jonathan Doney
Typeset by Inforum Typesetting, Portsmouth
Printed and bound by The Bath Press, Bath

Contents

Foreword	7
Introduction	9
Service history	10
War service	11
General arrangement and hull structure	11
Machinery	12
Accommodation	14
The Photographs	17
The Drawings	35
A. General arrangement	36
B. Hull construction	56
C. Machinery	74
D. Accommodation	88
E. Superstructure	107
F. Rig	116
G. Fittings	133
H. Ground tackle	140
I. Boats	142

Foreword

The *Queen Mary* project in Long Beach began in May 1967, with Cunard Line's announcement that the ship would be put up for sale. The city had previously intended to build a maritime museum in its downtown area, and the government officials concluded: what better place for a maritime museum than on the world's most famous ship! Because of the huge size of the liner, areas of the ship could be used for a hotel, convention facilities, shops and restaurants, as well as for the museum originally envisaged.

Long Beach submitted the winning bid of $3,450,000, and oversaw the Last Great Cruise, taking the *Queen Mary* around South America to Pier E in Long Beach on 9 December 1967. Diners Club was named the overall operators, and the job of converting the *Queen* to her new role was begun.

The *Queen Mary* was placed in the drydock in the Long Beach Naval Shipyard in April 1968 to have her underwater areas scraped and repainted. She then was moved back to Pier E for removal of the equipment from her machinery areas, including the five boiler rooms, two turbo-generating rooms, water softening plant and forward engine room. The after engine room and propeller shaft area were left intact for viewing on the tour.

Ship conversion had never been attempted before on this scale. Modifications included installing new air conditioning throughout the *Queen Mary*, and replacement of all fire, electrical, sewage, telephone and other services. The hull is now protected by a special cathodic system to prevent salt water corrosion.

The initial $10 million estimate for conversion, which included the purchase price, proved totally inadequate. Diners Club pulled out of the project just months before the *Queen*'s opening date of May 1971. The overall project cost about $65 million, though only about $20 million of this was spent for the ship herself. The remainder was used to extend the Long Beach Freeway to access the property, construct pier facilities, parking lots, etc.

The city of Long Beach quickly had to find new operators. They hired Specialty Restaurants to run the shops and restaurant operations, Pacific Southwest Airlines (PSA) for the hotel, and the Museum of the Sea for the tour. This method of split management failed for nine years at a loss of about $2 million per year. Attendance fell from 1.5 million the first year, levelling off at about 700,000 per year.

In September 1980, the Wrather Corporation became overall managers of the entire property, and as of January 1983 the *Queen Mary* was making a profit for the first time in Long Beach. The Spruce Goose, Howard Hughes's massive flying boat, opened in May 1983, which boosted attendance over the million mark again.

Today, the *Queen Mary*'s original elegant public rooms are used for private meetings and banquets, as is the Spruce Goose dome. The Hotel Queen Mary contains 345 staterooms, mostly the original cabin class staterooms with their original woods and fixtures.

Wrather Corporation was operating the property at a profit, but was bought out in January 1988 by the Walt Disney Company. At the time of this writing, the property is being brought up to Disney quality standards, while honouring the historical integrity of the *Queen Mary*. Long-range plans are being developed by the Disney 'imagineers' for using much more of the 285 acres of land and water which is included in the lease from the city. Our crew is looking forward to an even greater future for the *Queen Mary*.

I commend Ross Watton for the dedication he has shown in putting together this book, and the fine addition it makes to the Anatomy of the Ship series.

William M Winberg

Introduction

By the mid 1920s the Cunard Shipping Company were operating three ageing liners on the North Atlantic route. They were the *Mauretania* (1907), *Aquitania* (1914) and the *Berengaria* (1912), an ex-German liner taken as part of war remunerations. However, the increased competition from foreign shipping lines was eroding the company's business. American, French, Italian and German liners were all heavily subsidised by their respective governments, enabling them to build larger and faster ships, the main requisites of a successful passenger liner company. Consequently, they were snatching not only the much desired trade, but also the coveted and prestigious Blue Riband — the award for the fastest Atlantic crossing. This title had been irrefutably held for fourteen years by the *Mauretania*, but in July 1929 the new German liner *Bremen* secured the honour on her maiden voyage, with a passage of 4 days 17 hours and 42 minutes.

It was during 1926 that Cunard decided to try to regain some of their lost business with the proposed instigation of a two-ship express passenger service, sailing weekly, between Southampton and New York. This scheme was made feasible by numerous advances in marine engineering and naval architecture. Speed was the essential requirement, and to maintain a gruelling five-day schedule the ships would require an average speed of 28.5 knots. This figure was coupled with the desire to cater for three classes of passenger — cabin, tourist and third class — in order that the ships should be commercially viable. The Company's design team then began to assess the required dimensions; not surprisingly, it was calculated that the length would exceed 1000ft, with a gross tonnage of 80,000 tons. These dimensions were considered the barest minimum to provide the projected service.

Of course, building ships of such size would entail a great deal of planning, not only of the ship herself, but also of docking facilities both home and abroad — in particular dry-docking.

Several changes were made to the formative design, and then testing began on twenty-two 17ft long scale models, taking two years. This work was much simplified by the use of facilities provided by John Brown & Co Ltd of Clydebank, who had previously built thirty-two ships for the Cunard Line.

Some eight thousand experiments were conducted to assess the seakeeping qualities of the proposed ship, carried out in a special tank where the worst North Atlantic sea conditions could be simulated. Wind tunnel testing was used to find the optimum funnel arrangement and design to keep the upper decks clear of smoke.

Meanwhile, the type of boilers and propulsion machinery had still to be settled. It was not until mid-1929 that water-tube boilers were finally selected, for their greater efficiency.

One of the biggest problems facing the Cunard directors was the insurance of the liner during building and eventual service. The Cunard (Insurance) Act of December 1930 made the British government responsible for the excess over the insurance value of £2.7 million; the total amount was in excess of £4 million.

During May 1930 Cunard informed the owners of Southampton docks, the Southern Railway Company, that they would require a large dry-dock to take their new ship by October 1933. The SRC were understandably hesitant to outlay vast sums of money on such requirements for one ship, unless they could obtain a development grant. The two companies remained at stalemate for the rest of the year, each requiring assurance from the other, since Cunard made it clear they would not order the new boat without the new dock.

Another important consideration at the time was that the construction of the ship would bring work to the unemployment blackspot of Clydeside. The deadlock was finally broken when the railway company received a building grant from the government.

Across the Atlantic, in New York, agreement was also reached, after lengthy negotiation, to build a 1000ft pier, at a rent of £48,000 per year.

With these problems finally resolved, the formal shipbuilding contract was signed between Cunard and John Brown & Co Ltd on 1 December 1930, and the ship given the prosaic title of Number 534.

The first keel plates were laid on 27 December 1930, and work progressed well throughout the following year; it was even hoped that the ship would be launched ahead of schedule. Then the international depression took hold, and eventually made it impossible for Cunard to carry on with the new ship. The Government refused financial help. All work ceased at midday on Friday 11 December 1931, and the three thousand men employed on the vessel left, not knowing when, or even if, they would return. Nationwide, ten thousand people had been employed on work connected with the vessel.

During this dark period the dormant skeleton of the ship became a symbol of Britain's plight, but for David Kirkwood, Labour Member of Parliament for Dumbarton Burghs, it signified hope, and the resumption of work on the ship became his personal obsession. For two years he battled tirelessly on behalf of his constituents. The Prince of Wales, later to become King Edward VIII, showed considerable sympathy and went to Clydeside to see the situation for himself. On his return to London he made representations to the Government about restarting work on the stricken liner.

The Chancellor of the Exchequer, Neville Chamberlain, considered that the problem might be resolved if Cunard was to join forces with her rival company the White Star Line. The Government could then grant a loan to the newly amalgamated company so that work could be resumed on the liner.

The White Star Line was in a poor financial state, considerably worse than that of Cunard, and the latter were not overjoyed with the requirement for amalgamation. It was, however, their only option, and the merger went ahead on 19 May 1934. The new company was named Cunard White Star Ltd, and the Government made a loan of £9.5 million, a third of which was to be used to complete Number 534.

On 3 April 1934, four hundred men marched through the streets of Clydeside, led back to work by the Dalmuir Parish Pipe Band playing 'The Campbells are Coming'.

The moment the nation had awaited came on Wednesday 26 September 1934: the launch of Number 534 and the lifting of the veil of secrecy concerning her name. The Cunard ships had always received names ending -ia, while those of the White Star ships had ended -ic. Obviously, the new company would have to make a compromise, and a new name for a new era seemed fitting. The launching ceremony was to take place in the presence of King George V, Queen Mary and The Prince of Wales. The Queen would perform the act of sending the grey-painted hull on its way, and would thus become the first reigning monarch to name a merchant vessel; it was therefore more than fitting that the ship would be known as the *Queen Mary*.

TABLE 1: PARTICULARS OF THE QUEEN MARY, 1936

Length overall	1019ft 6in	
Length waterline	1004ft	
Beam	118ft	
Draught	38ft 10in	
Displacement	81,237 gross tons	
Speed	28.5 knots	
Shaft horsepower	212,000shp	
Complement	**1936**	**1957**
Cabin class	776	711
Tourist class	784	707
Third class	579	577
Officers and crew	1101	

TABLE 2: RECORD ATLANTIC CROSSINGS BY THE QUEEN MARY

Date	Passage	Distance (nm)	Time (days/hrs/min)	Average speed (knots)
May 1936	Cherbourg–Ambrose	3158	4.12.24	29.13
July 1936	Cherbourg–Ambrose	3098	4.8.37	29.61
July 1936	Ambrose–Cherbourg	3128	4.9.0	29.79
August 1936	Cherbourg–Ambrose	3097	4.7.12	30.01
	Bishop's Rock–Ambrose	2907	4.0.27	30.14
August 1936	Ambrose–Cherbourg	3129	4.6.20	30.57*
	Ambrose–Bishop's Rock	2939	3.23.57	30.63*
August 1938	Bishop's Rock–Ambrose	2907	3.21.48	30.99*
August 1938	Ambrose–Bishop's Rock	2938	3.20.42	31.69*

* Blue Riband record passage

SERVICE HISTORY

27 December 1930	Laid down
11 December 1931	All work ceased
3 April 1934	Work resumed
26 September 1934	Launch
24 March 1936	Departed Clydebank
27 March 1936	Arrived King George V Drydock, Southampton
15 April 1936	Left Southampton
18 April 1936	Began measured mile trials off Arran
20 April 1936	Berthed Southampton
12 May 1936	Officially handed over to Cunard White Star Line
25 May 1936	Visited by royal family
27 May 1936	Maiden voyage to New York
1 June 1936	Arrived New York
2 December 1936	End of first season; arrived at Southampton for drydocking
1 March 1940	Requisitioned for war service
21 March 1940	Departed New York, in grey war livery
17 April 1940	Arrived Sydney, Australia, for further war preparations
5 May 1940	Departed with 5000 Australian troops for Greenock
2 October 1941	Collided with and sank HMS *Curacoa*
5 August 1943	Conveyed Prime Minister Winston Churchill to Quebec Conference
5 September 1944	Conveyed Winston Churchill to Halifax, Nova Scotia
29 September 1946	Returned to Southampton to be demilitarised
31 July 1947	Sailed on first commercial trip since the war
8 May 1957	First call inside Cherbourg breakwater since 1939
6 July 1952	Lost Blue Riband title to the liner *United States*

1958	Stabilizers fitted
22 September 1967	Left New York for last time
27 September 1967	Arrived at Southampton for last time
31 October 1967	Sailed for Long Beach, California

WAR SERVICE

The *Queen Mary* was officially called up for war service on 1 March 1940, after languishing on the south side of Pier 90 in New York harbour since early September the previous year. She was given her war livery of grey paint and a skeleton crew, increased by some five hundred officers and men from the liner *Antonia*, also in port.

At this time came the first historic (though, under the circumstances, subdued) meeting between the *Queen Mary* and the latest addition to the Cunard White Star Fleet, her sister ship the *Queen Elizabeth*. The latter had secretly left the Clyde before completion for the relative safety of a neutral harbour. The larger *Queen Elizabeth* berthed on the north side of Pier 90, and with the world's second largest liner, the *Normandie* of France, at Pier 88, it was a true meeting of the Goliaths of ocean travel.

The *Queen Mary* was the first to depart, on 21 March, headed for Sydney harbour, where she spent two weeks of militarisation, having her elaborate furnishings removed. On 5 May she embarked 5000 Australian troops and transported them to Greenock. From there she ferried another 5000 troops to the Middle East, to reinforce the depleted garrison there.

Throughout 1941, Sydney Harbour was to be the *Queen Mary*'s base port in her role as troopship to the Middle East. With the advance of the Japanese, however, Australia began to look vulnerable. The *Queen Mary* returned to New York to have her troop-carrying capability increased to over 8000 men, and set out to transport American soldiers to Australia, arriving in Sydney on 28 March 1942.

After returning to New York, she had her area of operation changed to the North Atlantic and began shuttling American GIs to the European theatre of war. Throughout all these top secret movements, always in radio silence, the *Queen Mary* never saw enemy action. This was fortunate as the ship was inadequately armed against air attack, though she was later fitted with Oerlikon guns. She did, however, receive a radar outfit in 1942 and a degaussing coil around the ship to protect her against magnetic mines.

It was on 2 October 1942 that the worst incident of her war service and commercial career occurred, when she collided with and subsequently sank her anti-aircraft escort, the cruiser HMS *Curacoa*. This unfortunate incident happened off the northern coast of Ireland, on the homeward leg of her journey. As usual in open waters, the troop-carrying *Queen Mary*, travelling at a speed of 28.5 knots, was carrying out a set pattern of course alterations known as zig-zag No 8. This was to make her a less easy target for enemy submarines.

The reasons for the collision will never be fully understood, but obviously human error and negligence were contributing factors. The whole affair was kept secret during the war, but during later inquests it was finally decided that the more manoeuvrable escort should have kept clear of the *Queen Mary*, and that both ships had failed to take sufficient evasive action early enough. Whatever the reasons, the *Queen Mary* struck the cruiser at an acute angle 11ft from its stern, spinning the smaller ship around and then slicing it in two. Both fore and after ends of the ship sank within minutes, with the loss of 338 men. The *Queen Mary* had no option but to continue through the wreckage on her course, though she did signal to the escorting destroyers to rescue any survivors. In comparison, the damage to the *Queen Mary* was only slight and many of the crew did not even know the disaster had occurred.

Makeshift repairs were made on the Clyde and the *Queen Mary* then left for the United States and more substantial repairs at Boston. She spent the rest of the war carrying troops, operating between America and Britain, transporting troops down to the Suez and back across the Indian Ocean to Australia.

GENERAL ARRANGEMENT AND HULL STRUCTURE

Internally, the *Queen Mary* was designed with twelve decks, the first continuous uppermost deck being A deck, and the four decks immediately below this also travelled the entire length of the ship uninterrupted. The hull was divided into 160 watertight compartments below C deck, the bulkhead deck.

In catering for three classes of passenger, allocation of space was of paramount importance; it was necessary that the highest paying, the cabin class, should be provided with outboard rooms on the main A and B decks. Cabin class principal rooms, lounge and smoking rooms were situated on the promenade deck. The cabin class lounge had a height of over 30ft, made by incorporating large dome ceilings over the central portion. The promenade deckhouse extended over a length of 552ft and was sheltered by a glazed screen featuring large windows, over which the sun deck was raised to a height of 14ft. Twelve lifeboats were arranged on both sides of the sun deck, high enough to allow an open-air promenade for the cabin class passengers. Another tier of deckhouses at the fore end of the sun deck contained additional cabin class staterooms, while at the after end was the verandah grill. The sports deck featured three large tennis courts behind the forward funnel.

The tourist class passengers were mainly accommodated in the after part of the ship, on A, B, C, D and E decks. Their smoking room was situated on the promenade deck towards the after end, flanked by the semi-sheltered tourist class promenade. A similar arrangement existed on the main deck, where the larger of the two tourist class lounges could be found.

Third class passengers resided in the forward part of the vessel, with the majority of the cabins being situated on D and E decks. They were also provided with a lounge, on B deck, a smoking room on A deck and a garden lounge on the main deck.

The main dining facilities for all classes were situated on C deck in their respective parts of the ship; the kitchens were between the cabin class restaurant and tourist class dining saloon.

Besides passengers and their requisite amenities, spaces were provided for the carrying of cargo, particularly mail, both forward and aft on G and H decks. Motor vehicles could also be shipped forward on F deck, where the provision of derricks at the foremast made for easy disembarkation. After baggage spaces on F and G deck were serviced by two large high-speed lifts, as were the linen rooms on G deck — no laundry facilities were provided.

Oil fuel tanks flanked the boiler rooms and turbo-generator rooms, while an inner skin extended the length of both engine rooms. These main machinery spaces were housed centrally below E deck.

Keel The centre girder of the keel was made continuous and watertight throughout the double bottom. It was constructed from plates 30ft long by 6ft deep with a thickness of 1.04in, joined together by triple riveted double straps. The top angles were 5in × 5in and the bottom angles 7in × 7in; no buttstraps were used to join the 60ft lengths of angle bar. The centre girder was non-watertight aft of frame 71 and forward of frame 289; here lightening drainage and air holes were cut. There were three keel plates; the inner was 66in wide by 1.12in thick, the middle 51in by 1.20in and the outer 42in by 1.12in. There were no buttstraps over the extent of the three thicknesses, each being constructed from approximately 29ft lengths. The outer keel plates ran from frame 77.5 to frame 277.5, and beyond these points triple riveted buttstraps were employed on the inner and middle plates. The thickness of both these keel plates gradually reduced towards their ends. The inner finished at frames 25 and 338 at .92in, and the middle keel plate finished at frames 24 and 339 at a thickness of 1in.

Double bottom longitudinal girders The keel was flanked by seven longitudinal girders either side, spaced 7ft apart; two were continuous and watertight, and the others were intercostal and non-watertight. The former were .64in at their greatest thickness, with top, bottom and vertical angles of 6in × 6in. The intercostal side girders were generally .54in thick, with top and vertical angles of 3½in × 3½in and bottom angles of 4in × 3½in. The 4in side was riveted to the shell plating.

Transverse Frames These were spaced at 3ft intervals from frame 78 to frame 252, beyond which they gradually reduced to 2ft intervals. Throughout the double bottom these served as floors, being intercostally connected between the two continuous side girders. Lightening and air holes were cut in the non-watertight floor plates, and strengthening achieved with 6in × 3½in bulb angle stiffeners between each side girder. The thickness of the floor plates increased from .54in to .60in under the boiler bearers in the forward boiler room. Where the floor plates were continued from the tank margin up to D deck they were known as web frames — this usually occurred every third frame. Elsewhere within the double skin of the ship intermediate framing was of 12in × 4in × 4in channel bars on the outboard side, and 10in × 4in × 4in on the inboard side. Three longitudinal stringer plates, known as F, G and H, ran intercostally between the web and intermediate frames.

Within the oil fuel bunkers, intermediate framing was of 12in × 4in × 4in channel bars running up to E deck, and 11in × 4in × 4in above. Between D and E decks, 3ft wide webs were fitted over each web frame in the oil fuel bunker, and a 4ft wide web over the bulkheads in the oil fuel bunker. Forward and aft of the oil fuel bunkers, main channel frames decreased to 10in × 4in × 4in. The use of combined channel and web frames was adapted to withstand the strenuous conditions that prevail in the North Atlantic. Additional transverse strength was afforded by the divisional bulkheads within the fuel tanks.

Beams Every frame throughout the ship was fitted with a channel section beam; the largest, 11in × 4in × 4in, were under the promenade deck and main deck. Below these the size decreased to 10in and 9in. Where the span was greater than 29ft a back bar of 3½in × 3½in angle was fitted to every beam. A total of nine strong beams of rectangular section were also fitted in way of engine and funnel hatches. These were supported by large pillars, and also carried pillars to support the decks above.

Decks The promenade deck was the upper strength deck. It consisted of .67in thick steel plating overlayed with .63in HEL (high elastic limit) steel. This special steel allowed for a saving in weight without serious loss in strength. It was also employed in a similar fashion on the main and A decks. Elsewhere, decks employed stronger plates around their outer edges; these were of thick steel and constituted the strength of the deck. Longitudinal girders were fitted under every deck and consisted of plate steel, with channel bars back to back, running underneath the beams and supported by pillars — usually spaced three frames apart. All decks above the promenade deck incorporated three expansion joints to relieve the upper works from overloading. The weather decks and enclosed promenade areas were laid with Burma teak.

Shell plating The ship's side was plated with 1.14in thick steel, reducing to 0.76in at the forward and after ends and increasing to 1.25in down to the garboard strake. HEL steel was also employed on the upper parts of the ship, giving an increased thickness of 1.26in in the area between the main and promenade decks. All landings down to I stringer were triple riveted, and those below were double riveted.

MACHINERY

Boilers The four main boiler rooms each housed six Yarrow double-flow water-tube boilers, fitted with super heaters and air heaters. Boiler rooms No 2 and No 4 provided steam for the forward engine room, and No 3 and No 5, the after engine room. Steam was generated at a working pressure of 400psi at a temperature of 700°F.

Within the boiler, straight steel tubes connected the three water drums to the steam drum on top of the boiler casing. The two smaller 23in diameter water drums were arranged over the working face at the side of the boiler and flanking the superheater drum. Tubular steel airheaters straddled the steam drum, passing hot air down both sides of the furnace, underneath the combustion chamber, and into the double-sided casing to the air distributors at the oil-fired burners.

The boilers were operated under the forced-draught closed-stokehold system, by two pairs of electrically driven forced-draught fans arranged either side of each boiler room on E deck. Access to the boiler rooms was only via airlocks on E deck.

Auxiliary boilers No 1 boiler room generated superheated steam for the hotel turbo-generators and saturated steam for other domestic services throughout the ship. This was produced from three double-ended cylindrical Scotch-type boilers, operated by the closed ashpit system of forced draught. Their designed working pressure was 250 psi at a temperature of 200°F. Waste gases from these boilers was passed up through the front section of the forward funnel. Combustion air was produced by four single-inlet forced-draught fans, two on each side of the boiler room on E deck.

Turbines Two engine rooms housed the four turbine sets, which drove the four propeller shafts. The forward engine room turbines powered the outer shafts and the after engine room the inner two shafts. A turbine set had a maximum output of 50,000hp and was composed of one HP (high pressure), two IP (intermediate pressure) and one LP (low pressure) turbine. Each turbine drove its own pinion, which connected with the main gear wheel. The turbines were of the Parsons impulse-reaction type; each set contained 257,000 blades, while the LP rotors on their own weighed 42 tons and rotated at a maximum of 3000rpm. The second IP and the LP ahead turbines both incorporated a three-row impulse LP section for moving the ship astern.

The main gearing was the double-helical single-reduction type, and the main gear wheel had a diameter of 14ft. The HP and first IP turbine were at one end of the gear case, and the second IP and LP turbines at the other. This gearing reduced the rotation of each of the four-bladed propellers to a maximum of 200rpm. The propellers themselves were made of high-tensile manganese bronze, and each weighed 35 tons with a 20ft diameter. They were situated over 250ft from their respective engines, and the thrust was transmitted to the hull structure via a Michell single-collar thrust block, just aft of the turbine set.

Condensers and the Weir main closed-feed system Four Weir regenerative type main condensers were individually arranged alongside each LP turbine. The exhaust steam outlet from the LP turbine was connected to the condenser's steam inlet. However, the condenser could also receive exhaust steam directly from the second IP turbine when the LP turbine was isolated.

Each condenser contained 41,000sq ft of cooling surface, consisting of 13,780 cupro-nickel tubes, each 15ft 6in long. These condensers were designed to maintain a vacuum of 29in of mercury at the maximum, with a sea temperature of 60°F. Two 285hp circulating pumps provided 25,000 gallons of water per minute to each condenser, while one of eight 55hp Weir electrically driven water extraction pumps could remove the resulting condensate from the cooling system at a maximum of 550,000lb per hour. The vacuum for the efficient running of the condenser was produced by two Weir steam jet three-stage air ejectors. These removed the air and non-condensable gases.

The condensate was passed onto drain coolers, which raised its temperature from 84 to 115°F by the heat received from cooling the LP feed water heater drains. The LP feed water heater then raised the temperature from 115 to 205°F and received steam from the evaporators, turbo-feed pumps and the second IP turbine. The LP feed water heater was positioned on the suction side of the turbo-feed pump. On the discharge side of this pump was the IP feed water heater, which increased the feed water temperature from 205 to 320°F, and was heated with steam from the main turbines and drains from the HP feed water heater. The final stage of feed water heating was conducted in the HP heaters; these increased the temperature to 370°F. Eight steam-driven Weir turbo-feed pumps delivered the water at a pressure of 500 psi, discharging through the IP and HP heaters to the boiler feed regulators.

A large hot-well tank of 28 tons capacity was fitted in the forward engine room, and two 14-ton tanks occupied a similar position in the after engine room. These were for the make-up feed water.

Two auxiliary condensers and associated motor-driven pumps were fitted in the after engine room and one in the forward turbo-generator room. These handled the exhaust steam from the ship's galley, pantries and ventilation system, the condensate being stored in the forward turbo-generator room's hot well tank.

Four evaporators in the forward engine room, each with a capacity of 100 tons, converted fresh or sea water to additional feed-water for the boilers.

Turbo-generators and auxiliaries Power for the main engine auxiliaries was produced by four BTH (British Thomson-Houston) 1300kw turbo-generators housed in the after turbo-generator room. Three identical turbo-generators were contained in the forward turbo generator room and provided electricity for most of the ships domestic services — lighting, cooking, lifts and even the two swimming baths.

Each consisted of a 10-stage turbine and combined condenser driving a DC generator via single reduction gearing. These turbo-generators were kept functional with steam from the auxiliary boilers in No 1 boiler room. If necessary, either turbo-generator room could be used to provide power for all services. In addition there were two emergency generators, consisting of a Parsons eight-cylinder kerosene engine and BTH 75kw DC generators, housed on the after port side of B deck. These could be started immediately, and could provide power sufficient for all the ship's services for 36 hours.

Two electrically-driven circulating pumps gave the after turbo-generator room condensers a total of 4200 gallons of water per hour, while four electrically-driven extraction pumps removed the condensate at a maximum of 19,300lb per hour.

Similarly, two circulating pumps, three extraction pumps and three air ejectors served the forward turbo-generator room. Vacuum was maintained within these condensers at 28¾in mercury, with circulating water temperature of 60°F, by four Weir steam-jet air ejectors.

Feed water softening plant This installation was situated in a separate compartment forward of the auxiliary boiler room. The careful preparation of feed water was of paramount importance in maintaining the efficiency of the water tube boilers. Keeping these relatively free from scale deposits and corrosion over many months of constant steaming was vital for an express passenger liner service.

The plant was capable of producing 300 tons of softened water every day. Untreated water was stowed in the ship's double bottom and then pumped through the various stages of the softening plant to be stored in special tanks. Hydrated lime was made into a cream in a mixing tank, then the hard water was added and then passed onto duplicate reaction and precipitation tanks. The resulting sludge was discharged into the bilges and the treated water was sent through two quartz sand pressure filters. A further two Basex softening units, employing brining, removed any hardness still apparent in the water.

Steering Gear The *Queen Mary* was equipped with an electro-hydraulic four-ram unit, the largest steering gear built in Britain at that time; it weighed 180 tons. Three VSG (variable speed gear) Mk III size 50 electric pumping units maintained the pressure fluid within the four hydraulic cylinders, though only two were operational at any one time. Double hydraulic steering telemotor equipment was fitted in the forward wheel house, with another aft below the docking bridge. These were connected via electro-hydraulic servo gear consisting of two VSG Mk 111 size 1 pumps supplying fluid to duplicated cylinders which moved the main steering gear controls. The ship could also be steered by two handwheels within the steering gear compartment; one controlled the servo-gear and the other by-passed the servo-telemotor system. Finally, a Sperry gyro pilot was connected directly to the servo gear, for automatic steering along a pre-determined course.

Ventilation Efficient ventilation was crucial for passenger comfort and the ship's machinery. The two engine rooms alone required 400,000cu ft of fresh air every minute, entering through large diffusers. These air diffusers consisted of a series of graduated concentric cones which distributed the incoming air evenly over a large area.

Throughout most of the ship sound-proof fan rooms were installed, containing the fans and air-conditioning units for adjacent compartments. The incoming air could be heated or de-humidified and sent about the ship via ducting, giving each stateroom its own adjustable air system. Exhaust fans were also provided for the expulsion of stale air from the smoking rooms, lounges, bathrooms and lavatories. They also removed the heat and smell from kitchens, while supply fans completely regulated them with fresh air every 45 seconds. The entire ship installation included over 260 fans and air-conditioning units, which handled over 118,000,000cu ft of air every hour.

Five air-conditioning plants, with a total capacity of 7,000,000cu ft of air per hour, were also provided; two for the cabin class restaurant and the remainder for the cabin class lounge, tourist class dining saloon and hairdressing rooms. These plants were designed to cope with the extremes of climatic temperatures frequently encountered in the course of a transatlantic crossing.

Refrigeration Two vertical CO_2 evaporators, with compressors and electric motors, along with a reserve system of two CO_2 condensers, centrifugal pumps and electric motors, were situated abaft the after engine room on H deck. These supplied brine for the cold store compartments, cold cupboards and water coolers, via two Weir reciprocating pumps. The temperature was 15°F except in the ice-cream and frozen fish storerooms, where independent methyl-chloride compressors were used to obtain a 0°F temperature. Other independent refrigerators were provided throughout pantries, bars and cold cupboards.

ACCOMMODATION

Cabin class The largest room on the *Queen Mary* was the cabin class restaurant on C deck; with an overall length of 143ft, it spread across the entire width of the vessel. Along the central aisle the ceiling reached a height of 27ft. The colour scheme reflected the browns of autumn, with three shades of Brazilian peroba panels arranged in horizontal bands around the walls, and on the large structural columns silver-bronze (nickel silver) marquetry embellished the woodwork and framed the artificially illuminated windows of peach ripple glass. Seating was for 815 people on red-upholstered sycamore chairs. In the centre of the after wall, double bronze doors of a finely scrolled design were surmounted by a large painting depicting English countryside pursuits. On the opposing wall a decorative chart of the North Atlantic with a central clock revealed the ship's daily progress with the aid of illuminated crystals.

Many prominent artists of the era were commissioned to design paintings, murals, carvings and statuettes for the ship. These, combined with the richness of decor throughout, gave the ship the air of a stately home.

The main lounge was probably the focal point of the ship's social life; this large apartment was also used as a cinema and a ballroom. Seating was for over 400 people. It was decorated with maple burr, with dados of makore producing rich golden hues. At the after end of the room was a large stage with a grand proscenium featuring a burnished phosphor-bronze plaque. When this room was not being used for dancing, a heavy grade Wilton carpet of dark green and grey covered the parquet floor of oak and mahogany bands with Indian laurel.

The smoking room was designed much along the lines of that of an English gentlemen's club. It featured a unique large coal-burning travertine fireplace, flanked by two pierced and carved screens at the forward end of the room. A relaxed ambience was created, with English brown oak mural decor, and lower panels of quartered walnut burr.

Another restful room was the library, with its soft velvet curtains and deep pile carpets of grey, brown and slate blue. It contained over 1700 books in sliding glass-door bookcases set in alcoves. The walls were panelled with pigskin leather of a dark golden colour, used for its acoustic properties. The dado was of oak burr with sycamore rails and an ebonised oak skirting.

The observation lounge and cocktail bar at the forward end of the promenade deck had twenty-one 5ft high by 2ft wide windows, which allowed a panoramic view forward of the ship. The sheer of the deck in this area was concealed at the forward end by a raised platform with broad steps and a balustrade featuring carved motifs. Wall panelling was of maple burr, thinly banded with cedar wood. The compartment was dominated by the strong use of red on the metal enamelled light pylons, pillars and furnishings, and even the bar stools had red hide on their seats.

The verandah grill at the after end of the sun deck was used for dancing and the serving of *à la carte* meals; it also provided a cocktail bar and supper service. The dance floor was parquetry laid in sycamore with bordering lines of mahogany, peartree and ebonised hornbeam. A black carpet covered the two platforms at the sides of the room, which were separated from the dancing area by a silver-bronze ballustrade featuring etched designs on fluted glass panels. The walls were covered with large paintings, reflecting different forms of entertainment within the performing arts. Coloured lighting played an integral role in the compartment's chic night-club appearance.

Single and two-berth staterooms were provided, mostly positioned to receive natural light and ventilation from sidelights. Twelve private suites, consisting of sitting room, bedroom, bathroom, boxroom and servant's room, were available on the main deck. Other special staterooms were provided on the main deck and A deck; these were individually designed and featured peach glass and python skin fabrics. Furniture was made of hardwoods and veneered with a variety of exotic woods with names to match, such as amboyna, petula, pomla, and zebrano. Wooden wall panelling was used throughout the cabins in a wide variety to blend harmoniously with the furnishings of each room. Underneath the Wilton carpets and hand-made rugs, all decks were lined with linoleum. Wooden cot beds 3ft wide with upholstered box-spring bases were a feature of all the rooms, while in a two-berth cabin one bed could easily be converted into a divan. Other luxuries included a washbasin with hot and cold water (a feature of all the cabins on the *Queen Mary*) electric radiator and telephone.

Tourist class Two tourist class lounges, the main lounge and supplementary lounge, were provided on the main deck and A deck respectively. The principal lounge was 80ft long by 70ft wide. This contained a large parquet dance floor of oak and walnut lines radiating from octagonal panels. A large stage with a proscenium was at the after end of the room. Seating accommodation was for 210 people, but this could be increased to 388 when the room was used as a cinema. The upper walls featured a horizontal stripe design of green, ivory and silver appliqué leather, over a dado of thuya burr-figured birch and maple, Among the furniture were easy chairs and settees upholstered in fabrics of green, cream and black.

The lounge on A deck had an elm burr dado offset by silver-bronze metal bands. Above, the walls were panelled with Moselle-figured Canadian birch. This room also had a parquet floor of oak and walnut panels. Seating was for 100 people, on furniture of elm burr.

The tourist class dining saloon covered the full width of C deck and was 78ft long. It had a dado of light oak burr under silver grey courses of blistered maple. Both ends of the room featured eight glazed panels with attractive sand-blasted designs of cereals and fruit which were illuminated from behind. Dining chairs of light sycamore with ash burr bandings and French rose tapestry upholstery were provided, to seat 400 people.

All of the tourist class staterooms had washbasins, while 80 percent of the rooms were fitted with private toilets. Two mahogany bedsteads were augmented with folding upper berths, as these rooms often slept three or four people.

Third class The garden lounge was situated forward on the main deck and afforded a marvellous view from beam to beam, because of its semi-circular shape. The room was divided into five bays on both sides and the walls were panelled with weathered sycamore. Furniture consisted of Malacca framed chairs of green cane, interlaced with orange and black cane. The floor was a cinnamon coloured korkoid with green and brown stripes.

TABLE 3: PARTICULARS OF SHIP'S BOATS

Number	20	2	2
Type	motor lifeboat	motor lifeboat with wireless	motor lifeboat rigged as accident boat
Length	36ft	36ft	30ft
Beam	12ft 5in	12ft 5in	9ft 3in
Depth	5ft	5ft	3ft 10½in
Speed	6 knots	6 knots	6 knots
Engine	18bhp 2-cylinder diesel	18bhp 2-cylinder diesel	18bhp 2-cylinder diesel
Weight	18¾ tons full load	not known	not known
Life saving capacity	145	136	47
Construction	steel	steel	steel

TABLE 4: GROUND TACKLE

Number	4
Type	bower anchors
Pattern	Dreadnought stockless
Weight	16 tons
Length of cable	330 fathoms
Size of cable	4⅛in
Type of cable	stud-link chain

The third class smoking room was another semi-circular apartment with an all-round sea view forward, positioned on A deck. It contained five roomy recesses with built-in settees, augmented with armchairs and small tables. The korkoid tile design floor featured shades of green, brown and beige, with walls of figured oak veneer panels.

The lounge and cinema, on B deck, was divided by a 27ft wide central entrance; the two large halves could be used as a cinema. Each had eight large oval windows on the outboard side, with wall panels of cherrywood and three bands of dark Honduras mahogany. The korkoid floor was cinnamon with chocolate coloured stripes.

Like those in the other classes, the third class dining saloon occupied the full width of C deck and was about 90ft long. Finely ground sycamore panels covered the walls above a dado of coral-coloured mahogany. Seating was for 412 people, on chairs of polished Honduras mahogany. The floor was decorated in a design of korkoid in red, orange and cinnamon.

The third class staterooms were either a double or four-berth design with mahogany bedsteads. The upper berths were the Pullman folding type. All beds had internally sprung mattresses. There were polished hardwood built-in wardrobes, dressing tables and chairs. Every cabin had a washbasin with hot and cold water, mirror and overhead electric light. The floors were of a korkoleum purple marble design with a bedside rug and curtains of grey, blue and orange hues.

The Photographs

2. The *Queen Mary* nearing completion in the fitting-out basin. Plank stages are rigged around the intakes, which are receiving their final coat of paint. The starboard gangway derrick, squash court and the wireless telegraph leads in trunk are visible.
Popperfoto

3. View of the forward superstructure during fitting out. Doors for access to the space under the false flooring are especially visible around the forward superstructure just above the sundeck. *Popperfoto*

4. Looking aft from abreast the forward funnel; the workmen's wooden ladders are still in place. *Popperfoto*

5. Looking forward from the middle funnel. *Popperfoto*

6. The starboard side, looking aft from the 30ft lifeboat davit. A 36ft motor lifeboat is in the foreground. *Popperfoto*

7. Workmen reveal the size of the twin sirens on the forward funnel. *Popperfoto*

8. The forepeak and jackstaff. *Glasgow University Archives*

9. A view of the cable deck, looking aft. *Glasgow University Archives*

10. The cargo derrick table on the foremast, surrounded by the 6-ton electric cargo winches. *Glasgow University Archives*

11. The compass platform 1936, looking forward. The wireless direction finder and forward funnel floodlight are in the foreground and the standard compass and port searchlight are visible behind. *Queen Mary Historical Archives*

12. The after capstan deck. *Glasgow University Archives*

13, 14, 15. The *Queen Mary* on 24 March 1936, being led down the Clyde to anchor off Gourock, where she would pick up the rest of her lifeboats. Notice her shallow draught, to reduce the danger of running aground.
Maritime Photo Library

25

16. A port side view of the *Queen Mary* at the height of her wartime career, with full anti-aircraft armament. *Queen Mary Historical Archives*

17. The port side looking aft; 20 mm Oerlikon positions are visible on top of the boiler vents and deckhouses. *Queen Mary Historical Archives*

18. The after sun deck defence positions, showing the starboard 3 in HA gun and centre single Oerlikon, with Carley floats and life floats. *Queen Mary Historical Archives*

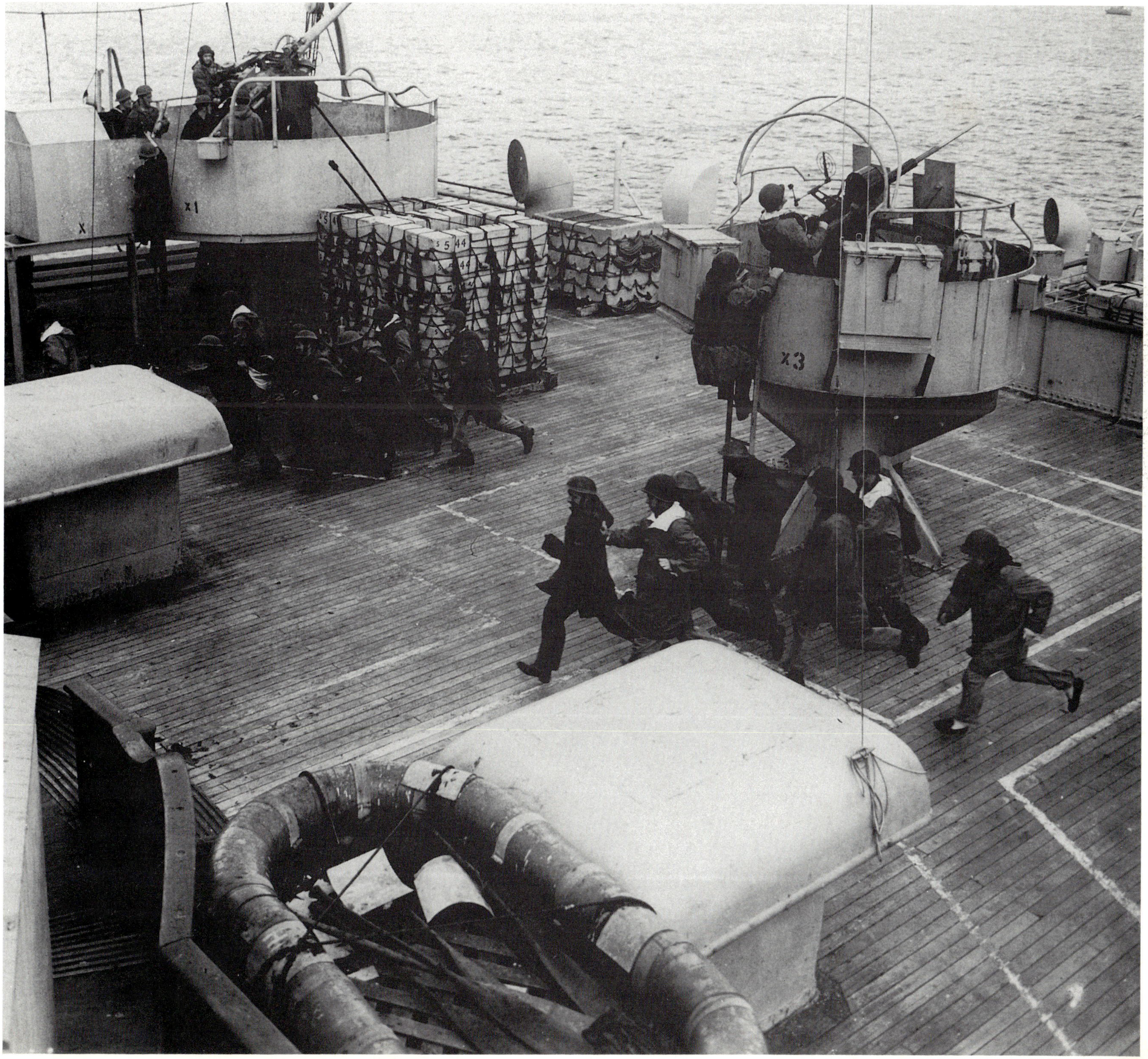
x1
x3

19. The *Queen Mary* leaving the King George V drydock on 3 May 1947, after repairs to her bow, which sustained damage from her collision with HMS *Curacoa*. The degaussing coil and radar outfit have also been removed. *CPL*

20. The *Queen Mary* receiving a final clean at the close of her post-war refit in early July 1947. The forward three large boiler vents still retain the strengthening brackets and pillars they received when anti-aircraft positions were fitted on top. The high wire screen around the deck games area has been removed and replaced by a metal screen between the first boiler vent and forward funnel. *CPL*

21. The radar outfit on the compass platform, seen in early July 1947. *CPL*

22. A post 1947 refit photograph showing the single extra lifeboat and its quadrant davits retained after the ship's war service. *Popperfoto*

23. The *Queen Mary* alongside at Southampton's Ocean Terminal in 1951. *Skyfotos Ltd*

30

24. The liner at sea during the early 1950s. *Skyfotos Ltd*

25. The windows of an extension to the deckhouse forward of the middle funnel are visible in this picture. *Skyfotos Ltd*

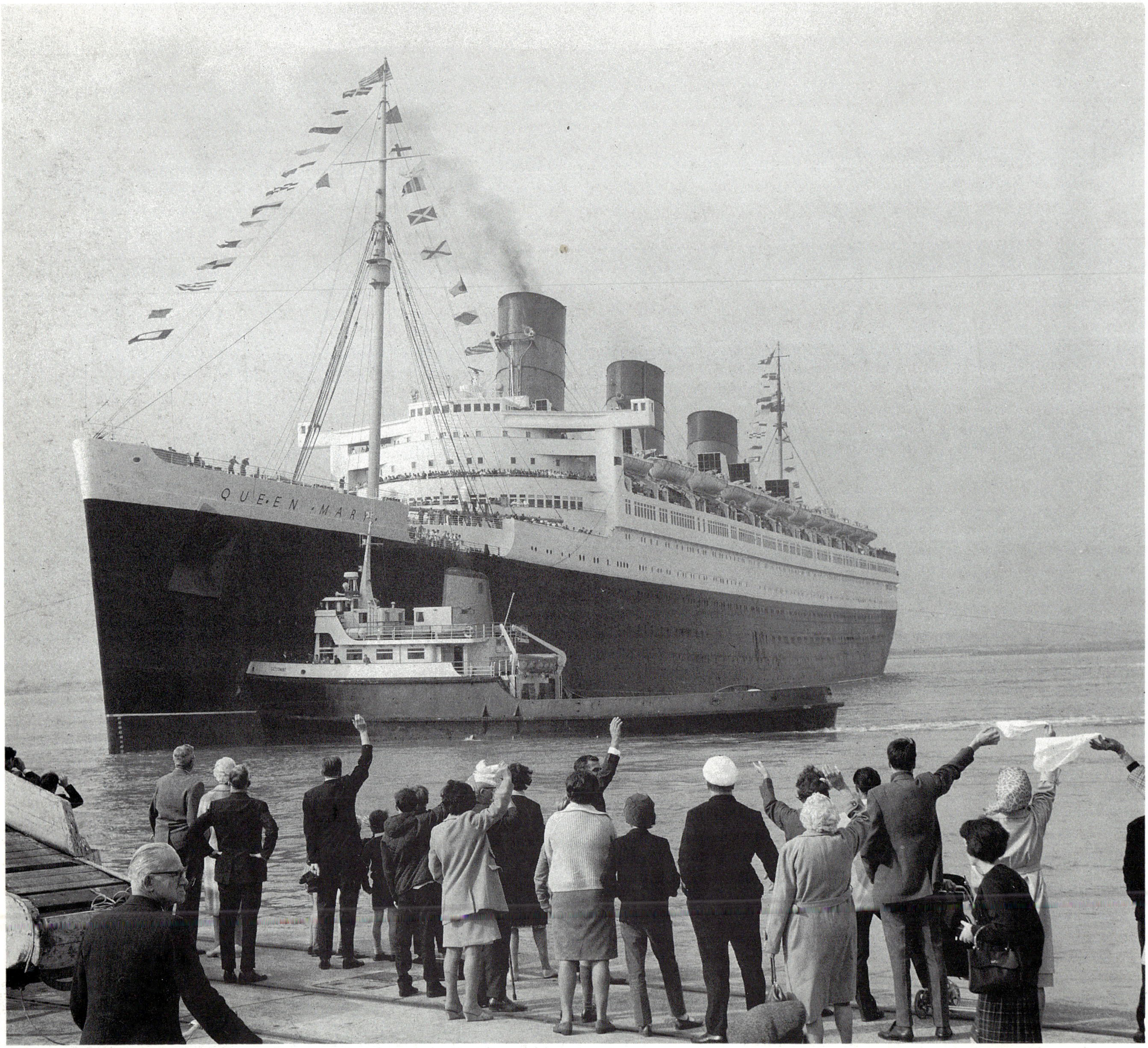
QUEEN MARY

26. (opposite) The *Queen Mary*'s last departure from Southampton, on 6 September 1967. *CPL*

27. The old liner leaving New York for the last time on 22 September 1967, after one thousand visits. The Manhattan skyline may have altered, but the city's high regard for the *Queen Mary* had not changed in over thirty years of service. She is bid farewell by tugs and pleasure craft. *CPL*

28. On 31 September 1967 the *Queen Mary*, flying her paying-off pennant, departs for Long Beach, California and her new home. Two double-decker buses are carried on the after part of the main deck. *CPL*

29. The *Queen Mary* is given an enthusiastic reception on her arrival at Long Beach on 9 December 1967. *Popperfoto*

The Drawings

A General arrangement

A1 GENERAL ARRANGEMENT AS COMPLETED, MARCH 1936 (all drawings in section A are 1/700 scale)

A1/1 External profile

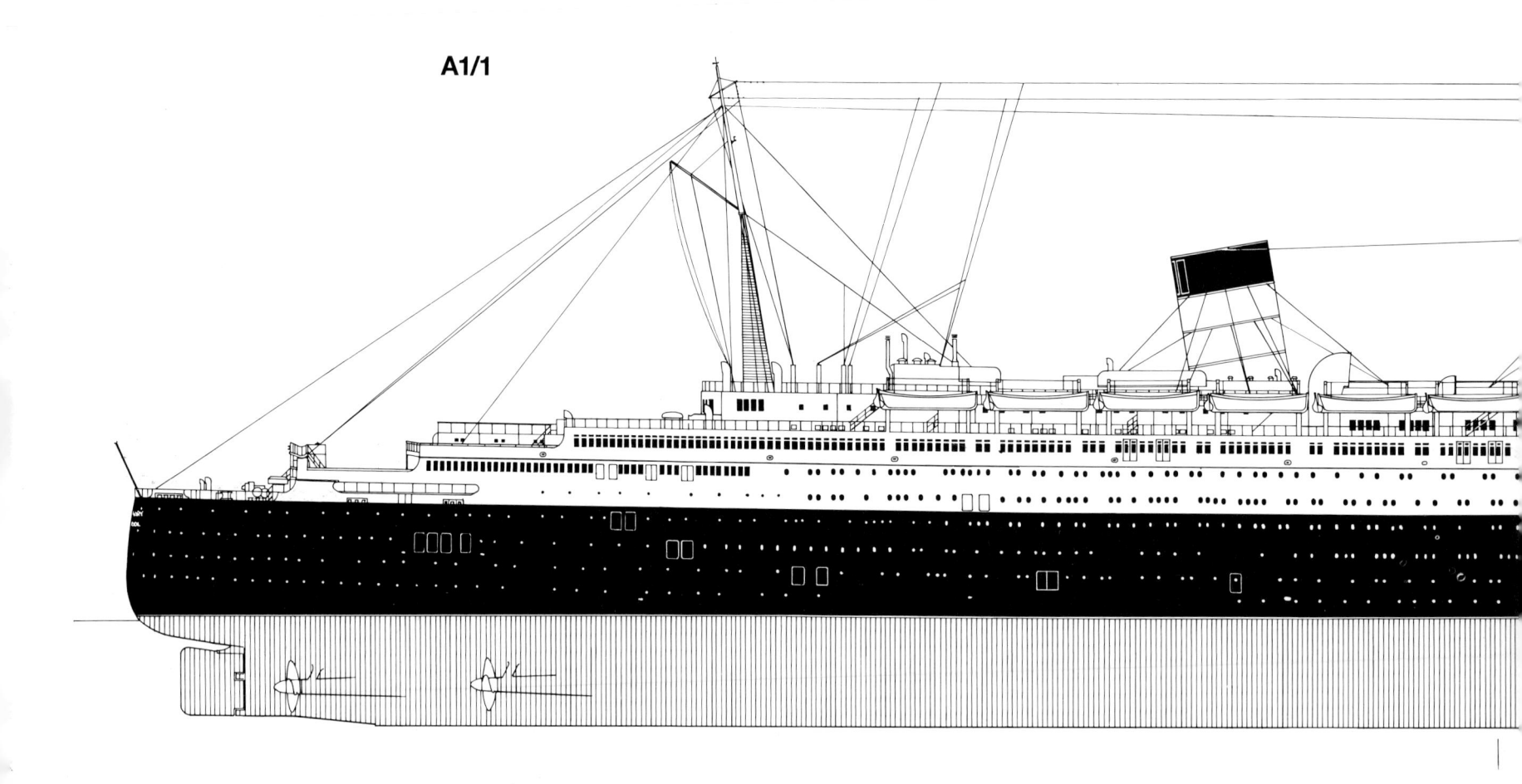

A1/1

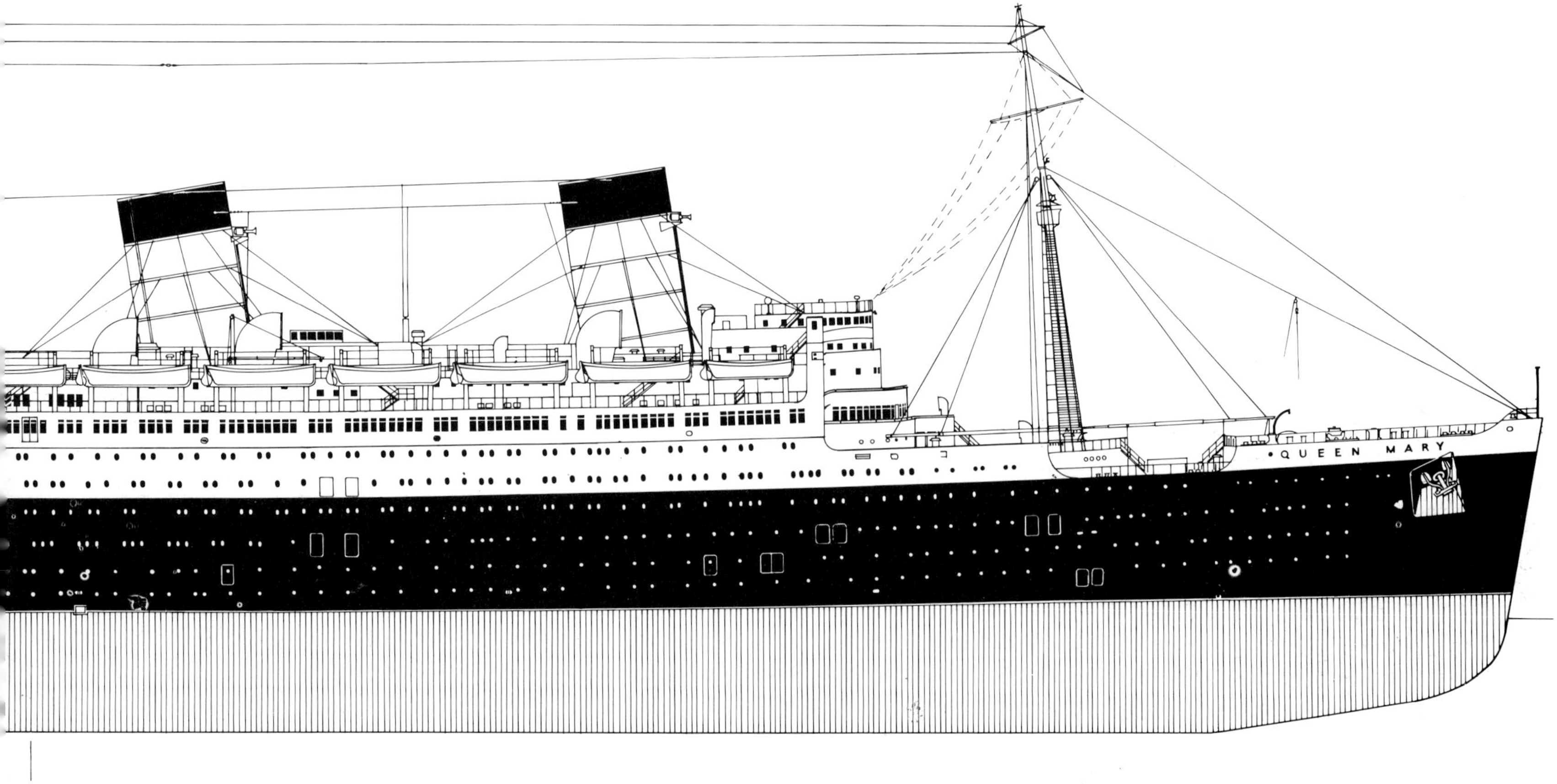
QUEEN MARY

A General arrangement

A1/2 Internal profile

1. Male hospital
2. Stewards's washplace
3. Stewards's accommodation
4. Steering gear compartment
5. Steering gear trunk
6. Docking bridge
7. Wheelhouse
8. Deck stores
9. Tourist class accommodation
10. Leading stewards' accommodation
11. Watertight compartment
12. After peak tank
13. Tourist lounge
14. Stores entrance
15. Baggage space
16. Tunnel
17. Cinema box
18. Bar
19. Engineers' and tourist accommodation
20. Tourist swimming bath
21. Tourist class entrance
22. Furniture store
23. Verandah grill
24. Tourist class library
25. Tourist class dining saloon
26. Linen store
27. Engineers' accommodation
28. Refrigerator machinery compartment
29. Cabin class accommodation
30. Cabin class smoking room
31. Champagne and white wine store
32. After engine room
33. Ballroom
34. Galley space
35. Stores
36. Forward engine room
37. Vent unit spaces
38. Tank room
39. Oil tanks
40. Hatch pantries
41. Cabin class lounge
42. Cabin class dining saloon
43. No 5 boiler room
44. After turbo-generator room
45. No 4 boiler room
46. Air conditioning plant
47. Squash court
48. Main hall
49. Cabin class library
50. Deck games locker
51. Wireless telegraph receiving room
52. Wireless telegraph operators' accommodation
53. Balcony
54. Cabin class swimming pool
55. Swimming pool tank
56. Cofferdam
57. No 3 boiler room
58. Forward turbo-generator room
59. No 2 boiler room
60. Chartroom
61. Captain and officers' accommodation
62. Cocktail lounge
63. Third class garden lounge
64. Third class dining saloon
65. No 1 boiler room
66. Third class and crew accommodation
67. Water softening plant
68. Motor car or cargo space
69. Drinking water tank
70. Cargo space
71. Third class smoke room
72. Mail space
73. Capstan machinery space
74. Third class entrance
75. Paint store
76. Seamen's accommodation
77. Trimming tank
78. Chain locker
79. Oil fuel compartment
PS. Pipe space
EH. Engine hatch
FH. Funnel hatch

A1/2

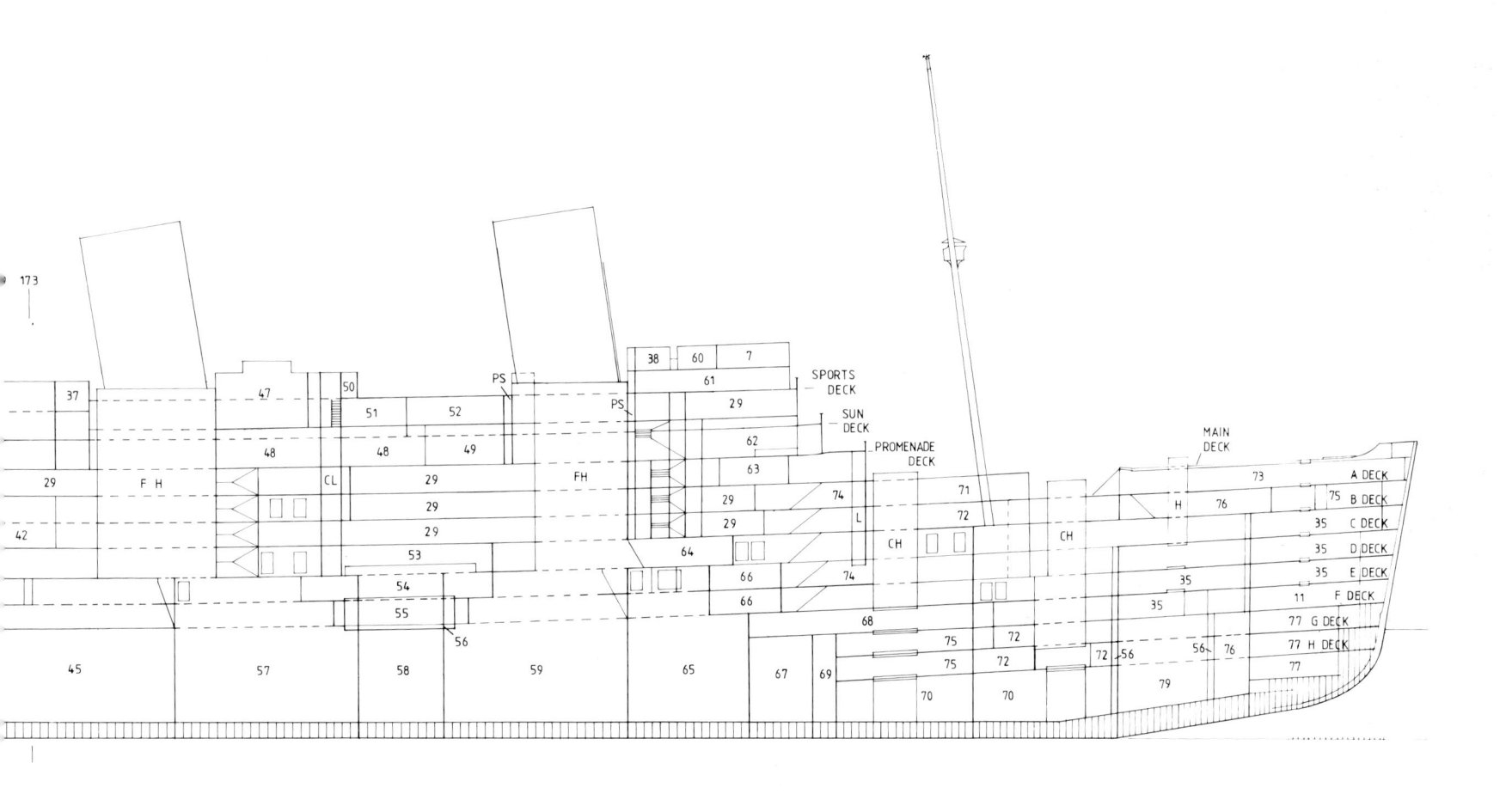

CH Cargo hatch
CL Cabin lift
EL Engineers' lift
TL Tourist lift

A General arrangement

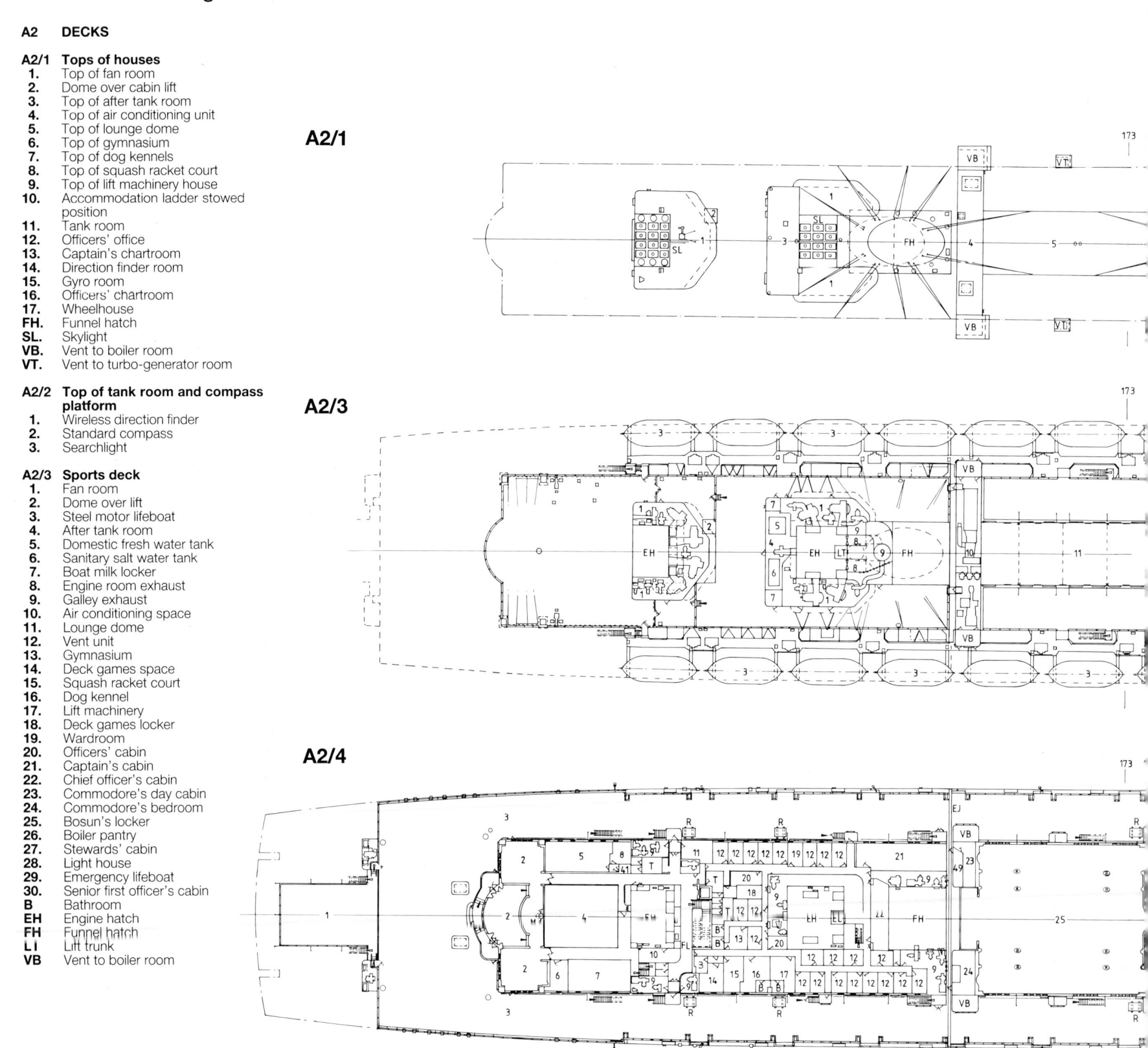

A2 DECKS

A2/1 Tops of houses
1. Top of fan room
2. Dome over cabin lift
3. Top of after tank room
4. Top of air conditioning unit
5. Top of lounge dome
6. Top of gymnasium
7. Top of dog kennels
8. Top of squash racket court
9. Top of lift machinery house
10. Accommodation ladder stowed position
11. Tank room
12. Officers' office
13. Captain's chartroom
14. Direction finder room
15. Gyro room
16. Officers' chartroom
17. Wheelhouse
FH. Funnel hatch
SL. Skylight
VB. Vent to boiler room
VT. Vent to turbo-generator room

A2/2 Top of tank room and compass platform
1. Wireless direction finder
2. Standard compass
3. Searchlight

A2/3 Sports deck
1. Fan room
2. Dome over lift
3. Steel motor lifeboat
4. After tank room
5. Domestic fresh water tank
6. Sanitary salt water tank
7. Boat milk locker
8. Engine room exhaust
9. Galley exhaust
10. Air conditioning space
11. Lounge dome
12. Vent unit
13. Gymnasium
14. Deck games space
15. Squash racket court
16. Dog kennel
17. Lift machinery
18. Deck games locker
19. Wardroom
20. Officers' cabin
21. Captain's cabin
22. Chief officer's cabin
23. Commodore's day cabin
24. Commodore's bedroom
25. Bosun's locker
26. Boiler pantry
27. Stewards' cabin
28. Light house
29. Emergency lifeboat
30. Senior first officer's cabin
B   Bathroom
EH Engine hatch
FH Funnel hatch
LI Lift trunk
VB Vent to boiler room

40

A2/2

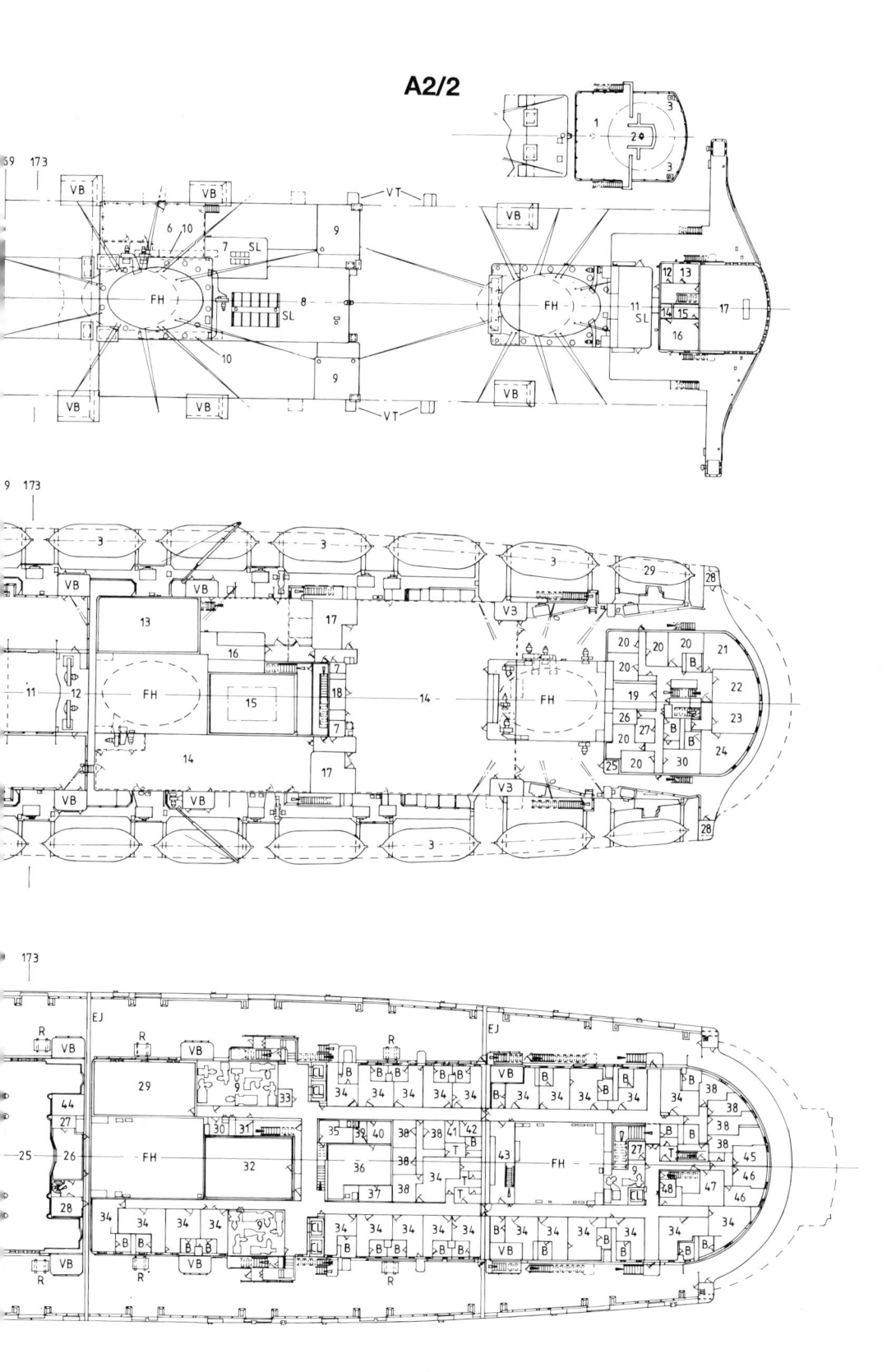

A2/4 Sun deck
1. Dome over tourist lounge
2. Verandah grill
3. Cabin promenade
4. Dome over smoking room
5. Wireless telegraph transmitting room
6. Bar
7. Verandah grill kitchen
8. Wireless telegraph electrician's cabin
9. Vent units
10. Scullery
11. Gardener's store
12. Engineer's cabin
13. Engineer's office
14. Chief engineer's bedroom
15. Chief engineer's day room
16. Staff chief engineer's cabin
17. Senior second engineer's cabin
18. Stewards' cabin
19. Chief electrician's cabin
20. Auxiliary switchboard
21. Engineers' wardroom
22. Service lift machinery
23. Boat engineer's workshop
24. Gangway lifting gear store
25. Lounge
26. Cinema operating room
27. Generator
28. Rewinding room
29. Gymnasium
30. Gymnasium attendant's room
31. Court attendant's room
32. Squash racket court
33. Telephone cabinet
34. Cabin class berth
35. Passenger office
36. Wireless receiving room
37. Emergency battery room
38. Wireless telegraph operator's cabin
39. Accepting office
40. Clerical office
41. Wireless telegraph spare gear
42. Stewards' service locker
43. Cabin deck and bedroom pantry
44. Locker
45. Editor's cabin
46. Bank official's cabin
47. Press reception room
48. Dark room
49. Paint washing tank
B   Bathroom
M   Mast
R   Raft (4)
CL   Cabin lift
EJ   Expansion joint
EL   Engineer's lift
FL   Food lift
FH   Funnel hatch
EH   Engine hatch
VB   Vent to boiler room

41

A General arrangement

A2/5 Promenade deck
1. Docking bridge
2. Dome over tourist lounge
3. Tourist promenade
4. Cinema operating box
5. Vent units
6. Gas bottles
7. Generator room
8. Rewinding room
9. Tourist smoking room
10. Bar
11. Vestibule
12. Tourist entrance
13. Tourist deck pantry
14. Smoking room
15. Cabin class sheltered promenade
16. Pantry
17. Ballroom
18. Long gallery
19. Starboard gallery
20. Public room pantry
21. Lounge
22. Chair stowage
23. Writing room
24. Main hall
25. Tobacconist
26. Book shop
27. Library
28. Drawing room
29. Shop
30. Rug locker
31. Dressing room
32. Lectures
33. Children's playroom
34. Studio
35. Paint washing tank
36. Observation lounge and cocktail bar
37. Darkroom
38. Locker
GD Gangway doors
SL Service lift
TL Tourist lift
EL Engineers' lift
EH Engine hatch
FH Funnel hatch
VB Vent to boiler room

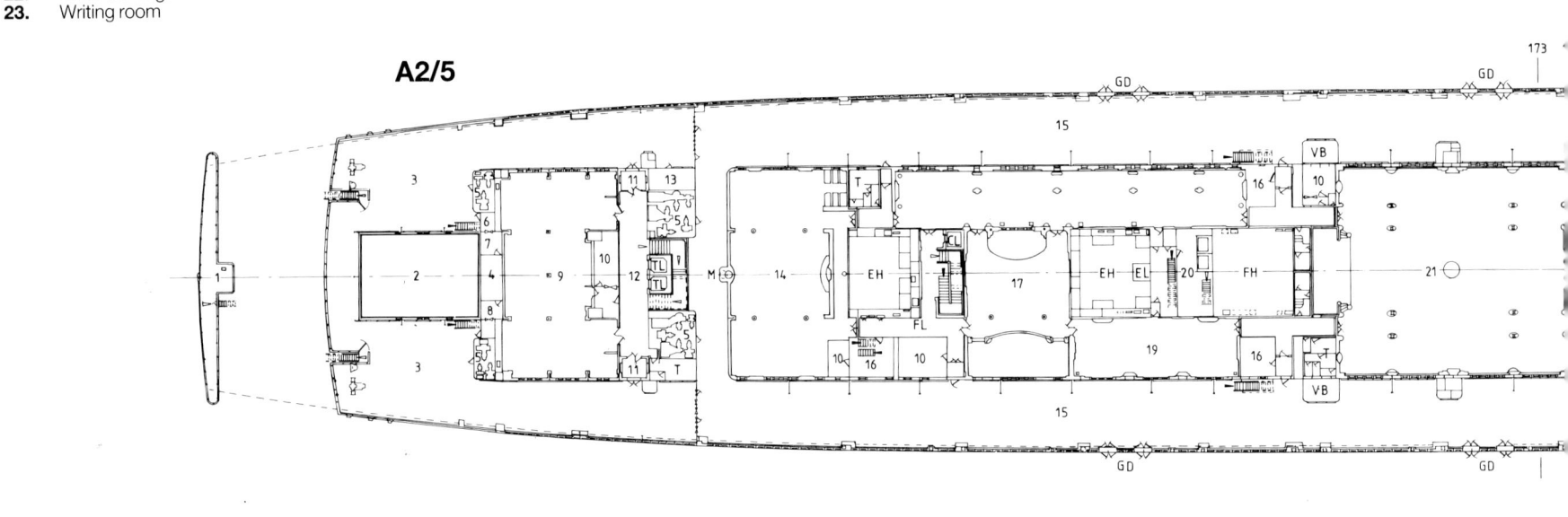

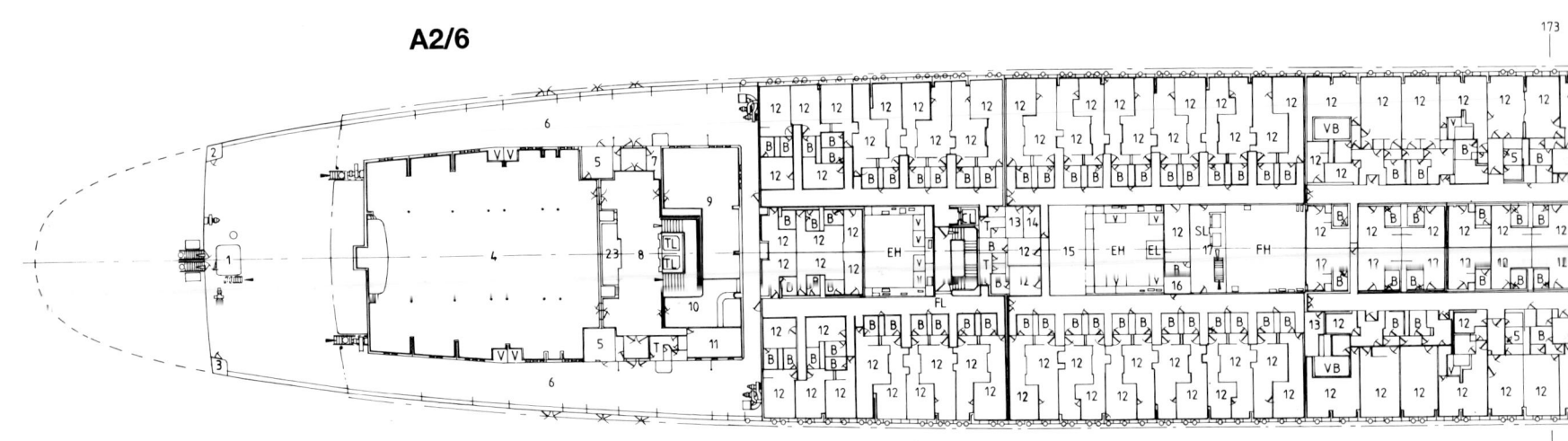

A2/5

A2/6

42

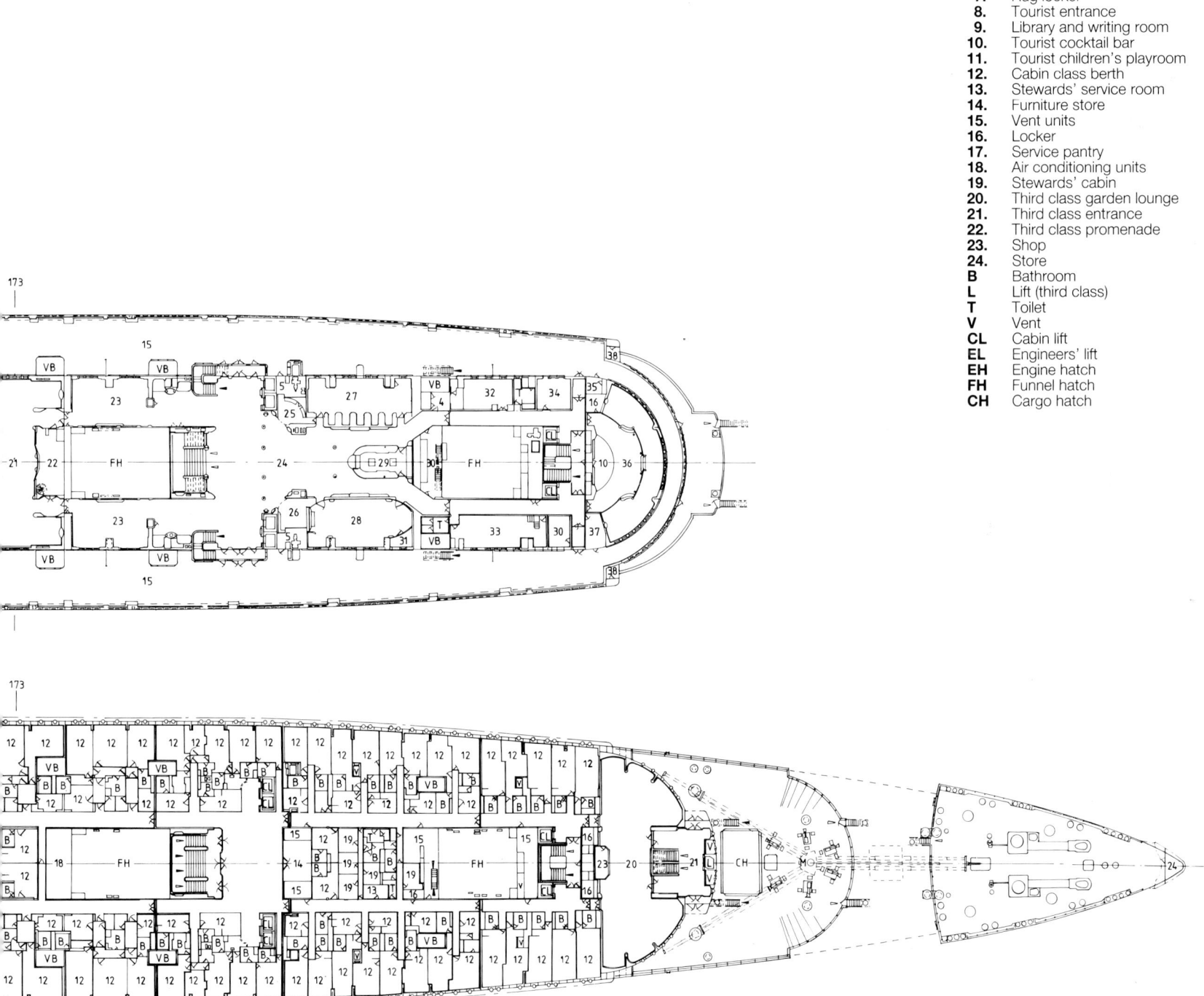

A2/6 Main deck
1. Wheelhouse
2. Games locker
3. Quartermaster's locker
4. Tourist lounge
5. Pantry
6. Tourist promenade
7. Rug locker
8. Tourist entrance
9. Library and writing room
10. Tourist cocktail bar
11. Tourist children's playroom
12. Cabin class berth
13. Stewards' service room
14. Furniture store
15. Vent units
16. Locker
17. Service pantry
18. Air conditioning units
19. Stewards' cabin
20. Third class garden lounge
21. Third class entrance
22. Third class promenade
23. Shop
24. Store
B   Bathroom
L   Lift (third class)
T   Toilet
V   Vent
CL Cabin lift
EL Engineers' lift
EH Engine hatch
FH Funnel hatch
CH Cargo hatch

A General arrangement

A2/7 A deck
1. Oil tank
2. Telephone box
3. Deck locker
4. Film locker
5. Tourist promenade
6. Tourist lounge
7. Vent units
8. Bar
9. Pantry
10. Tourist entrance
11. Tourist class berth
12. Cabin class berth
13. Thermotank room
14. Air conditioning units
15. Stewards' service room
16. Auxiliary switchboard
17. Valet service room
18. Cabin bedroom service pantry
19. Furniture locker
20. Music reproduction room
21. Dome over restaurant
22. Chief purser
23. Sitting room
24. Purser's private office
25. Bank
26. Mail and parcel office
27. Waiting room
28. Doctor
29. Consulting room
30. Cabin class entrance
31. Purser's office
32. Typing room
33. Safe deposit room
34. Stewards' cabin
35. Barber's shop
36. Third class entrance
37. Third class smoke room
38. Rope store
39. Switchboard
40. Capstan machinery
EH Engine hatch
FH Funnel hatch
CH Cargo hatch
H   Hatch
M   Mast
V   Vent
VB Vent to boiler room

A2/7

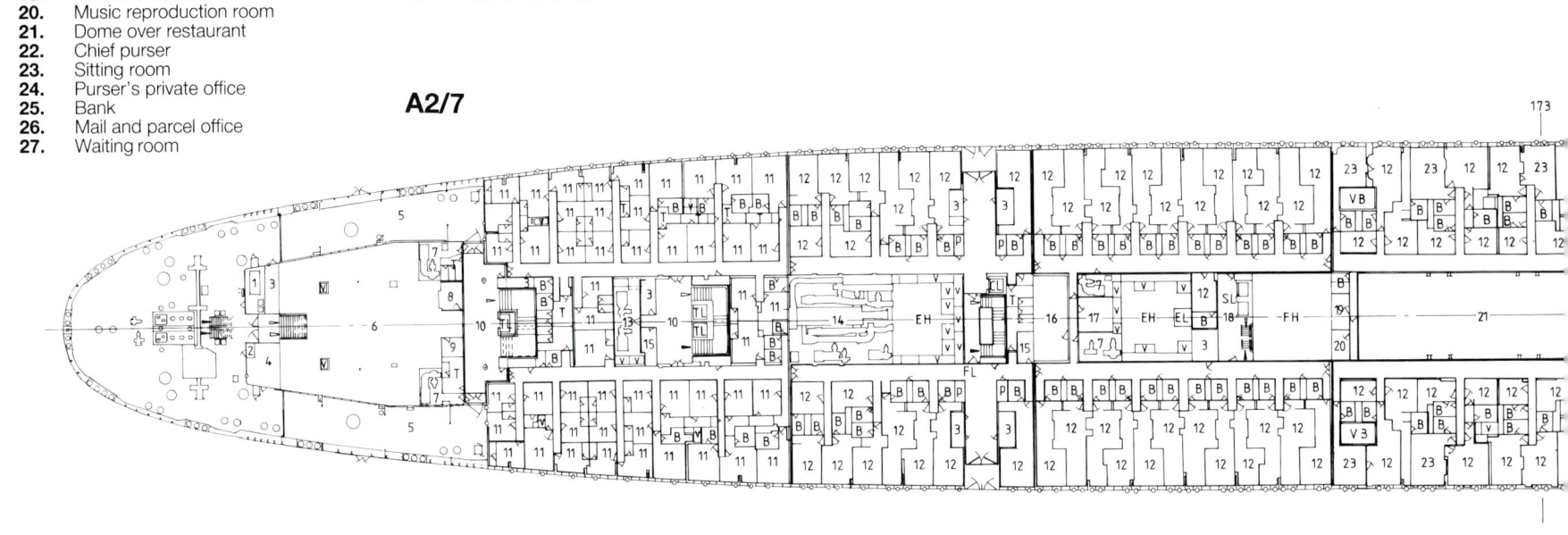

A2/8

A2/8 B deck
1. Male hospital
2. Female hospital
3. Hospital attendant's cabin
4. Nurses' cabin
5. Capstan machinery
6. Steering gear trunk
7. Rope store
8. Vent units
9. Tourist class berth
10. Emergency dynamos room
11. Stewards' ironing room
12. Stewardesses' cabin
13. Tourist entrance
14. Auxiliary switchboard
15. Locker
16. Gents' hairdresser
17. Shop
18. Assistant doctor
19. Consulting room
20. Lift machinery
21. Stewards' service room
22. Telephone exchange battery room
23. Cabin class berth
24. Cabin bedroom service pantry
25. Dome over restaurant
26. Cabin entrance
27. Air conditioning plant
28. Ladies' hairdresser
29. Third class children's playroom
30. Dressing room
31. Rewinding room
32. Scroll room
33. Cinema operating box
34. Third class cinema
35. Third class lounge
36. Mail handling space
37. Mail chute
38. Seamen's accommodation
39. Seamen's washplace
40. Seamen's drying room
41. Seamen's WC
42. Lamp room
43. Paint store
- **EH** Engine hatch
- **FH** Funnel hatch
- **CH** Cargo hatch
- **H** Hatch
- **B** Bathroom
- **T** Toilet
- **M** Mast
- **V** Vent
- **EL** Engineers' lift
- **SL** Skylight
- **TL** Tourist lift
- **VB** Vent to boiler room

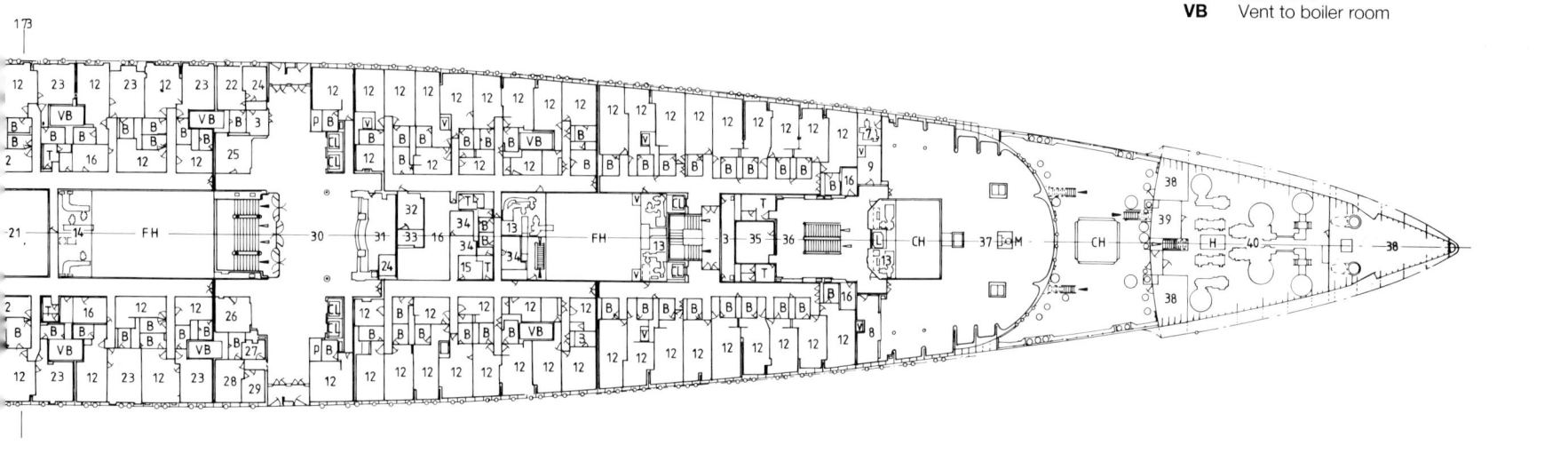

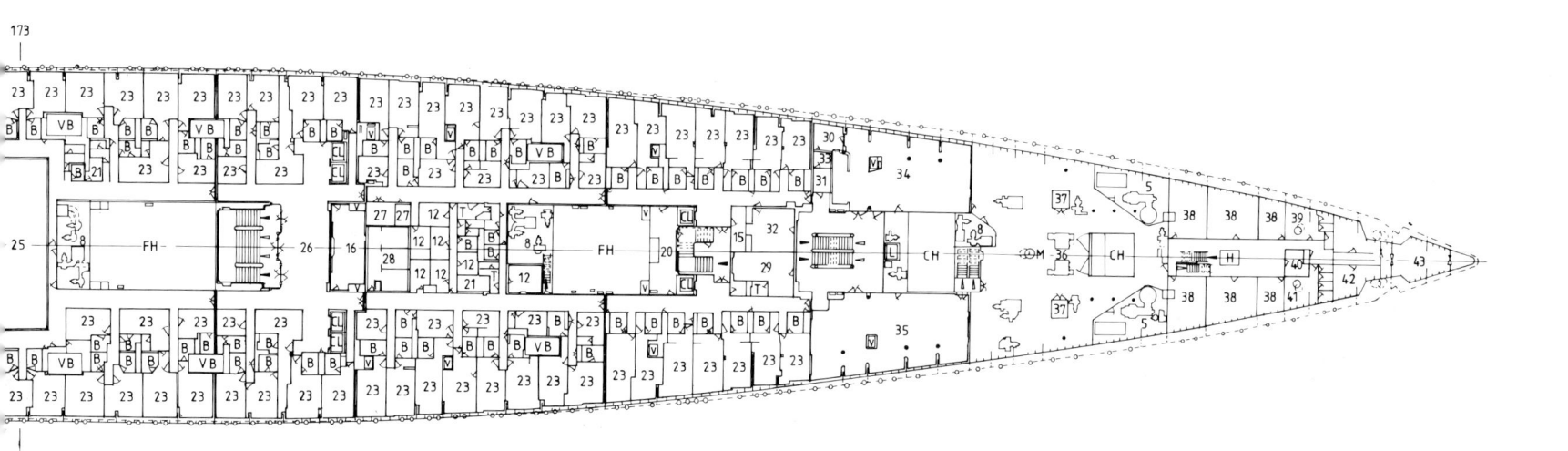

45

A General arrangement

A2/9 C deck

1. Stewards' washplace
2. Stewards' WCs
3. Leading stewards' washplace
4. Leading stewards' WCs
5. Steering gear trunk
6. Leading stewards' acommodation
7. Interpreter's cabin
8. Chef's cabin
9. Chief baker's cabin
10. Restaurant manager's cabin
11. Barkeeper's cabin
12. Crew's bar
13. Stores and baggage entrance
14. Lift motor
15. Rope store
16. Tourist bedroom service pantry
17. Vent unit
18. Tourist entrance
19. Locker
20. Tourist office
21. Bandsmen's cabin
22. Tourist class berth
23. Typing room
24. Bank
25. Chief tourist steward's cabin
26. Baggage master's cabin
27. Tourist dining saloon
28. Baker's shop
29. Bread room
30. Tourist bar
31. Tourist plate scullery
32. Storekeeper's cabin
33. Tourist glass and china room
34. Annexe
35. Vegetable preparing room
36. Auxiliary switchboard
37. Tourist kitchen
38. Tourist cold pantry
39. Ice pantry
40. Chef's larder
41. Tourist fruit and salad room
42. Larder for salads and hors d'oeuvres
43. Pantry
44. Saloon kitchen
45. Stillroom pantry
46. Confectioner's shop
47. Cold larder
48. Cabin class coffee room
49. Grill kitchen
50. Fruit room
51. Wine room
52. Cabin class china pantry
53. Scullery
54. Saloon dispensary bar
55. Private dining room
56. Glass pantry
57. Linen locker
58. Restaurant
59. Vestibule
60. Cloak room
61. Foyer
62. Towel locker attendant
63. Kitchen scullery
64. anteroom
65. Frigidarium
66. Heating element
67. Calidarium
68. Steam room
69. Fountain
70. Massage parlour
71. Electric baths
72. Balcony
73. Chief steward's day cabin
74. Chief stewards' writing office
75. Chief steward's bedroom
76. Staff purser's cabin
77. Assistant purser's cabin
78. Tourist director's cabin
79. Senior assistant purser's cabin
80. Third class saloon pantry
81. Third class dining saloon
82. Third class entrance
83. Bosun's cabin
84. Bosun's mate's cabin
85. Fire patrol men's cabin
86. Lamp storekeeper's cabin
87. Quartermaster's cabin
88. Quartermaster's mess
89. Master-at-arms's cabin
90. Chief master-at-arms's cabin
91. Third class office
92. Third class cabin
93. Mails and baggage entrance
94. Mail chute
95. Boys' mess

A2/9

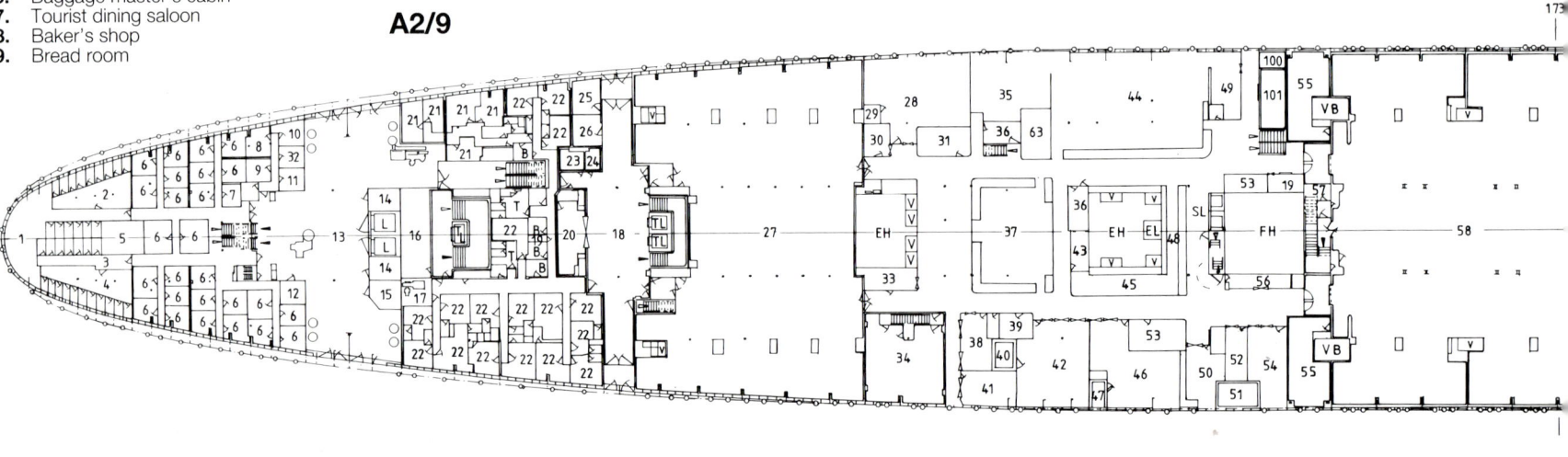

A2/10

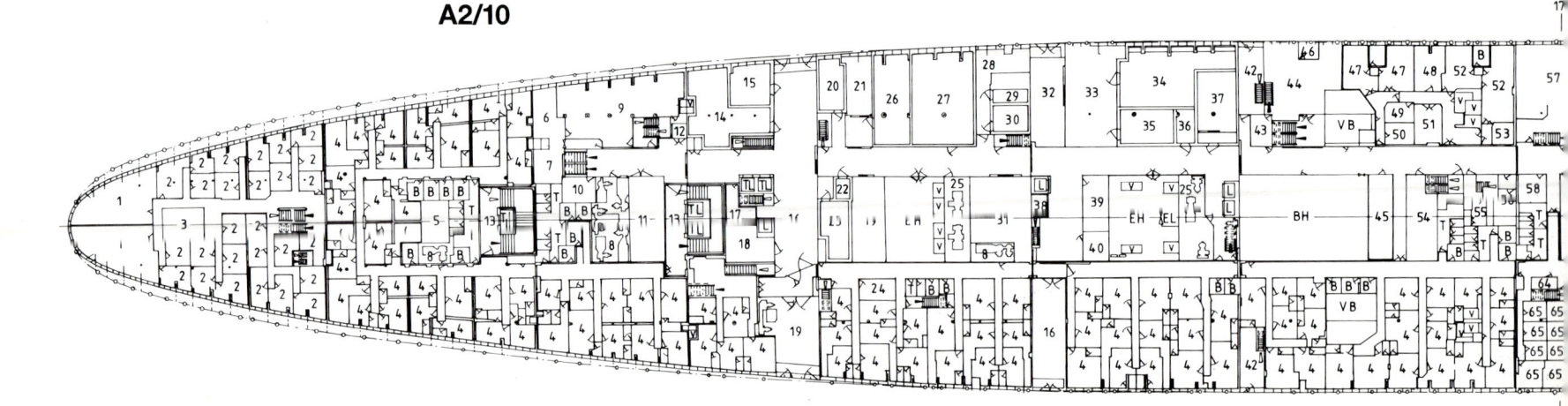

96. Seamen's mess
97. Seamen's cabin
98. Carpenter's store
99. Store
100. Chef's office
101. Silver room
102. Chief steward's office
103. Fire station
104. Chief third class steward's cabin
RD Revolving door
EH Engine hatch
FH Funnel hatch
CH Cargo hatch
H   Hatch
EL Engineers' lift
SL Service lift
TL Tourist lift
B   Bathroom
V   Vent
VB Vent to boiler room

A2/10 D deck
1. Stewards' accommodation
2. Leading stewards' accommodation
3. Steering gear trunk
4. Tourist class berths
5. Baggage lift trunk
6. Scullery
7. Pantry
8. Vent units
9. Engineers' dining room
10. Firestation
11. Mail assembling space
12. Mail chute
13. Tourist stairway
14. Ales and stout store
15. Ice store
16. Stores entrance
17. Chief engineer's office
18. Flour store
19. Soiled linen space
20. Ice cream store
21. Ripening room
22. Kosher meat store
23. Butter and milk store
24. Assistant chief steward's cabin
25. Engine room fans compartment
26. Fruit room
27. Vegetable and salad room
28. Fish preparing space
29. Fresh fish store
30. Frozen fish store
31. Linen drying and sorting room
32. Meat preparing space
33. Butcher's shop
34. Fresh meat and poultry house
35. Frozen meat and poultry house
36. Cold meats
37. Bacon, eggs and storekeeper's provisions
38. Second engineer's office
39. Empty cans store
40. Second steward's store
41. Lift machinery
42. Oil filling station
43. Wine and vinegar store
44. Grocery store
45. Root vegetable and charcoal store
46. Office
47. Female hospital ward
48. Dispensary
49. Dispenser's cabin
50. Nurses' cabin
51. Operating theatre
52. Male hospital ward
53. Hospital attendants' cabin
54. Potato store
55. Engineer's laboratory
56. Boot room
57. Printer's shop
58. Carpenter's shop
59. Chief printer's cabin
60. Printers' cabin
61. Plumbers' cabin
62. Carpenters' cabin
63. Chief carpenter's cabin
64. Locker
65. Third class berth
66. Firemen and trimmers' dining room
67. Greasers' dining room
68. Cabin class swimming pool
69. Writer's office
70. Drying room
71. Swimming pool attendant's room
72. Leading greasers' mess
73. Third class bar
74. Galley switchboard room
75. Kosher kitchen
76. Third class and crew's galley
77. Donkeyman and storekeeper's cabin
78. Electricians' cabin
79. Refrigerator attendant's cabin
80. Bosun's mess
81. Plumber's mess
82. Jewish cabin
83. Jewish supervisor's cabin
84. Engine room petty officer's cabin
85. Store
EH Engine hatch
CH Cargo hatch
BH Boiler hatch
H   Hatch
T   Toilet
B   Bathroom
VB Vent to boiler room

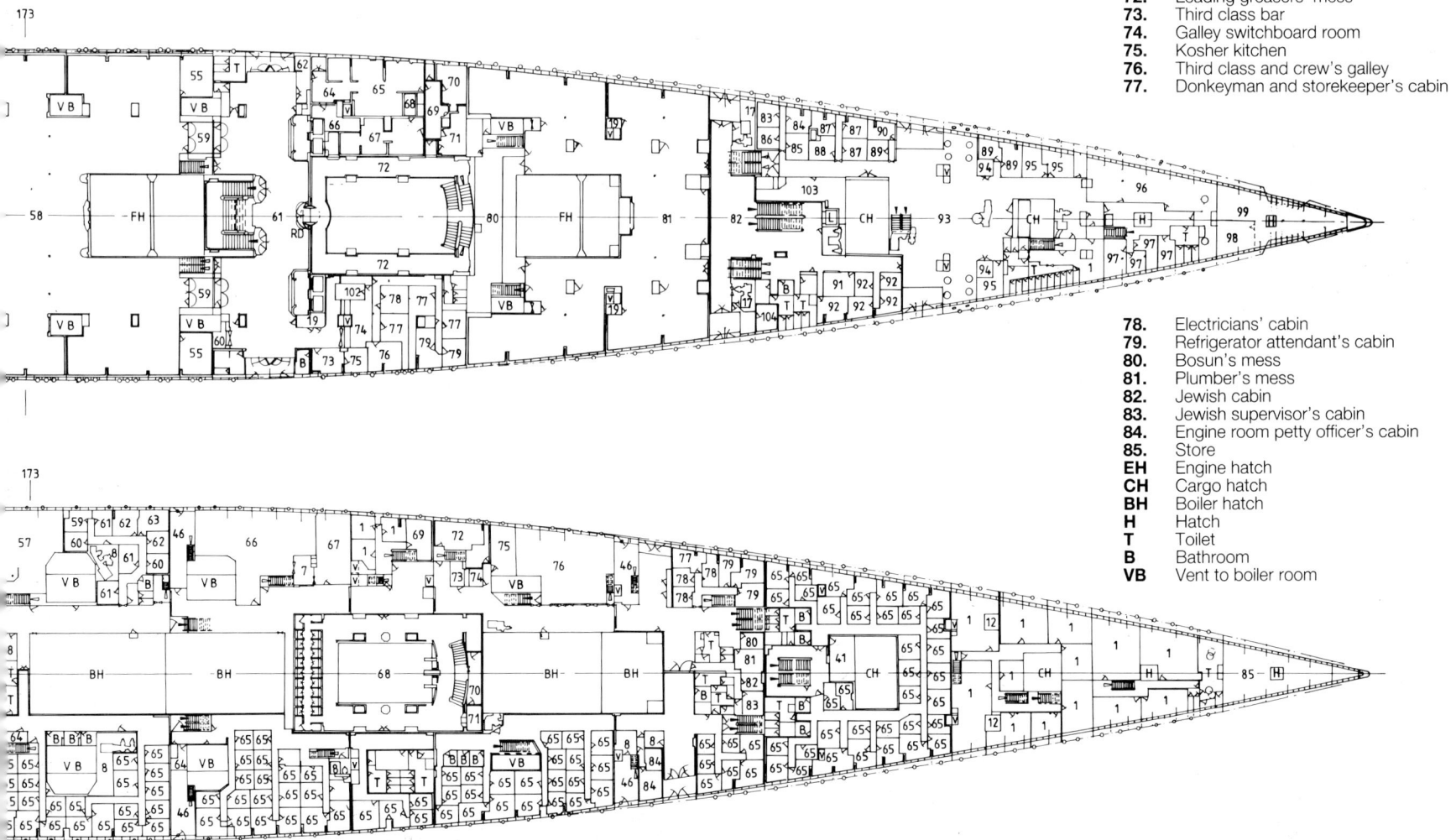

47

A General arrangement

A2/11 E deck

1. Stewards' accommodation
2. Steering gear trunk
3. Tourist class berth
4. Baggage lift trunk
5. Tourist class entrance
6. Engineers' accommodation
7. Stewardesses' accommodation
8. Mail chute
9. Engineers' washplace
10. Engineers' change room
11. Auxiliary switchboard
12. Dome over engine room condenser
13. Plan room
14. Plumbers' workshop
15. Plumbers' spares store
16. Electricians' workshop
17. Electrical store
18. Engineers' tank
19. Engineers' workshop
20. Dry tank
21. Ready use reserve feedtank
22. Lift motor space
23. Engineers' store
24. Storekeeper's office
25. Airlock
26. Tea and coffee store
27. Cereals and pickles store
28. Fan room
29. Air conditioning plant
30. Third class berth
31. Boiler makers' store
32. Vent unit
33. Crew's barber shop
34. Swimming pool tank
35. Greasers' cabin
36. Firemen's cabin
37. Electrical attendant's cabin
38. Leading stokers' cabin
39. Storekeeper's cabin
40. Trimmers' cabin
41. Firemen and trimmers' washplace
42. Mail discharge space
43. Specie room
44. Store
45. Low pressure generator room
46. Low pressure battery room

EH	Engine hatch
BH	Boiler hatch
CH	Cargo hatch
H	Hatch
EL	Engineers' lift
L	Lift
B	Bathroom

A2/11

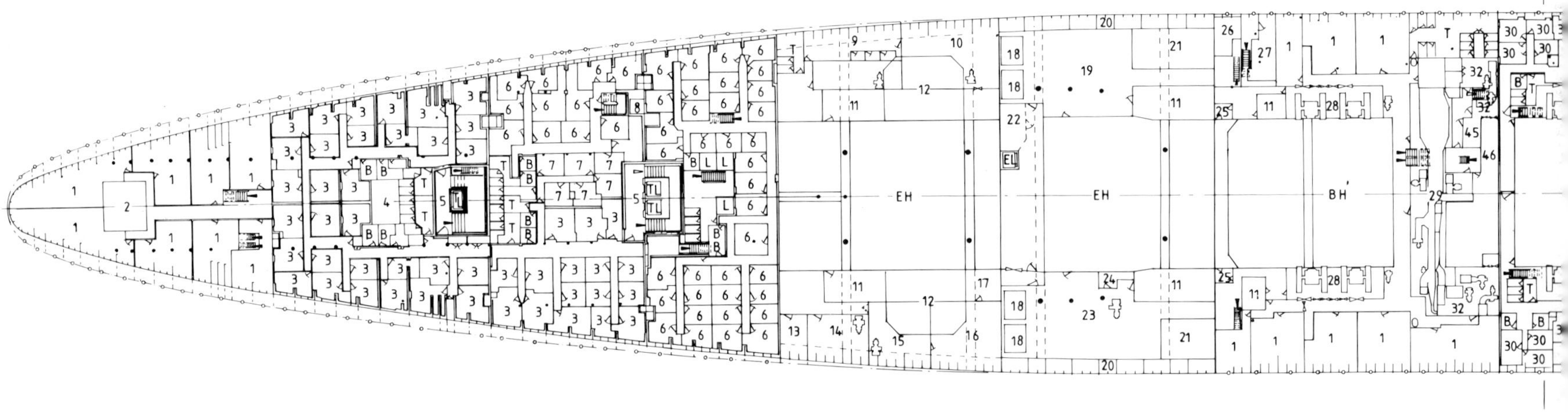

A2/12

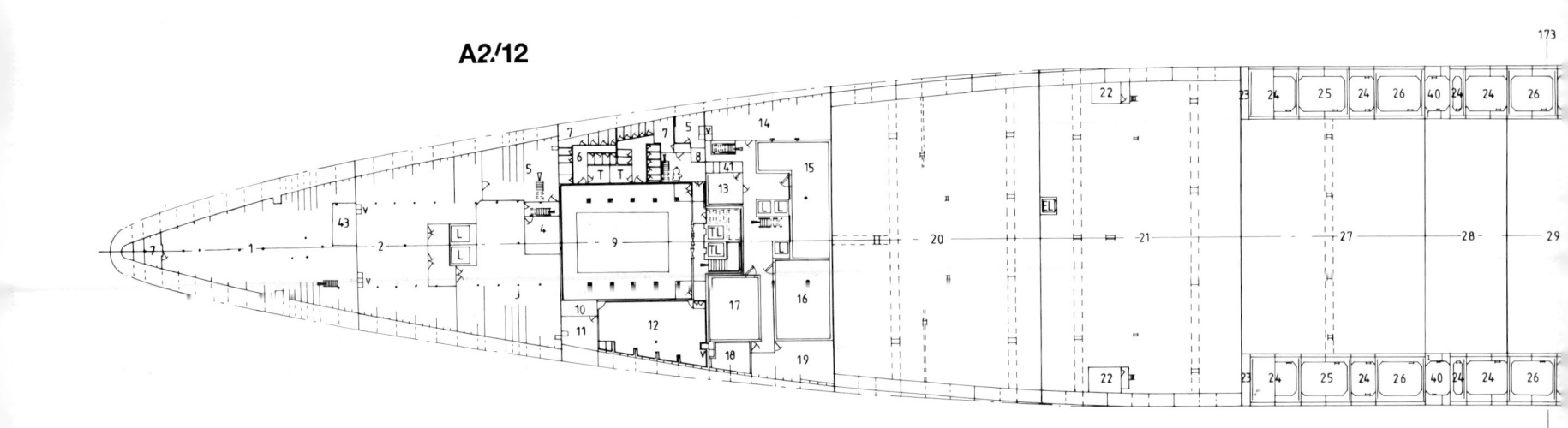

A2/12 F deck
1. Steering gear compartment
2. Baggage room
3. Space for bar refuse (empties)
4. Lift machinery
5. Furniture and joiners' store
6. Dressing boxes
7. Store
8. Mail chute
9. Tourist swimming bath
10. Swimming bath attendant's room
11. Drying room
12. Tourist gymnasium
13. Tobacco and cigarette store
14. Red wines and spirits store
15. Champagne and white wine store
16. Minerals store
17. Lager beer store
18. Chocolate and kiosk store
19. Glass and crockery store
20. After engine room
21. Forward engine room
22. Sewage plant
23. Cofferdam
24. Oil fuel tank
25. Overflow tank
26. Settling tank
27. No 5 boiler room
28. After turbo-generator room
29. No 4 boiler room
30. No 3 boiler room
31. Forward turbo-generator room
32. No 2 boiler room
33. No 1 boiler room
34. Motor cars or cargo space
35. No 2 hatch
36. Registered mail room
37. Mail space
38. No 1 hatch
39. Expansion trunk
40. Top of sewage tank
41. Cigar store
42. Escape from water-softening room
43. Switchboard
V   Vent

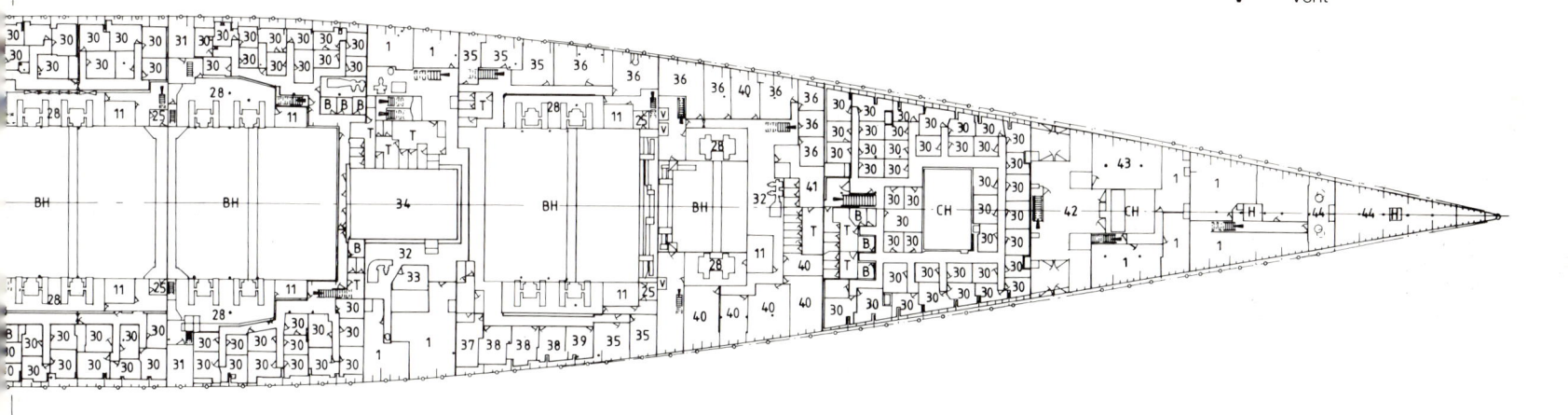

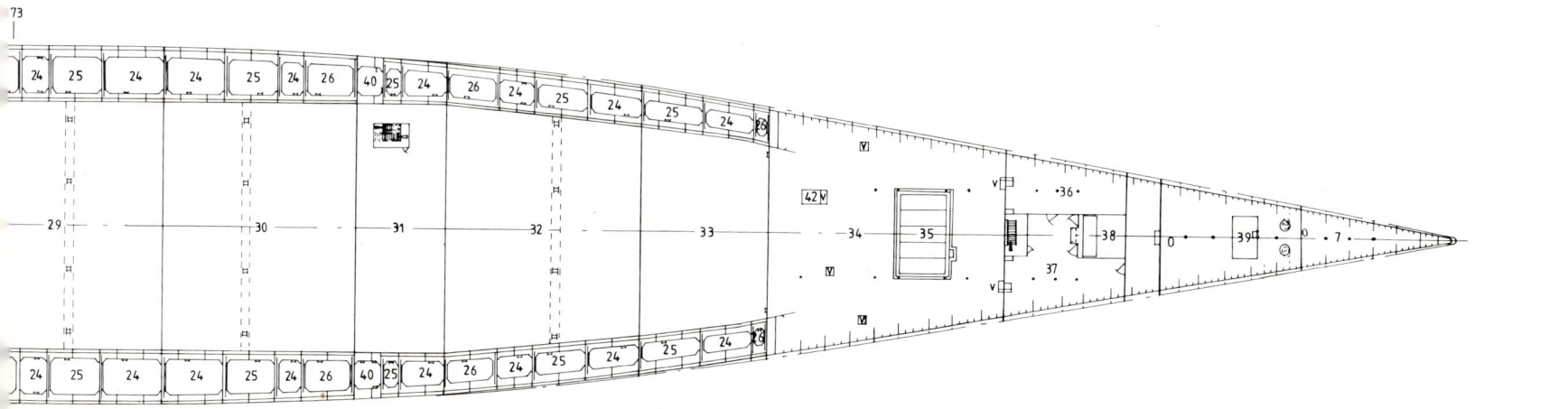

A General arrangement

A2/13 G deck

1. Watertight compartment
2. Baggage space
3. Tourist swimming bath tank
4. Cherbourg mail space
5. Cherbourg mail and baggage space
6. Lift motor
7. Linen store
8. After engine room
9. Forward engine room
10. Dry tank
11. Cofferdam
12. Oil fuel tank
13. Overflow tank
14. Settling tank
15. No 5 boiler room
16. Sewage tank
17. After turbo generator room
18. No 4 boiler room
19. No 3 boiler room
20. Forward turbo generator room
21. No 2 boiler room
22. No 1 boiler room
23. Water-softening room
24. Domestic water tank
25. Fresh drinking water tank
26. Baggage or cargo space
27. No 2 hatch
28. Mail space
29. No 1 hatch
30. Deep tank
31. Chain locker
32. Forepeak

A2/13

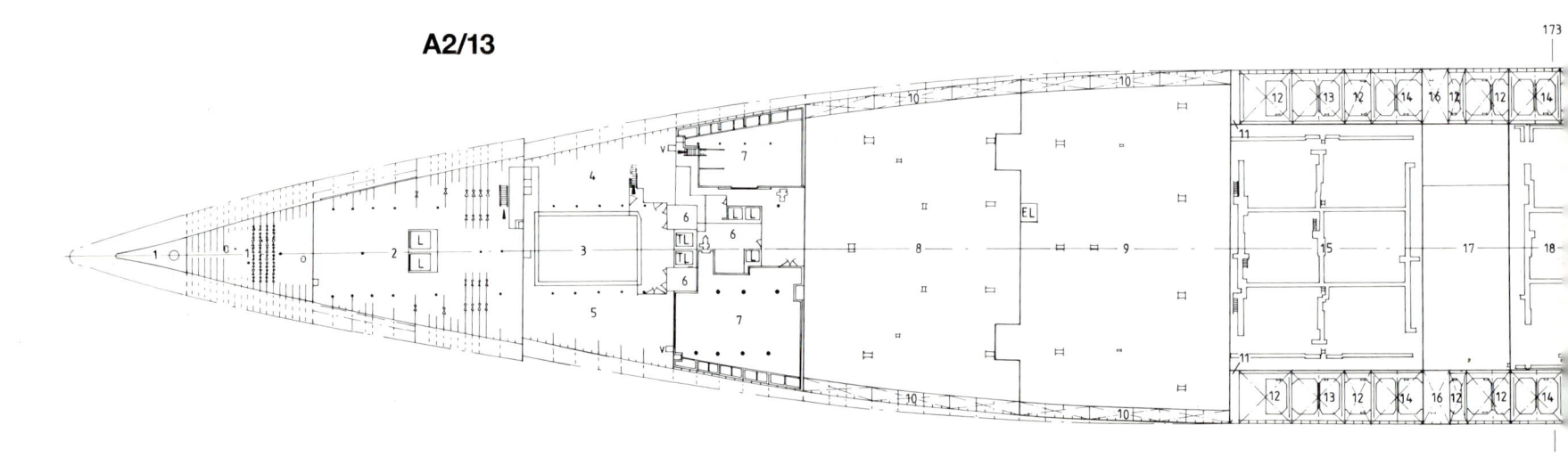

A2/14

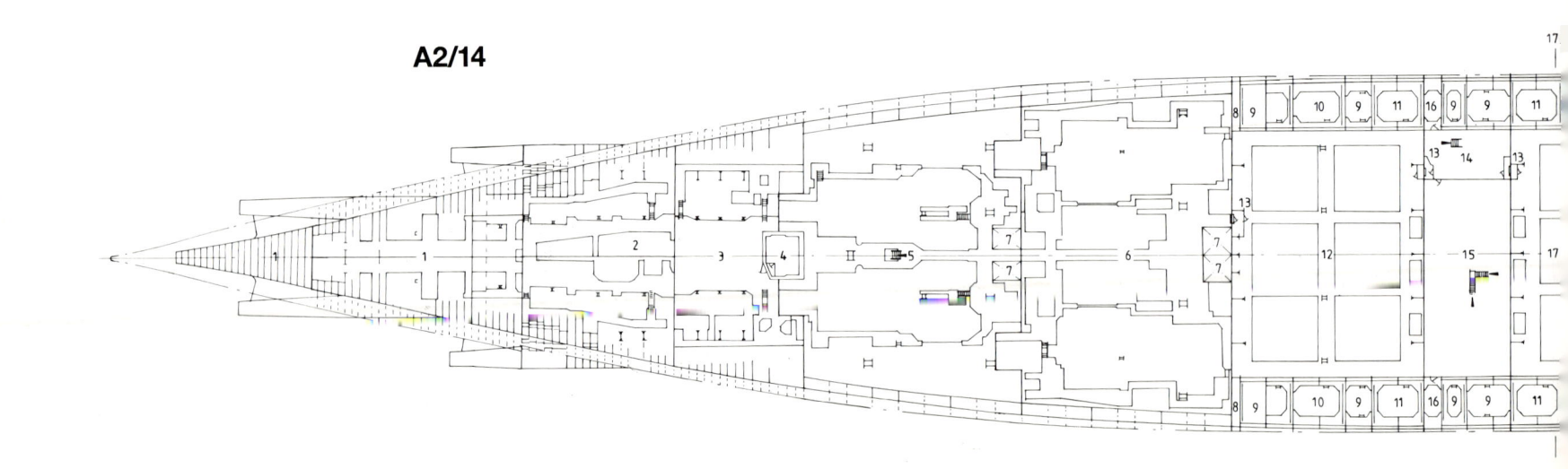

50

A2/14 H deck
1. Watertight compartment
2. Sewage tanks
3. Refrigerating machinery space
4. Evaporator room
5. After engine room
6. Forward engine room
7. Main feed tank
8. Cofferdam
9. Oil fuel tank
10. Overflow tank
11. Settling tank
12. No 5 boiler room
13. Airlocks
14. Pump compartment
15. After turbo-generator room
16. Sea valves recess
17. No 4 boiler room
18. No 3 boiler room
19. Forward turbo-generator room
20. No 2 boiler room
21. No 1 boiler room
22. Domestic water tank
23. Fresh drinking water tank
24. Water softening room
25. Baggage or cargo space
26. No 2 hatch
27. Mails space
28. No 1 hatch
29. Deep tank
30. Chain locker
31. Trimming tank

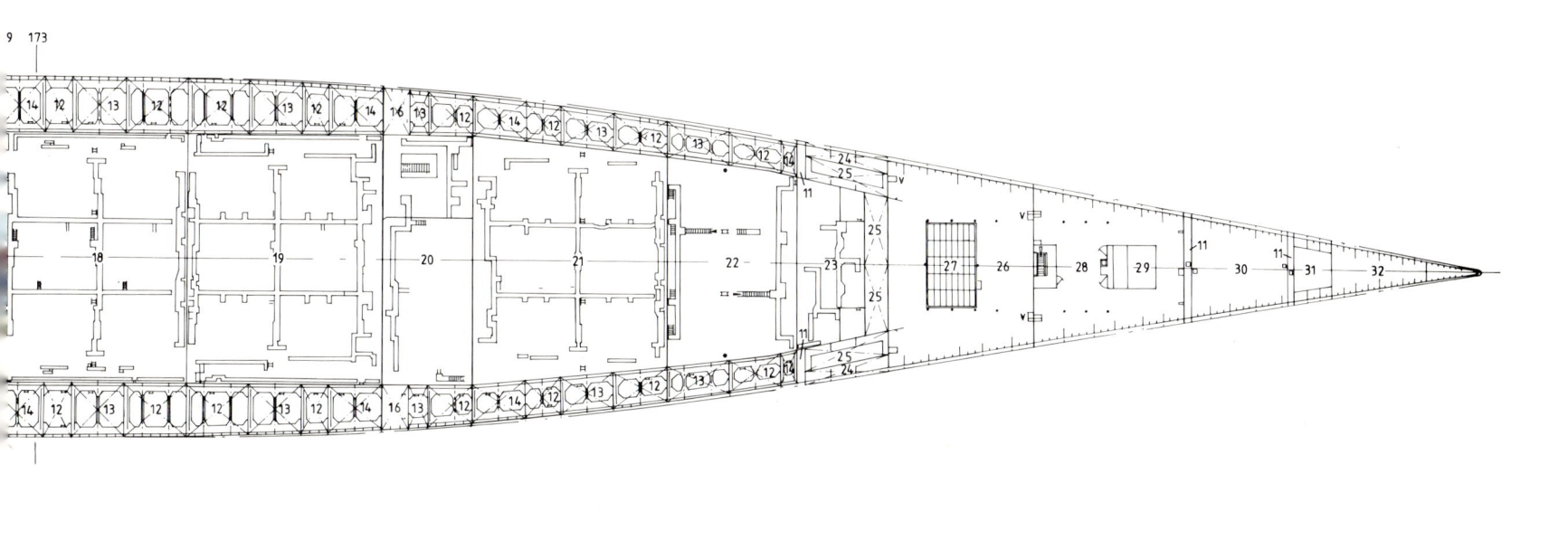

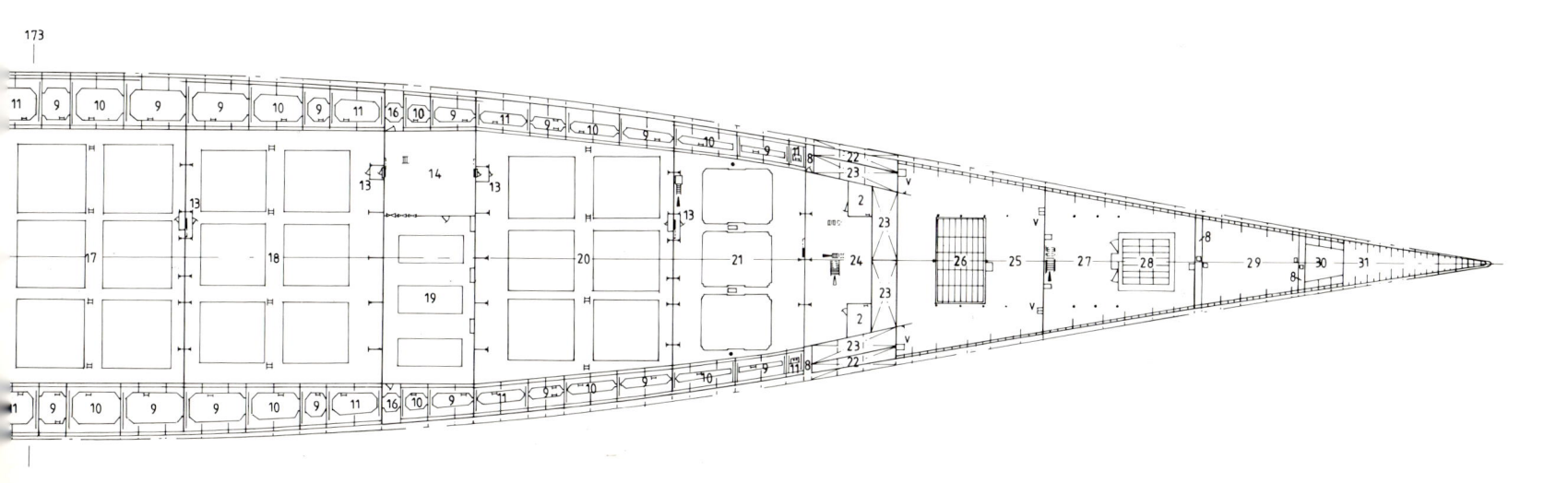

A General arrangement

A2/15 Tank top
1. Domestic water or water ballast
2. After engine room
3. Water ballast
4. Cofferdam
5. Oil drains
6. Reserve feed hotwell overflow tank
7. Forward engine room
8. No 5 boiler room
9. Reserve feed tank
10. After turbo-generator room
11. No 4 boiler room
12. No 3 boiler room
13. Forward turbo-generator room
14. No 2 boiler room
15. No 1 boiler room
16. Water-softening room
17. Fresh drinking water tank
18. No 2 cargo hold
19. No 1 cargo hold
20. Oil fuel or water ballast
21. Deep tank
22. Chain locker
23. Trimming tank

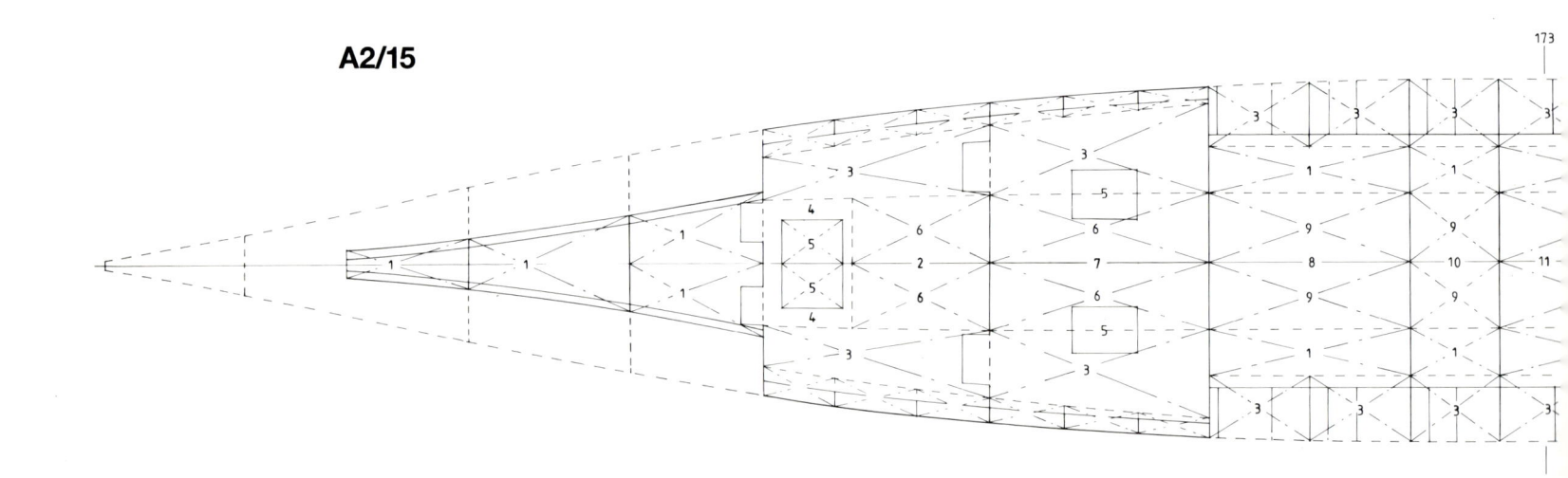

A2/15

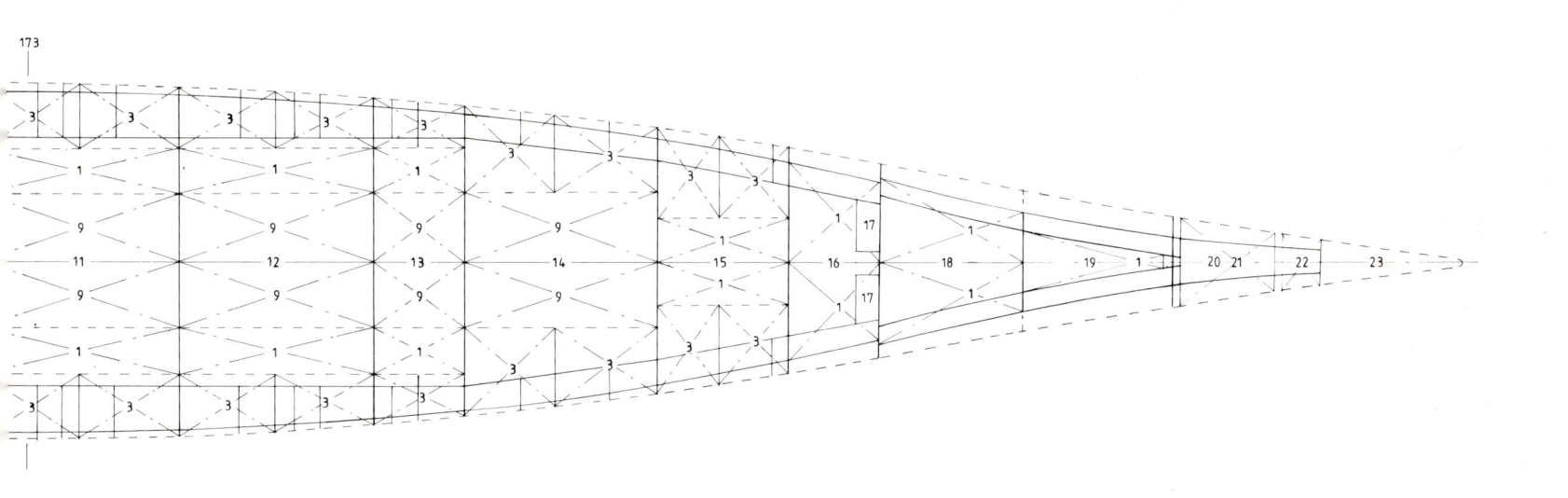

A General arrangement

A3/1

A3 WARTIME APPEARANCE, LATE 1942 TO 1945

A3/1 Plan

A3/2 External profile

1. 20mm Oerlikon position
2. 3in HA gun
3. Extra lifeboats
4. Carley floats
5. Life floats dispersed about upper decks
6. Type 273 radar office and aerial
7. Degaussing coil
8. 6in gun
9. 40mm Bofors twin Mk1
10. Mk 51 director
11. Rocket launcher
12. Armour plating

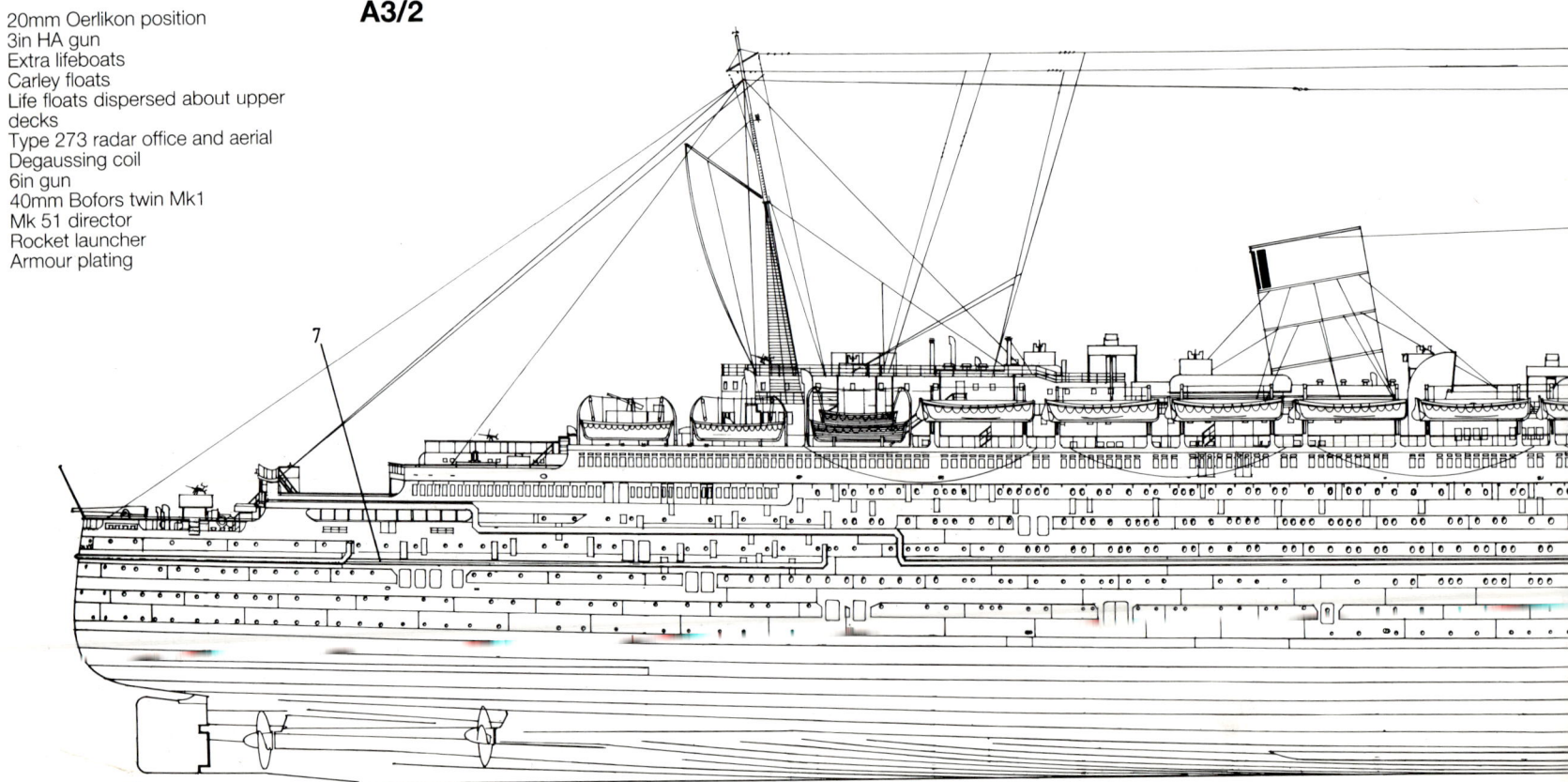

A3/2

54

55

B Hull construction

B1 LINE AND BODY PLAN

B1/1

B1/1 Lines (1/400 scale)

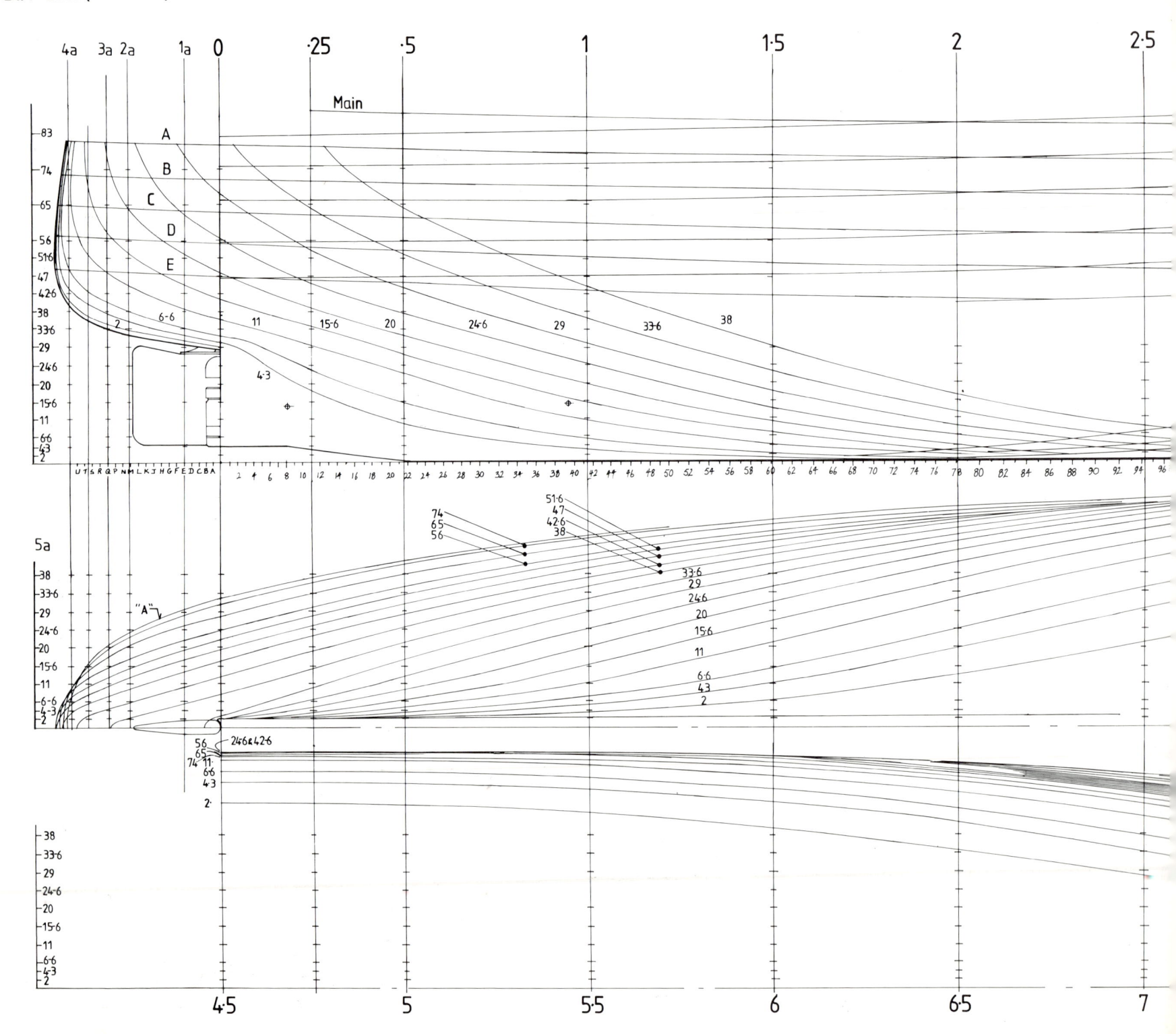

57

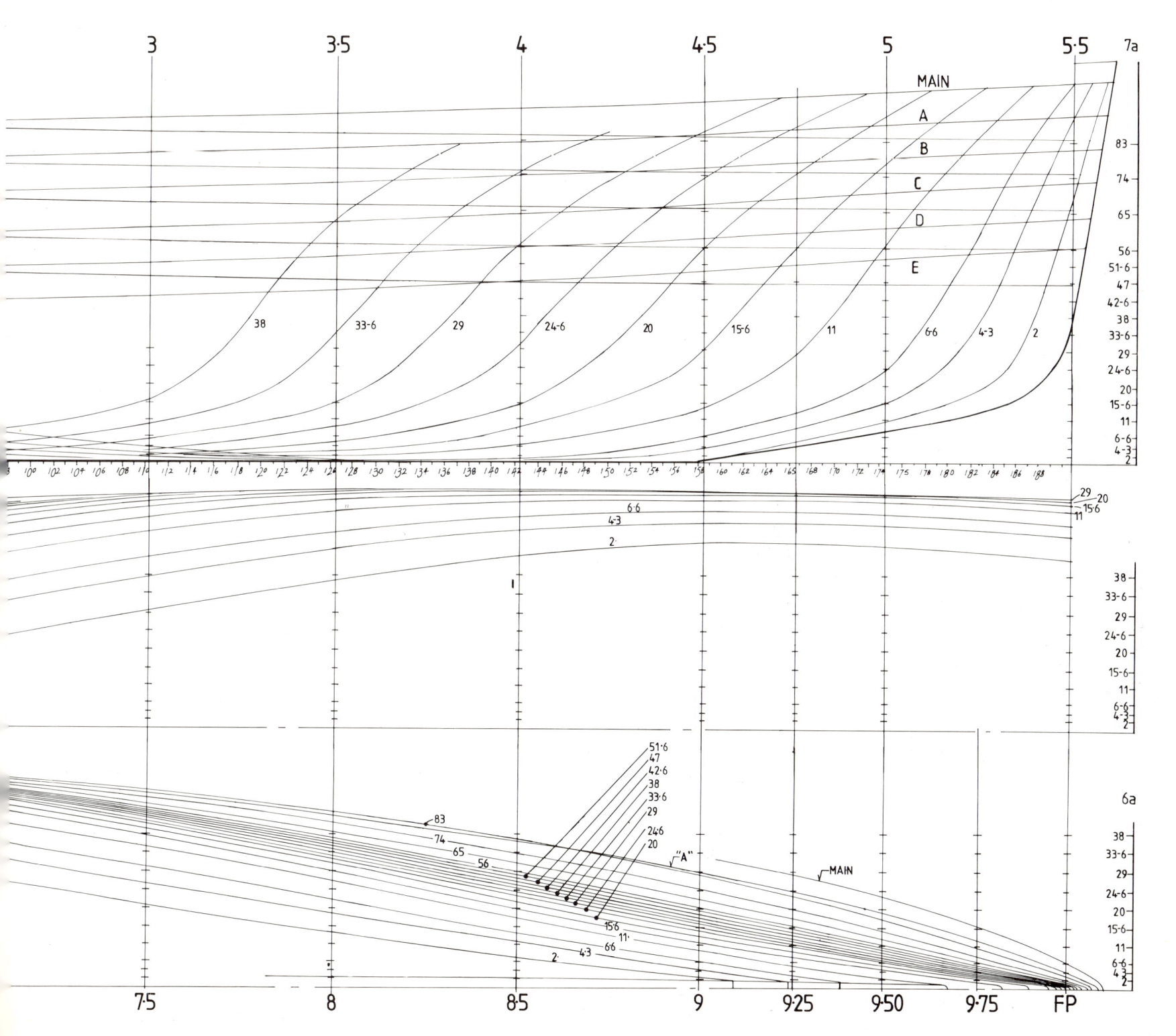

B Hull construction

B1/2 Body plan (1/200 scale)

- **1a.** 10ft aft of 0 (after perpendicular)
- **2a.** 20ft aft of 0
- **3a.** 30ft aft of 0
- **4a.** 40ft aft of 0
- **5a.** Buttock lines
- **6a.** Bow lines
- **7a.** Waterlines
- **8a.** 7½in double riveted lap
- **9a.** 6¾in double riveted lap
- **10a.** 9½in triple riveted lap
- **11a.** 12in riveted lap
- **12a.** Promenade deck
- **13a.** Centreline of sidelights

B2 FLAT KEEL PLATE AND CENTRE GIRDER (all drawings 1/200 scale except as noted)

- **B2/1** After end side elevation
- **B2/2** Plan
- **B2/3** Middle section side elevation
- **B2/4** Plan

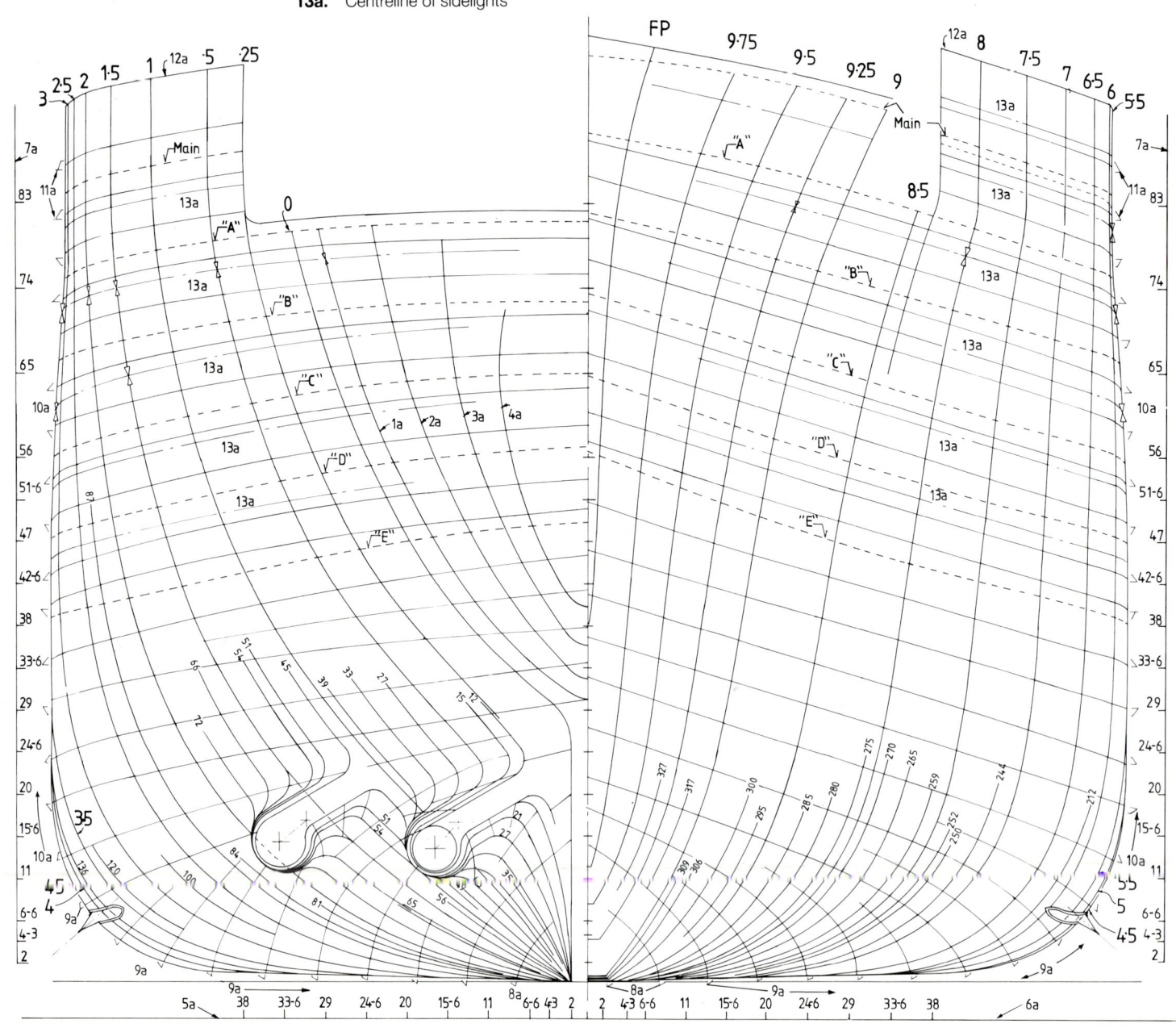

B1/2

B2/1

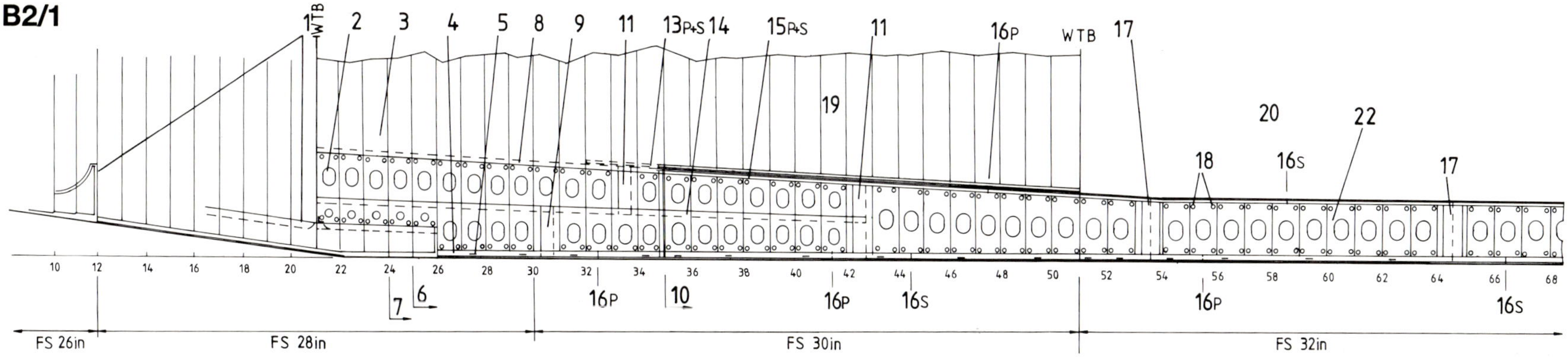

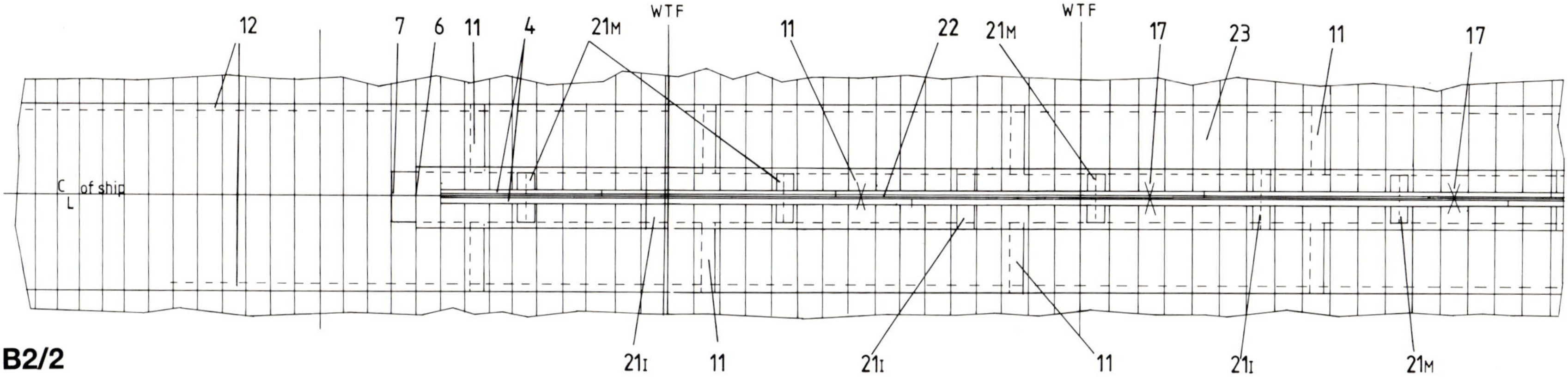

B2/2

B2/3

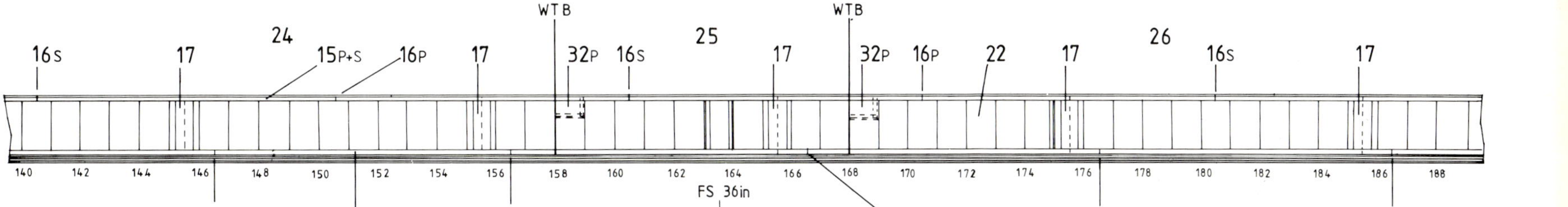

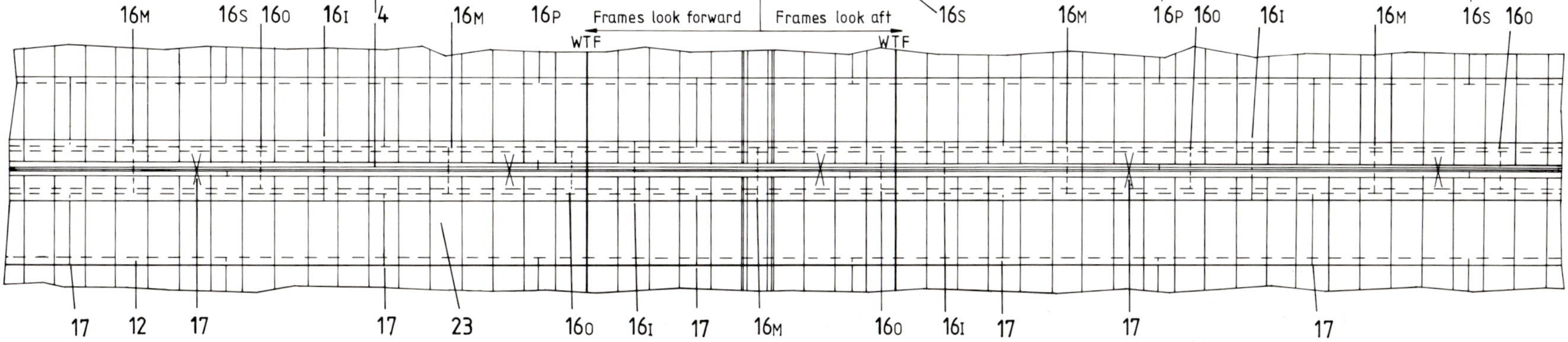

B2/4

B Hull construction

B2/5 Forward end side elevation

B2/6 Plan

1. Stern frame
2. Lightening holes
3. Centre longitudinal bulkhead
4. Bottom centre girder angle
5. Drainholes
6. End of inner keel plate
7. End of middle keel plate
8. Riveted seam
9. Triple riveted lap
10. End of double bottom
11. Quadruple riveted lap
12. Riveted landing
13. Angle bar to tank top
14. Riveted lap
15. Top centre girder angle
16. Butts
17. Triple riveted double buttstraps
18. Airholes
19. Tunnel
20. Fresh water tanks
21. Triple riveted buttstrap
22. Centre girder
23. Garboard strake
24. No 5 boiler room
25. No 3 auxiliary machinery room
26. No 4 boiler room
27. Cargo
28. Deep tank
29. Chain locker
30. End of outer keel plate
31. Steam casting
32. Drainwell
FS Frame spacing
WTB Watertight bulkhead
WTF Watertight floor
OTB Oil-tight bulkhead
S Starboard
P Port
I Inner keel plate
M Middle keel plate
O Outer keel plate

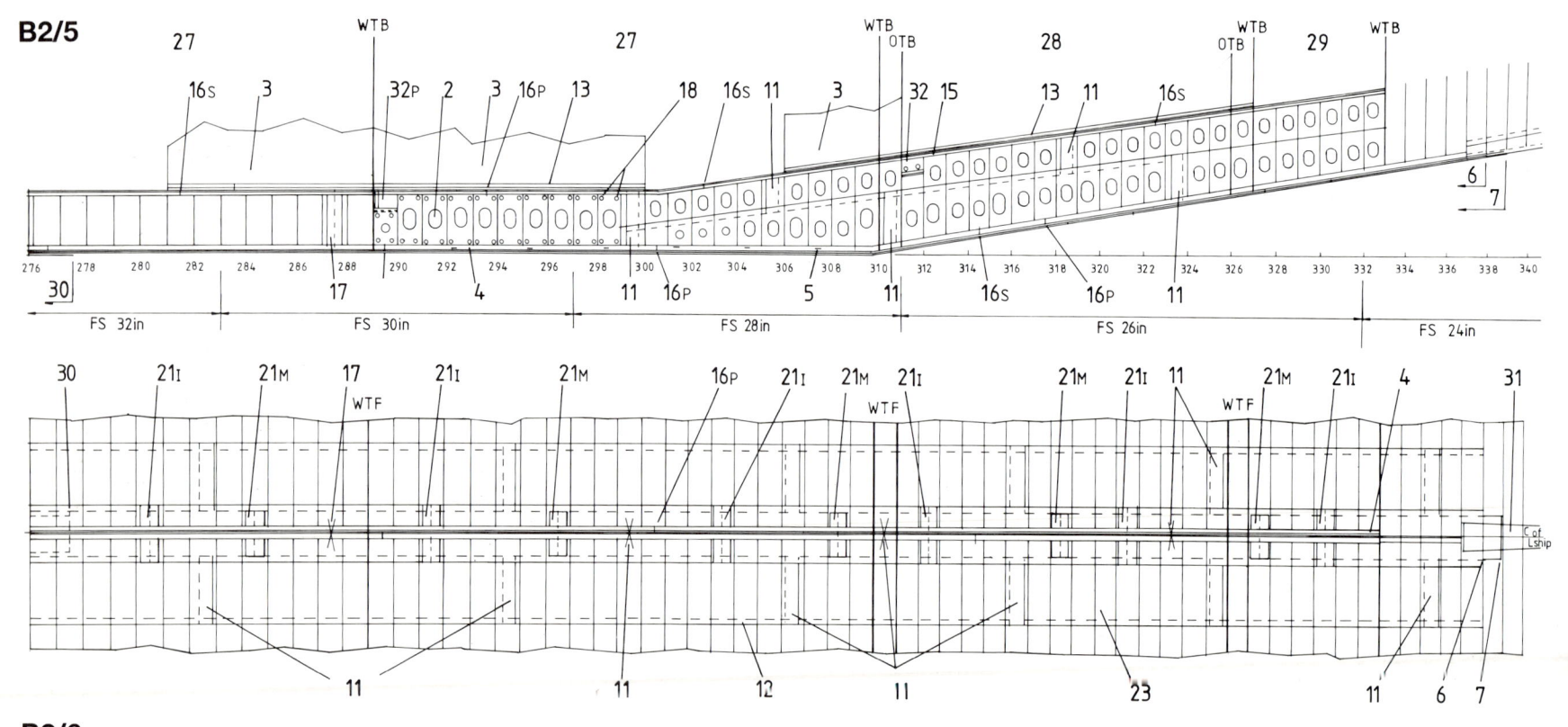

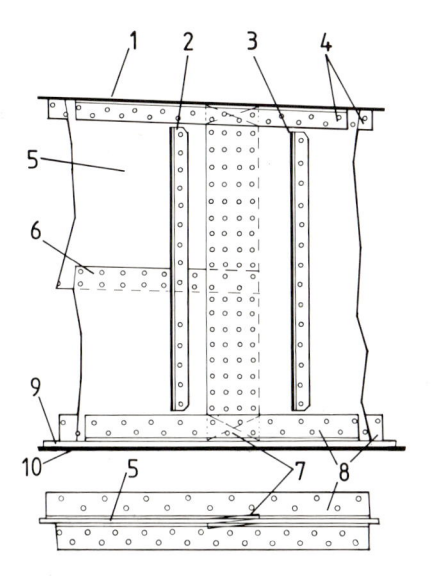

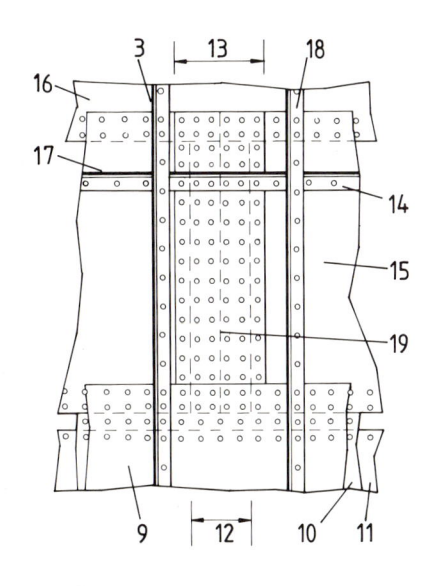

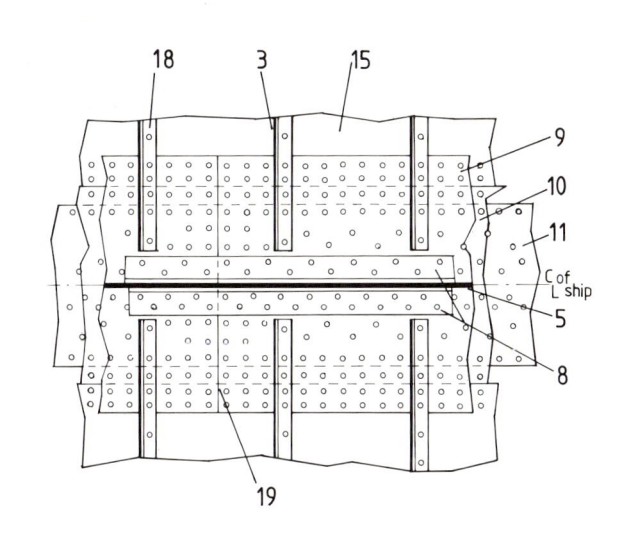

B2/7

B2/8

B2/9

B2/7 Elevation, showing quadruple riveted butt lap on the centre girder at the forward and after ends (1/50 scale)

B2/8 Plan of triple riveted double buttstraps straps on garboard strake (1/50 scale)

B2/9 Plan of riveted butts in way of inner, middle and outer keel plates (1/50 scale)

B2/10 Section through centre girder (1/50 scale)

B2/11 Elevation of centre girder riveted double buttstraps (1/50 scale)

1. Tank top
2. Vertical floor angle
3. Vertical floor plate
4. Centre girder top angle
5. Centre girder
6. Riveted lap
7. Scarphed butt
8. Centre girder bottom angle
9. Inner keel plate
10. Middle keel plate
11. Outer keel plate
12. Outer buttstrap
13. Inner buttstrap
14. Intercostal girder angle
15. Garboard strake
16. Shell plating
17. Intercostal girder plate
18. Frame angle
19. Butt joint
20. Lightening holes
21. Airhole
22. Vertical floor plate top angle
23. Double butt strap
24. Middle keel buttstrap
25. Inner keel buttstrap
26. Drainwell
27. Angle bar
28. Watertight floor

B2/10

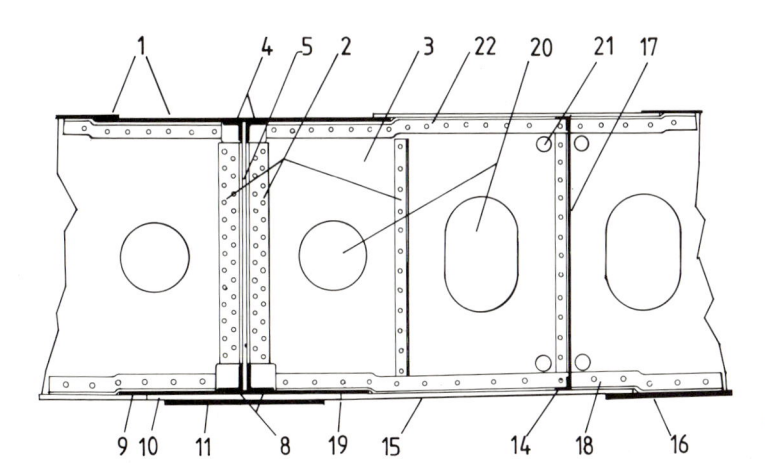

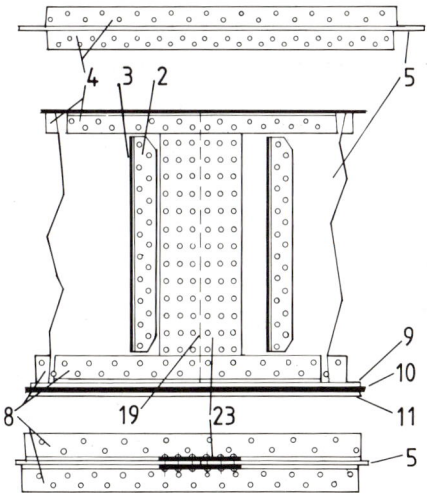

B2/11

61

B Hull construction

B2/12 Section through keel plates in way of buttstraps at forward and after ends (1/50 scale)

B2/13 Plan (1/50 scale)

B2/14 Section through forward end buttstraps (A) frame spacing 26in and 28in (B) frame spacing 30in (1/50 scale)

B2/15 Connection of watertight floors to centre girder forward and after ends (1/50 scale)

B2/16 Connection of watertight floors to centre girder between frames 55 and 255 (1/50 scale)

B2/17 Section through garboard strake butt lap at forward and after ends (1/50 scale)

B2/18 Plan of drainwell bottom (1/50 scale)

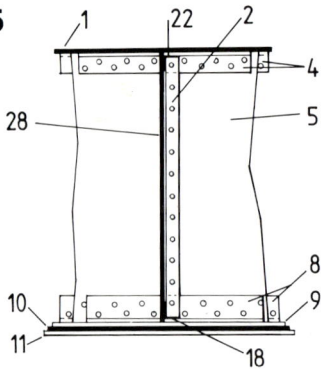

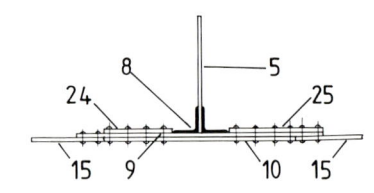

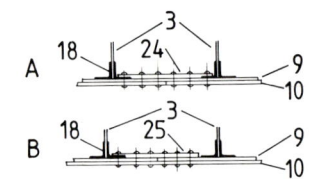

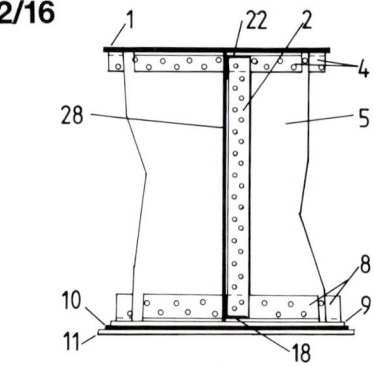

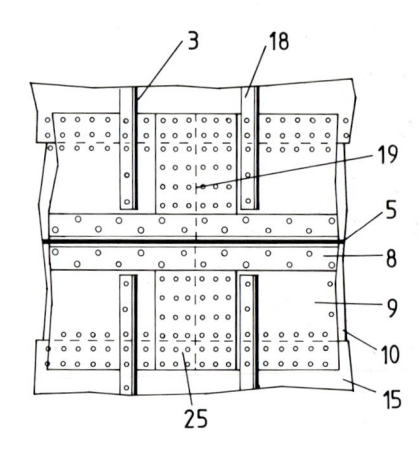

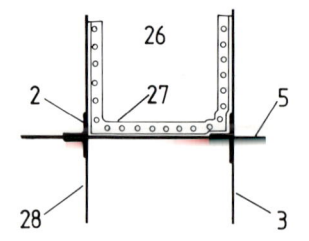

1. Tank top
2. Vertical floor angle
3. Vertical floor plate
4. Centre girder top angle
5. Centre girder
6. Riveted lap
7. Scarphed butt
8. Centre girder bottom angle
9. Inner keel plate
10. Middle keel plate
11. Outer keel plate
12. Outer buttstrap
13. Inner buttstrap
14. Intercostal girder angle
15. Garboard strake
16. Shell plating
17. Intercostal girder plate
18. Frame angle
19. Butt joint
20. Lightening holes
21. Airhole
22. Vertical floor plate top angle
23. Double butt strap
24. Middle keel buttstrap
25. Inner keel buttstrap
26. Drainwell
27. Angle bar
28. Watertight floor

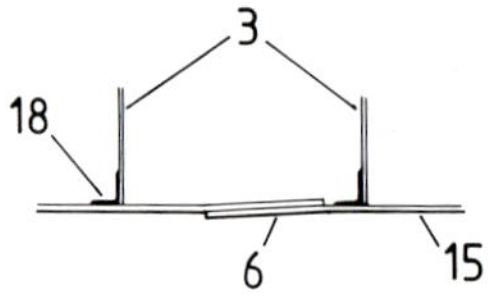

B2/19 General view showing vertical floor plates

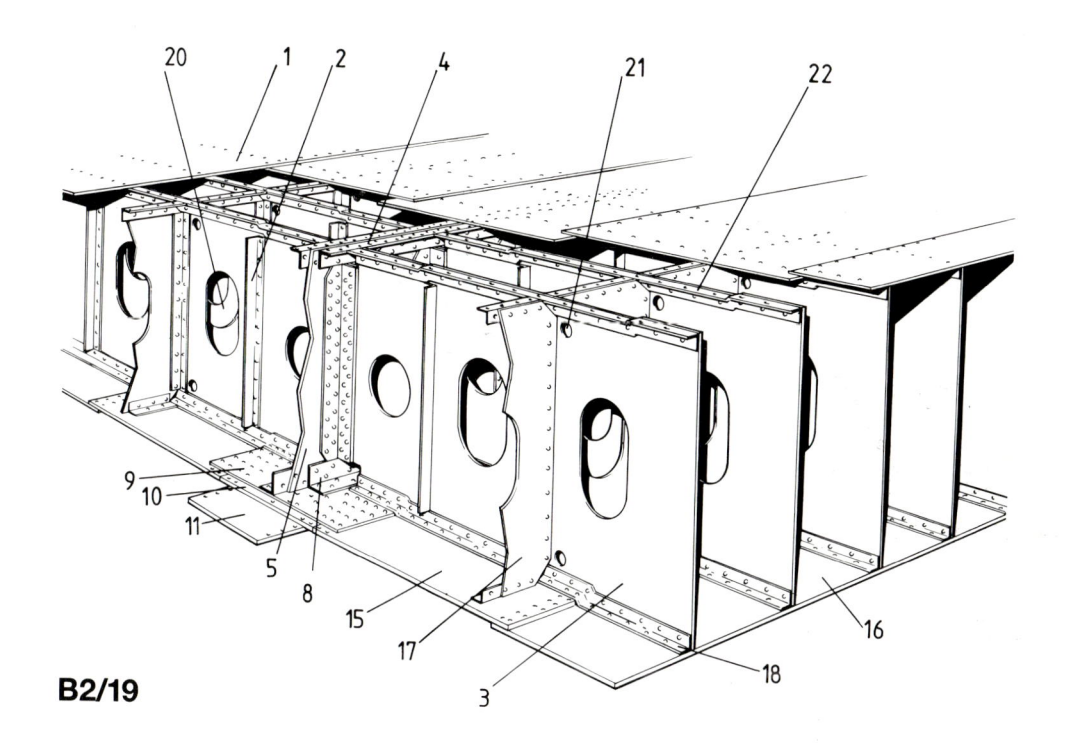

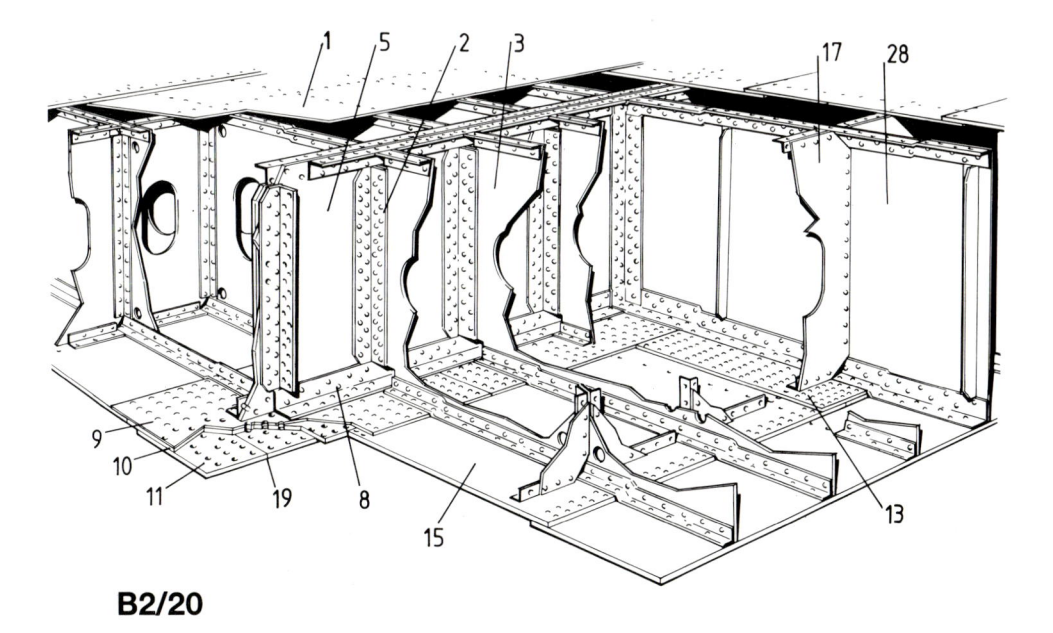

B2/19

B2/20 General view showing centre girder and watertight floor plate

B2/20

63

B Hull construction

B3 STRUCTURAL ARRANGEMENTS
(1/1400 scale)

1. 3½in × 3½in shell angle
2. 4in × 4in shell angle
3. 5in × 5in shell angle
4. 6in × 6in shell angle
5. 8in × 8in shell angle
6. 3½in × 3½in stringer angle
7. 4in × 4in stringer angle
8. 5in × 5in stringer angle
9. 6in × 6in stringer angle
10. 8in × 8in stringer angle
11. Curtain plate
12. 9in × 3in × 3in channel beam
13. 9in × 3½in × 3½in channel beam
14. 10in × 3½in × 3½in channel beam
15. 10in × 4in × 4in channel beam
16. 11in × 4in × 4in channel beam
17. No camber
18. 6in camber in full beam
19. 6in camber in width of deckhouse
20. Strong beams
- **EH** Engine hatch
- **EJ** Expansion joint
- **FH** Funnel hatch
- **G** Girder
- **H** Hatch
- **L** Lift
- **P** Pillar
- **S** Stairs
- **WTB** Watertight bulkhead
- **OTB** Oil-tight bulkhead

Steel plating thickness of deck is denoted in hundredths of an inch. Where two figures are given this indicates doubling of steel plating

- **B3/3** Sports deck
- **B3/4** Sun deck
- **B3/5** Promenade deck
- **B3/6** Main deck
- **B3/7** A deck

B3/1 Side elevation, showing web framing and bulkheads

B3/2 Side elevation, showing watertight bulkheads

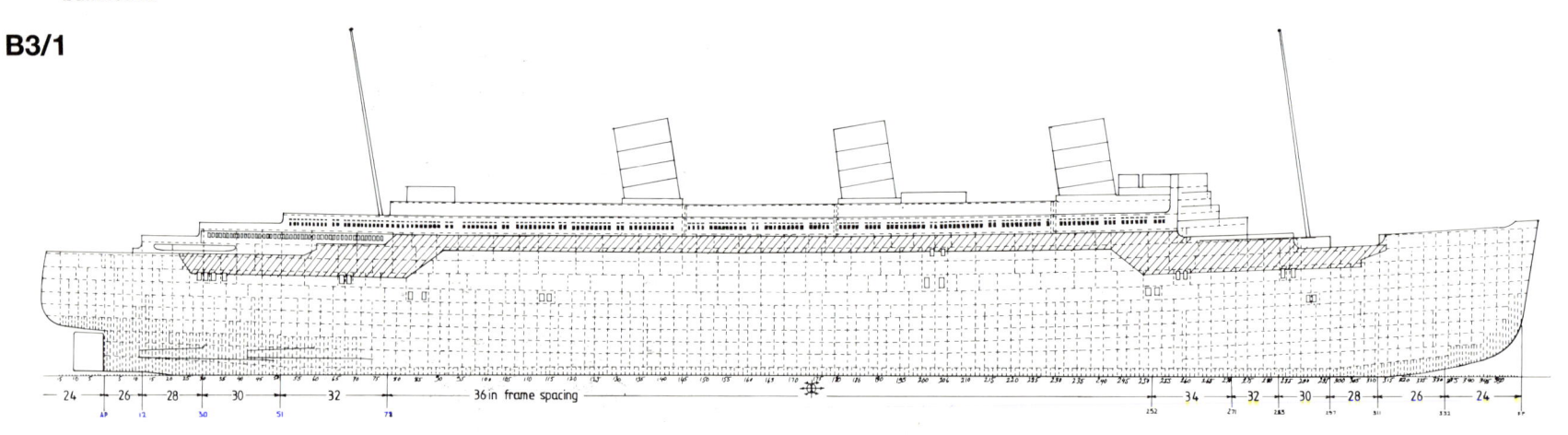

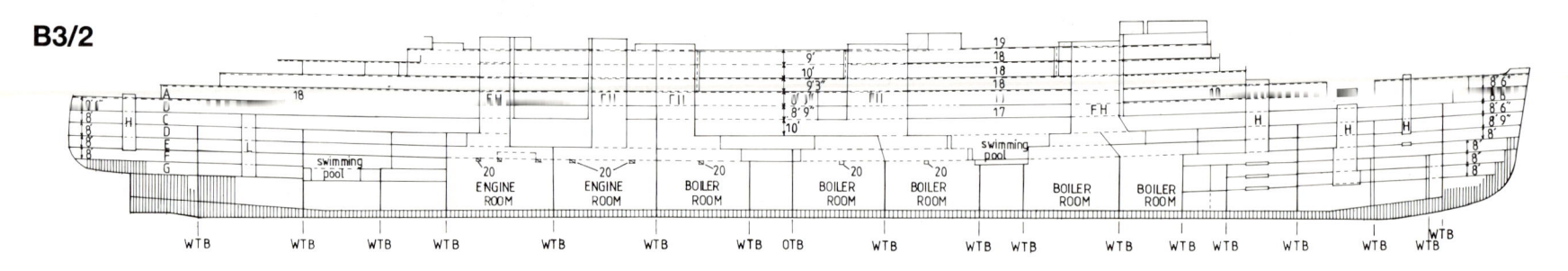

B3/1

B3/2

B3/3

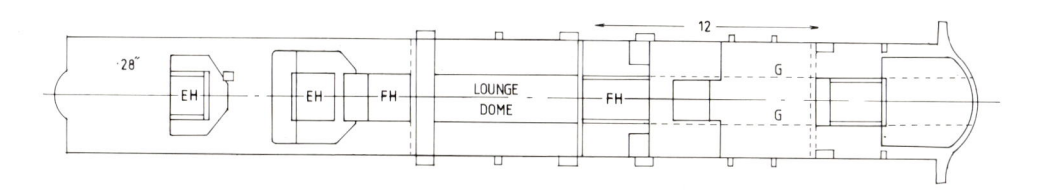

B3/4

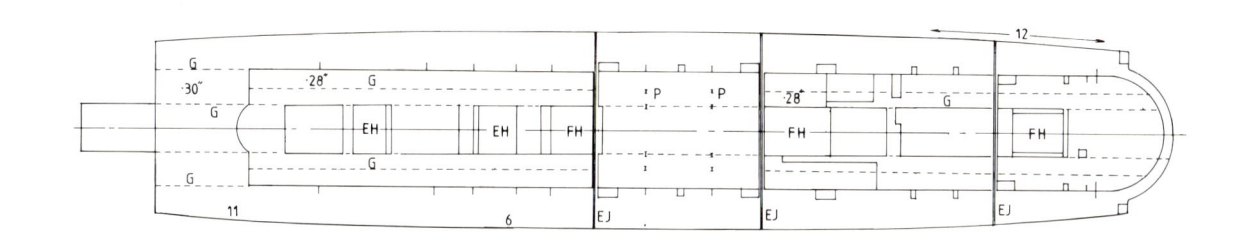

B3/5

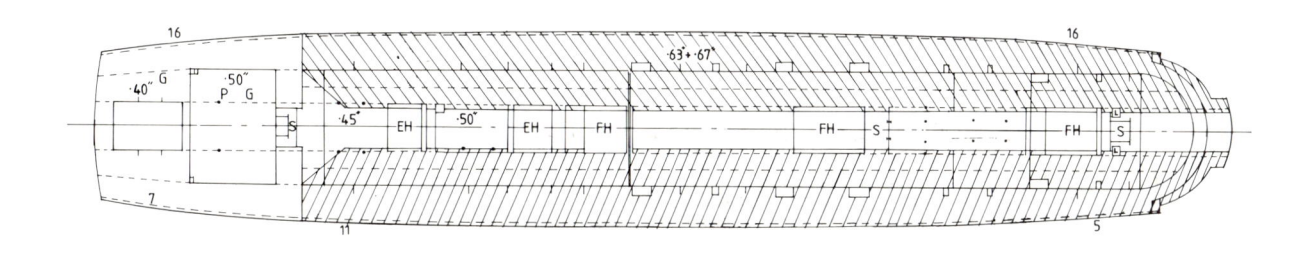

B3/6

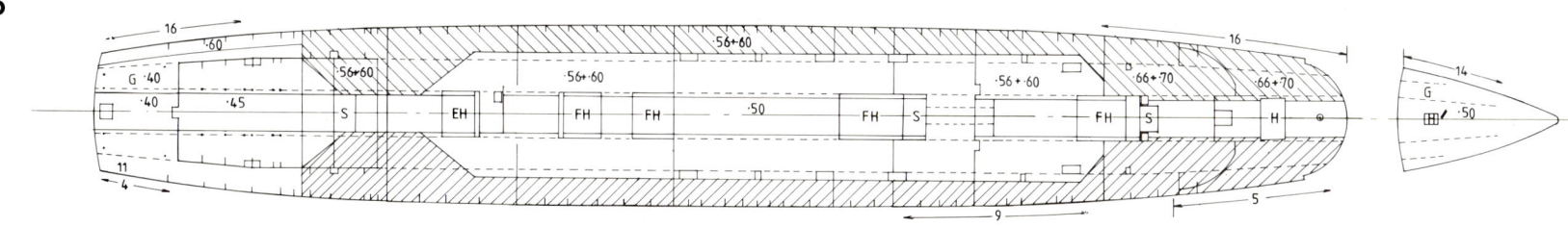

B3/7

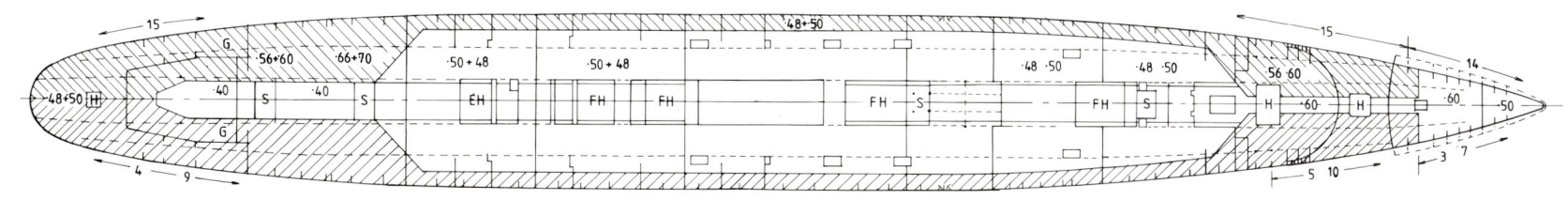

65

B Hull construction

B3/8   B deck
B3/9   C deck
B3/10 D deck
B3/11 E deck

1. 3½in × 3½in shell angle
2. 4in × 4in shell angle
3. 5in × 5in shell angle
4. 6in × 6in shell angle
5. 8in × 8in shell angle
6. 3½in × 3½in stringer angle
7. 4in × 4in stringer angle
8. 5in × 5in stringer angle
9. 6in × 6in stringer angle
10. 8in × 8in stringer angle
11. Curtain plate
12. 9in × 3in × 3in channel beam
13. 9in × 3½in × 3½in channel beam
14. 10in × 3½in × 3½in channel beam
15. 10in × 4in × 4in channel beam
16. 11in × 4in × 4in channel beam
17. No camber
18. 6in camber in full beam
19. 6in camber in width of deckhouse
20. Strong beams
EH   Engine hatch
EJ   Expansion joint
FH   Funnel hatch
G   Girder
H   Hatch
L   Lift
P   Pillar
S   Stairs
WTB Watertight bulkhead
OTB Oil-tight bulkhead

B3/8

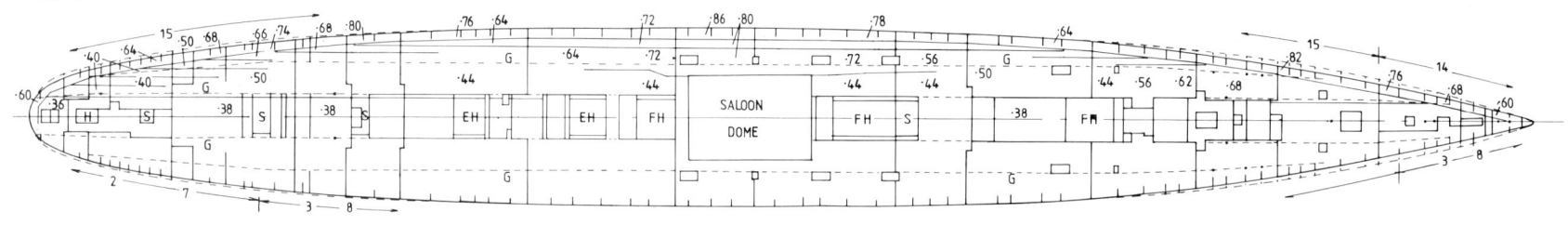

B3/9

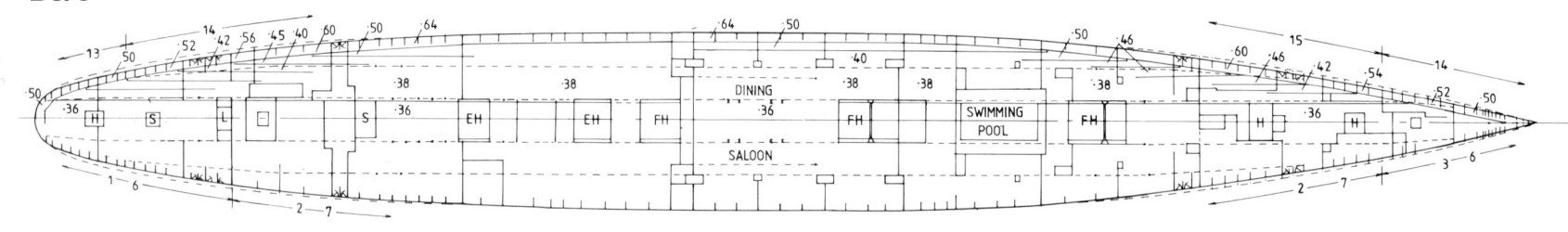

B3/10

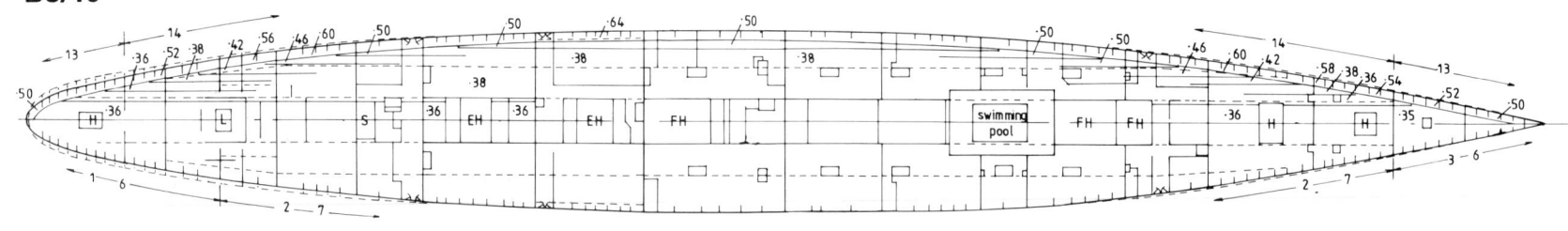

B3/11

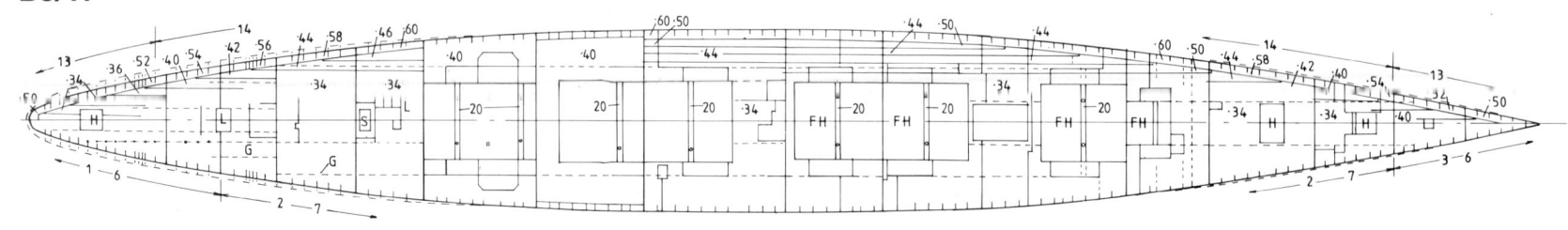

Steel plating thickness of deck is denoted in hundredths of an inch. Where two figures are given this indicates doubling of steel plating

B3/12 F deck

B3/13 G deck

B3/14 H deck

B3/15 Tank top

B3/12

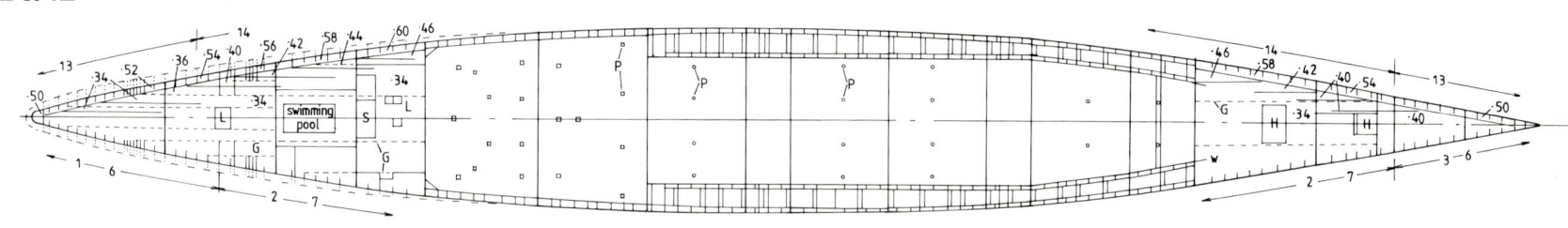

B3/13

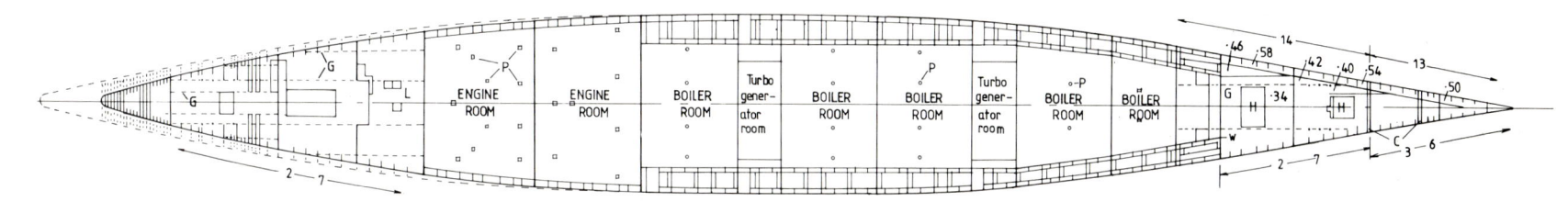

B3/14

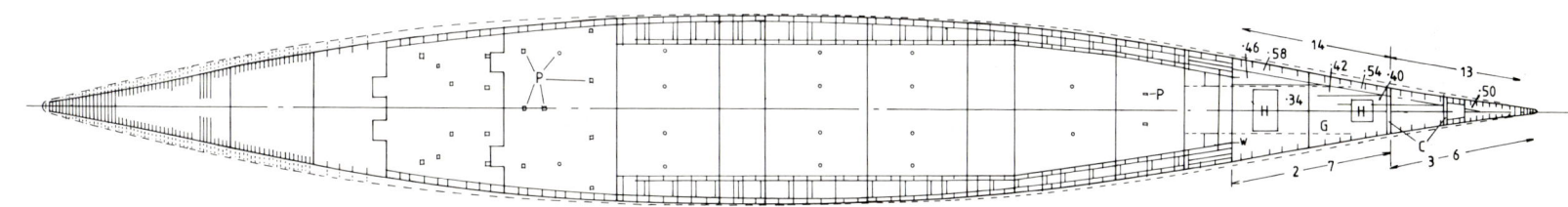

B3/15

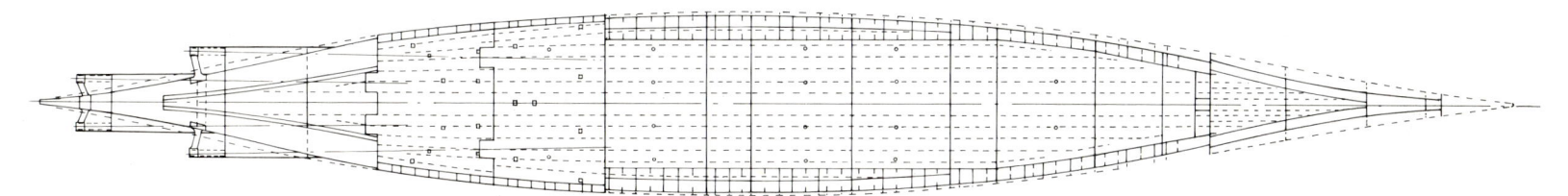

67

B Hull construction

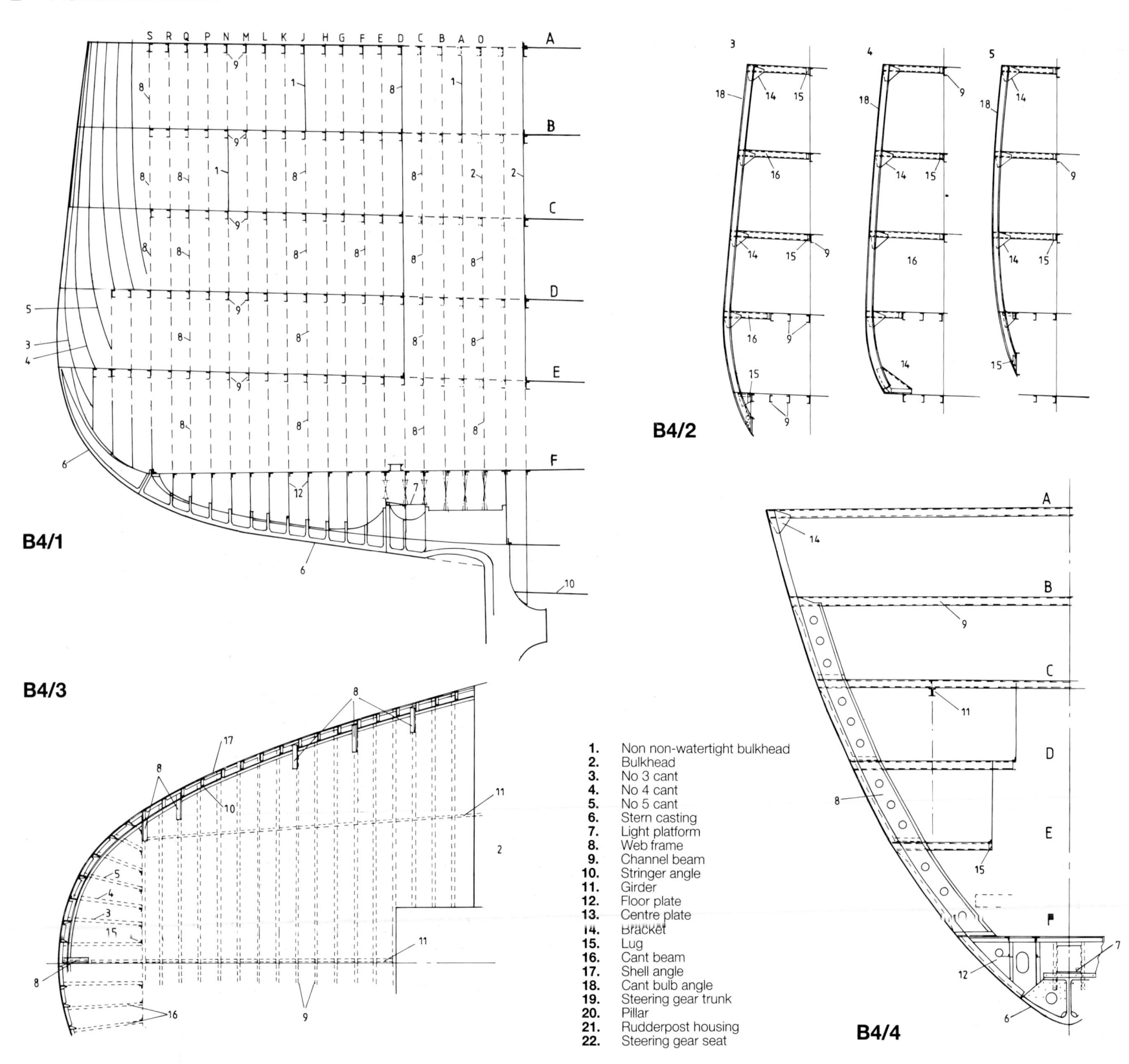

B4/1

B4/2

B4/3

1. Non non-watertight bulkhead
2. Bulkhead
3. No 3 cant
4. No 4 cant
5. No 5 cant
6. Stern casting
7. Light platform
8. Web frame
9. Channel beam
10. Stringer angle
11. Girder
12. Floor plate
13. Centre plate
14. Bracket
15. Lug
16. Cant beam
17. Shell angle
18. Cant bulb angle
19. Steering gear trunk
20. Pillar
21. Rudderpost housing
22. Steering gear seat

B4/4

B4 STERN CANTS AND AFTER END FRAMING (1/150 scale)

B4/1 Side elevation

B4/2 Stern cants

B4/3 Plan of C deck

B4/4 Section at frame C (looking aft)

B4/5 Section of centre cant (looking to port)

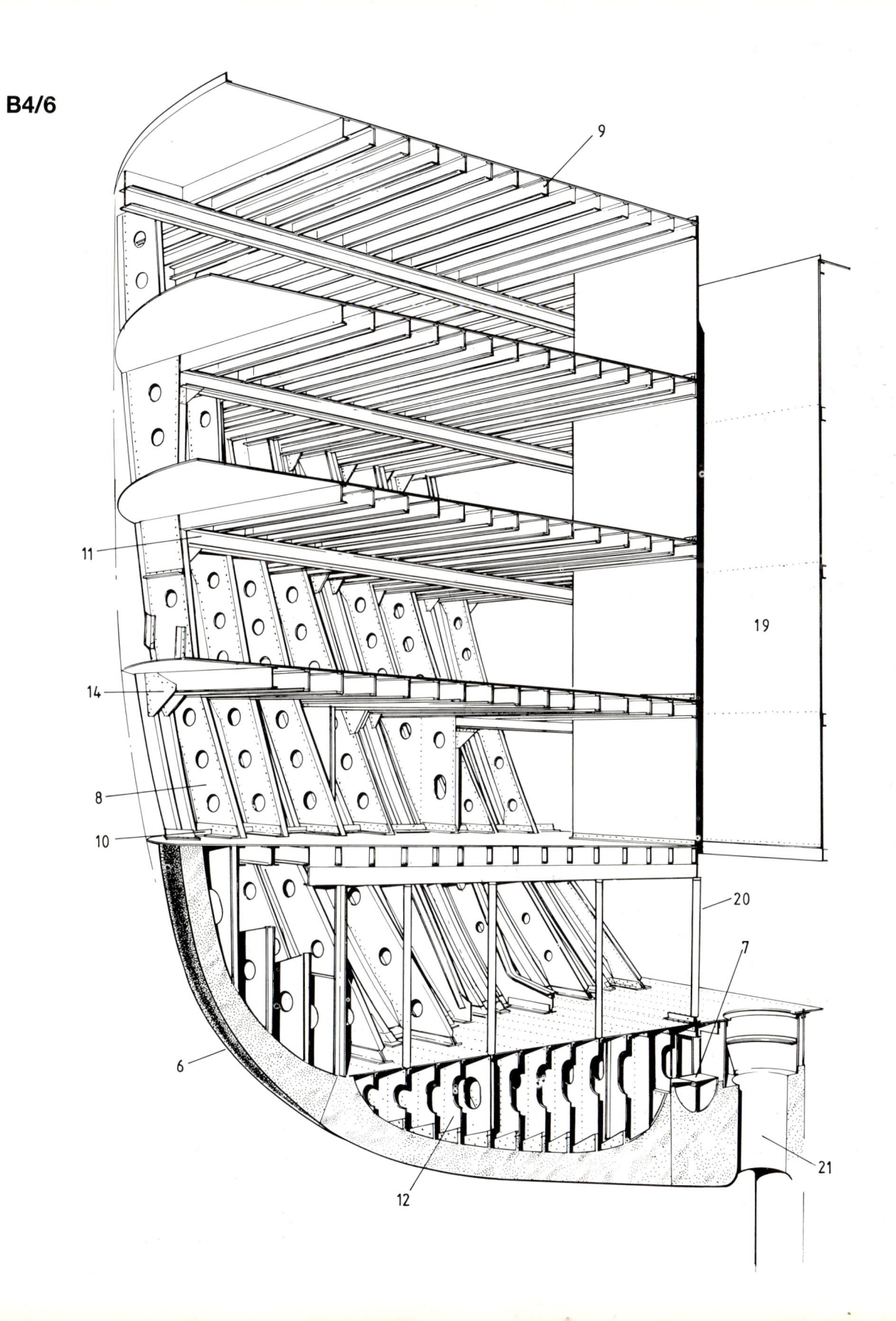

B4/6 Cutaway perspective view with stern cants removed

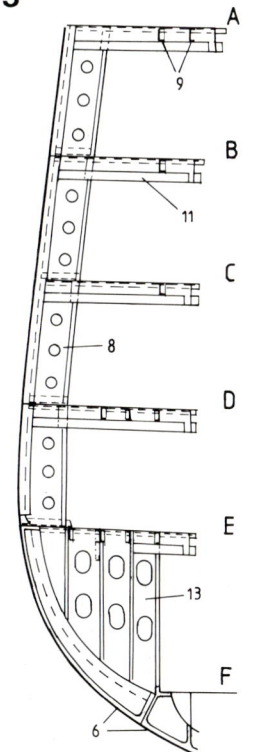

B Hull construction

B4/7 Cutaway perspective view with stern cants and interior bulkheads in place

1. Non non-watertight bulkhead
2. Bulkhead
3. No 3 cant
4. No 4 cant
5. No 5 cant
6. Stern casting
7. Light platform
8. Web frame
9. Channel beam
10. Stringer angle
11. Girder
12. Floor plate
13. Centre plate
14. Bracket
15. Lug
16. Cant beam
17. Shell angle
18. Cant bulb angle
19. Steering gear trunk
20. Pillar
21. Rudderpost housing
22. Steering gear seat

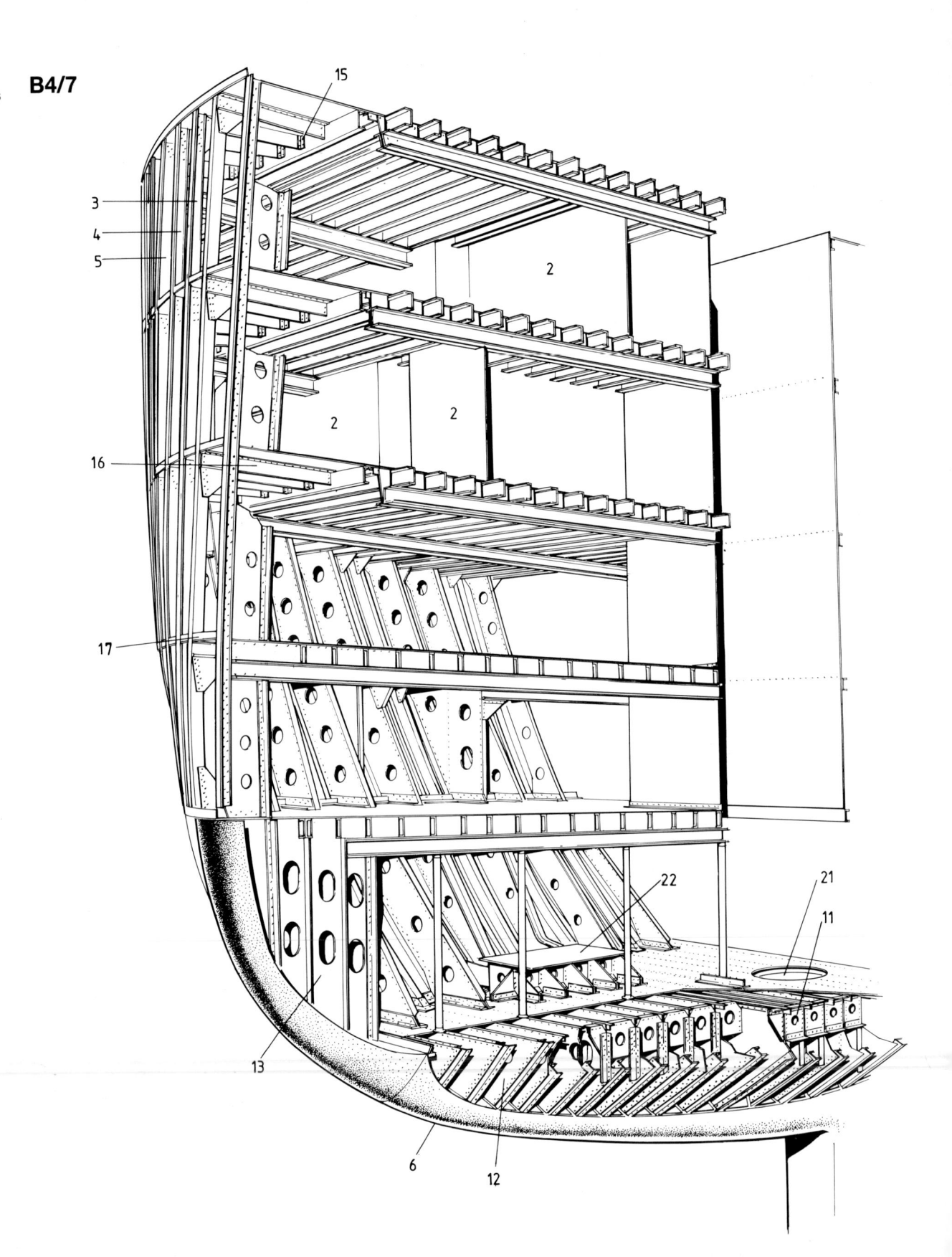

B5 MIDSHIPS HULL STRUCTURE

B5/1 Section where promenade deck is strength deck (1/200 scale)

1. Casing top
2. Funnel hatch
3. Wood deck planking
4. Deck plating
5. Casing
6. Stiffener
7. Web
8. Channel beam (every frame)
9. Waterway
10. Curtain plate
11. Fixed toplight
12. Sliding window
13. Deckhouse plating
14. Tube pillar (3 frames apart)
15. Bracket
16. Beam knees
17. Longitudinal girders
18. Side plating (doubled)
19. Shell angle
20. Web frame
21. Channel frame
22. Deck plating (doubled)
23. Side plating
24. Shelf plate
25. Bulkhead
26. Stringer
27. Margin plate
28. Girder plate (intercostal)
29. Girder plate (continuous)
30. Centre girder
31. Inner bottom
32. Floor plates
33. Bilge keel
34. Boiler room
35. Oil fuel bunker

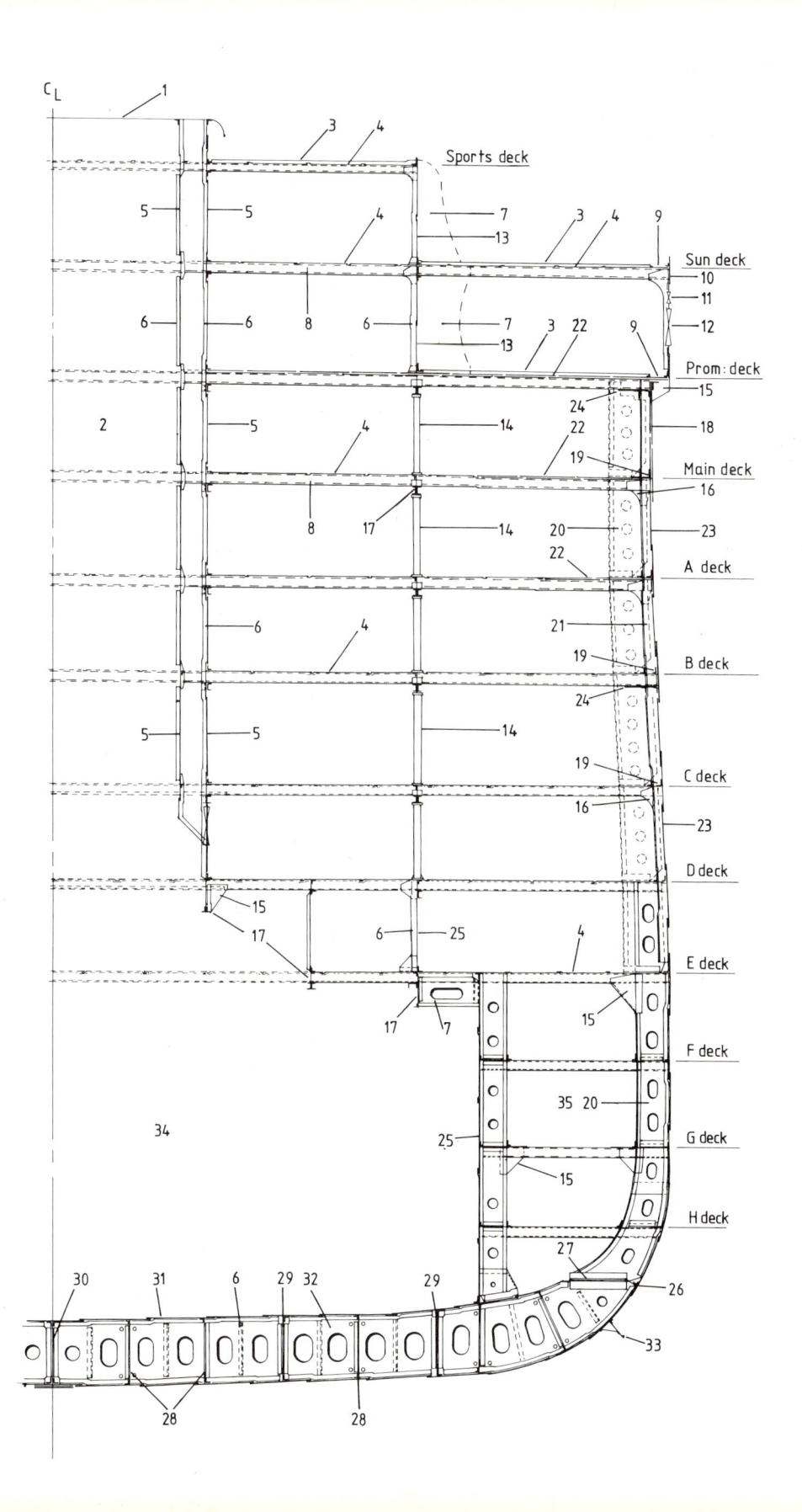

B Hull construction

B5/2 Section where main deck is strength deck (perspective view, no scale)

B5/2

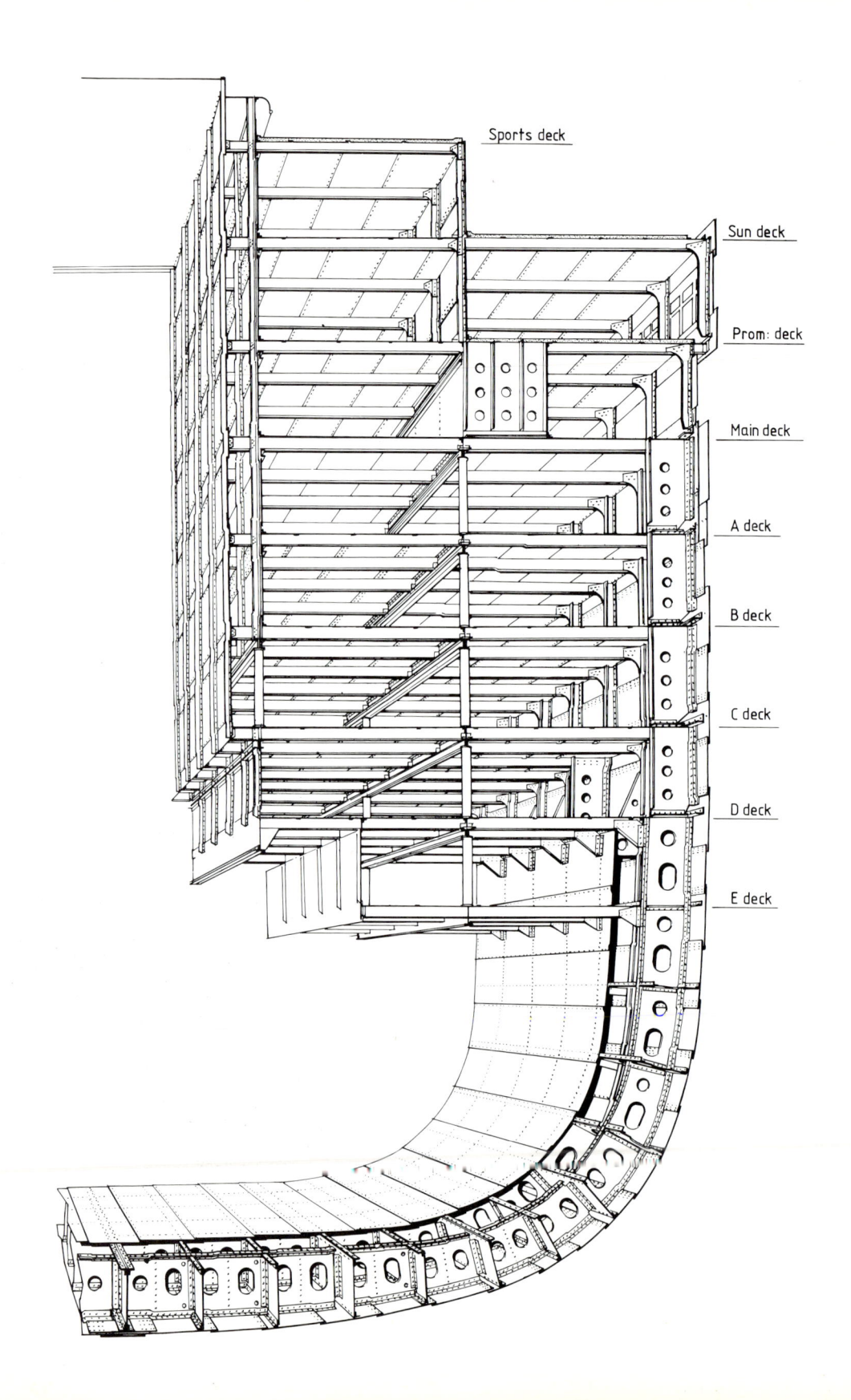

Sports deck
Sun deck
Prom: deck
Main deck
A deck
B deck
C deck
D deck
E deck

**B6 FRAMING IN WAY OF DOUBLE
SKIN (no scale)**   **B6**

1. Channel frame
2. Angle bar
3. Channel bar
4. Web plate
5. Stringer plate
6. Lug
7. Side plating
8. Inter plating
9. Bracket

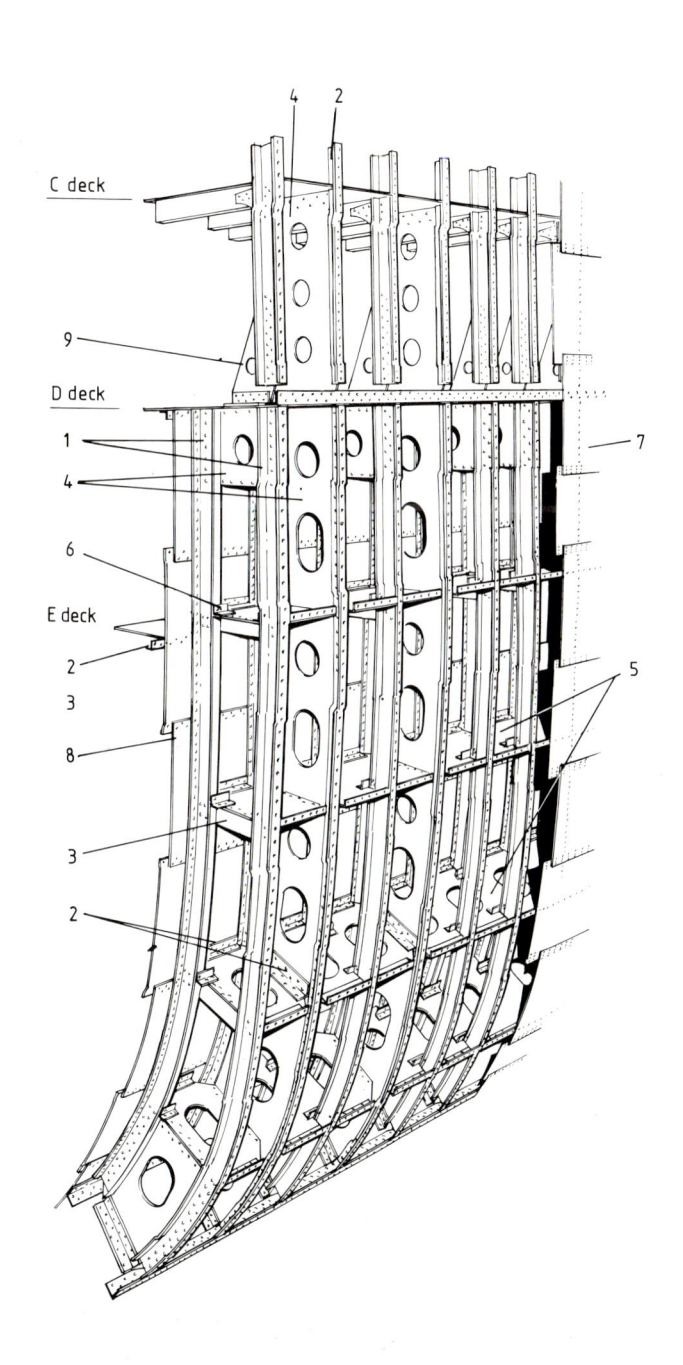

C Machinery

C1 FORWARD AND AFTER MAIN ENGINE ROOMS (1/300 scale)

C1/1 Longitudinal section

C1/2 Plan

1. Forward main engine room
2. After main engine room
3. Low pressure turbine
4. High pressure turbine
5. Condenser
6. Low pressure feed heater
7. High pressure feed heater
8. Main circulating pumps
9. Main circulating pump controller
10. Gear case
11. Thrust block
12. Oil cooler circulating pump
13. Oil cooler circulating pump starter
14. Oil coolers
15. Turning gear resistance and controller
16. Intermediate pressure turbines
17. Drain cooler
18. Forced lubrication pumps
19. Forced lubrication pump starter
20. Bilge well
21. Oil drain tank
22. Air ejectors
23. Extraction pumps
24. Main feed tanks
25. Turbo feed pumps
26. Feed filter
27. Intermediate feed heater
28. Lift
29. Sewage plant
30. Entrance to engine room port and starboard
31. Evaporators
32. Drain well
33. Controls
34. Starters
35. Watertight door
36. Main circulating discharge valves
37. Vents
38. Bilge injection
39. Main circulating inlet valves
40. Fire and wash deck pump
41. House for sewage plant
42. Sanitary pump
43. Air cooler starter
44. Emergency bilge pump control
45. Emergency bilge pump
46. Distiller and filter
47. Ballast pump
48. Assistant feed pump
49. Manoeuvring valves
50. Manoeuvring wheels
51. Main steam pipes
52. Door in lift
53. Frame 93
54. Frame 95
55. Frame 101
d   D deck
e   E deck

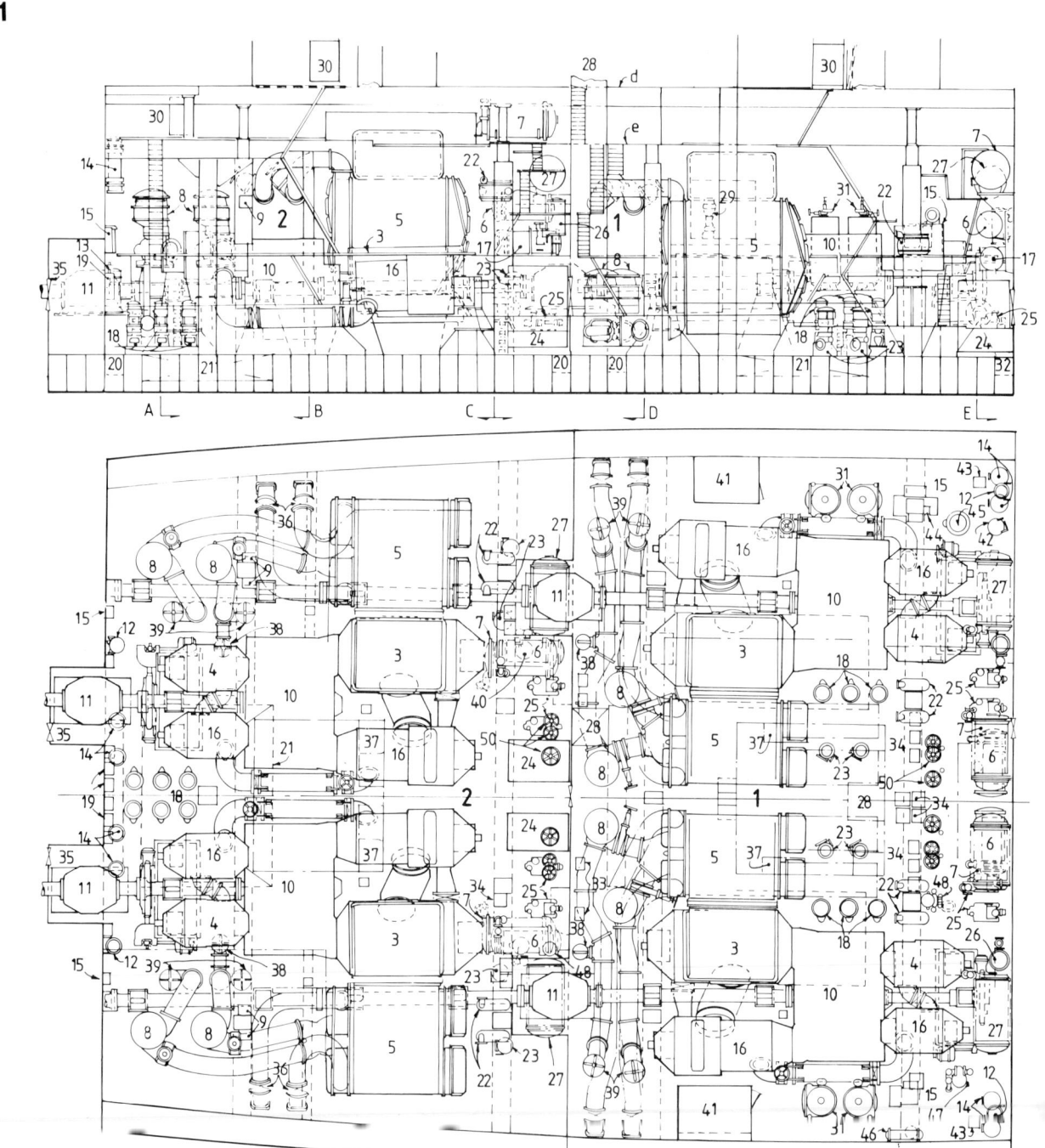

C1/1

C1/2

74

C1/3 Section at A (looking forward)
C1/4 Section at B (looking aft)
C1/5 Section at C (looking aft)
C1/6 Section at C (looking forward)
C1/7 Section at D (looking aft)
C1/8 Section at E (looking forward)

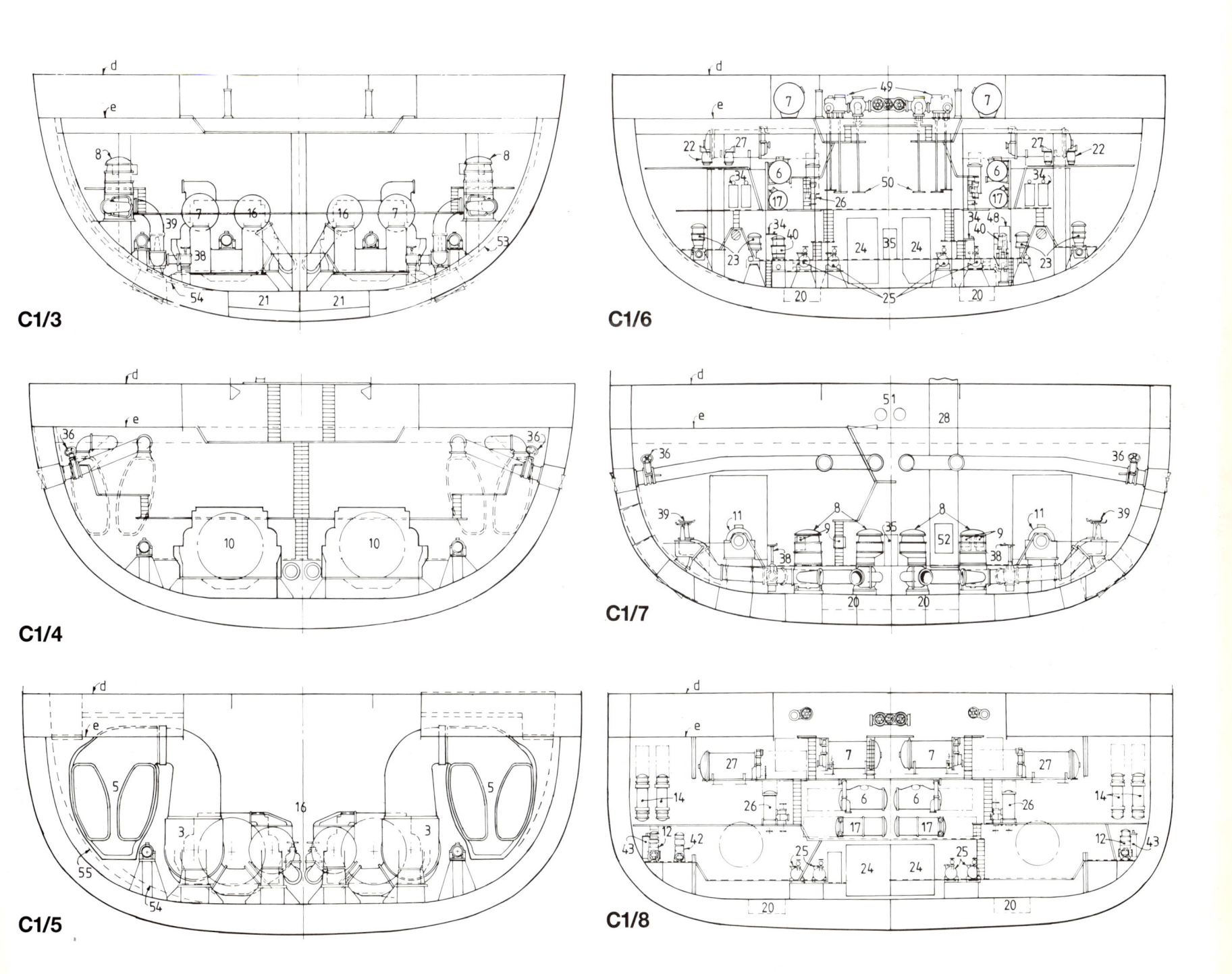

C1/3

C1/4

C1/5

C1/6

C1/7

C1/8

75

C Machinery

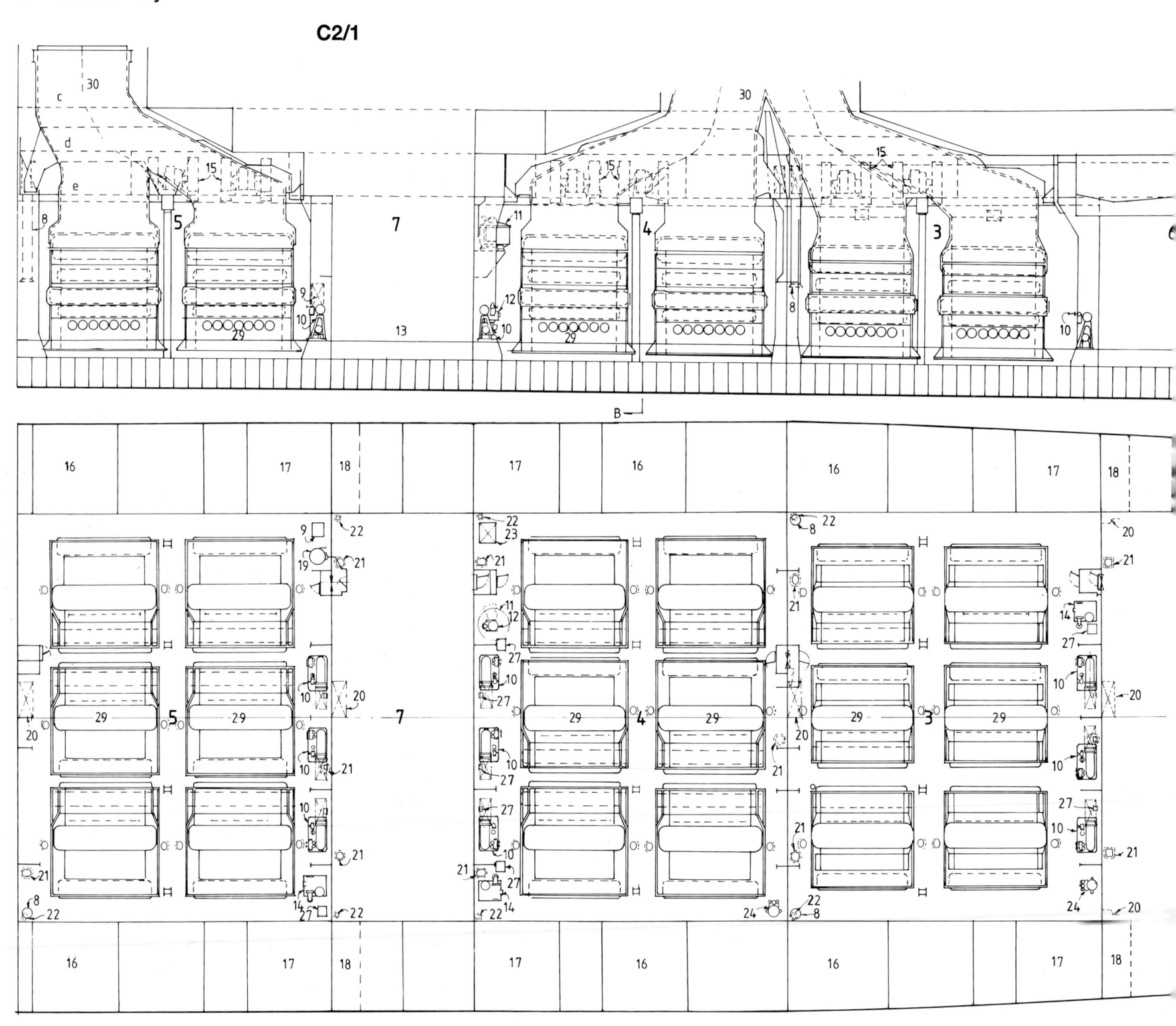

C2/1

C2/2

C2 MAIN AND AUXILIARY BOILER ROOMS (1/300 scale)

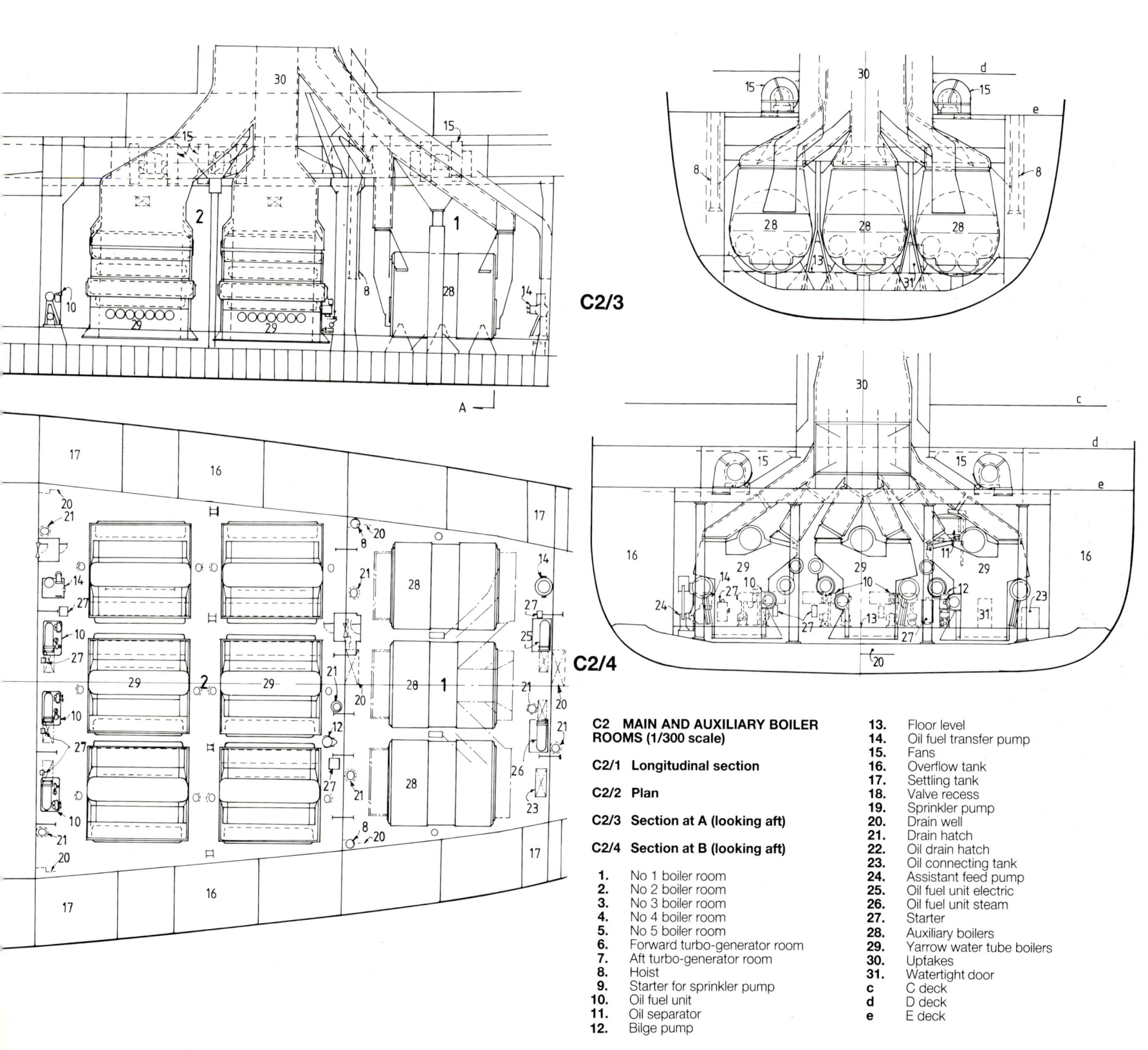

C2/1 Longitudinal section
C2/2 Plan
C2/3 Section at A (looking aft)
C2/4 Section at B (looking aft)

1. No 1 boiler room
2. No 2 boiler room
3. No 3 boiler room
4. No 4 boiler room
5. No 5 boiler room
6. Forward turbo-generator room
7. Aft turbo-generator room
8. Hoist
9. Starter for sprinkler pump
10. Oil fuel unit
11. Oil separator
12. Bilge pump
13. Floor level
14. Oil fuel transfer pump
15. Fans
16. Overflow tank
17. Settling tank
18. Valve recess
19. Sprinkler pump
20. Drain well
21. Drain hatch
22. Oil drain hatch
23. Oil connecting tank
24. Assistant feed pump
25. Oil fuel unit electric
26. Oil fuel unit steam
27. Starter
28. Auxiliary boilers
29. Yarrow water tube boilers
30. Uptakes
31. Watertight door
c C deck
d D deck
e E deck

77

C Machinery

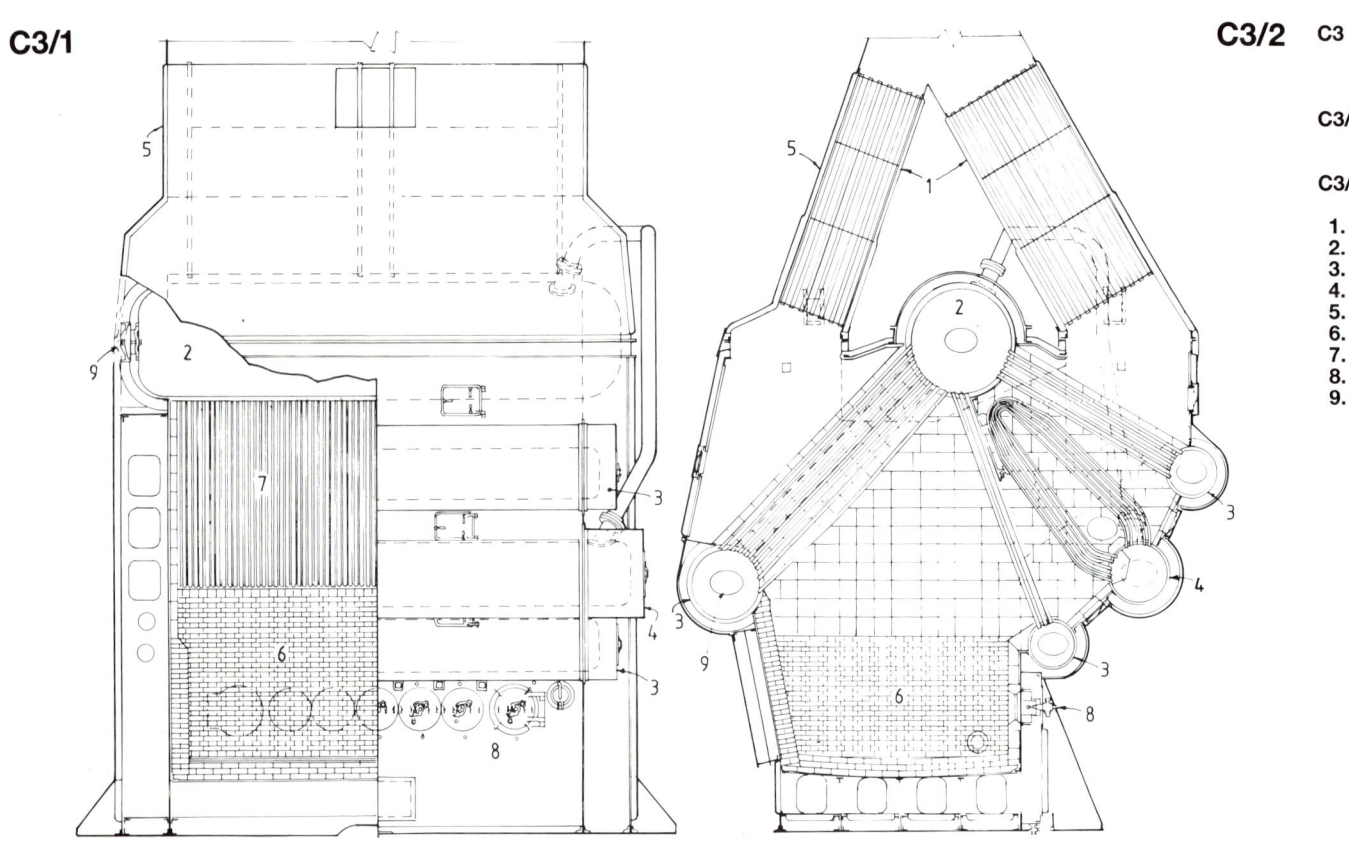

C3/1

C3/2

C3 YARROW DOUBLE FLOW MAIN WATER-TUBE BOILER (1/100 scale)

C3/1 Profile (half-section and outside view)

C3/2 Transverse section

1. Air heaters
2. Steam drum
3. Water drum
4. Superheater drum
5. Stiffening angles
6. Fire bricks
7. Water tubes
8. Oil fuel sprayers
9. Manhole door

C4

78

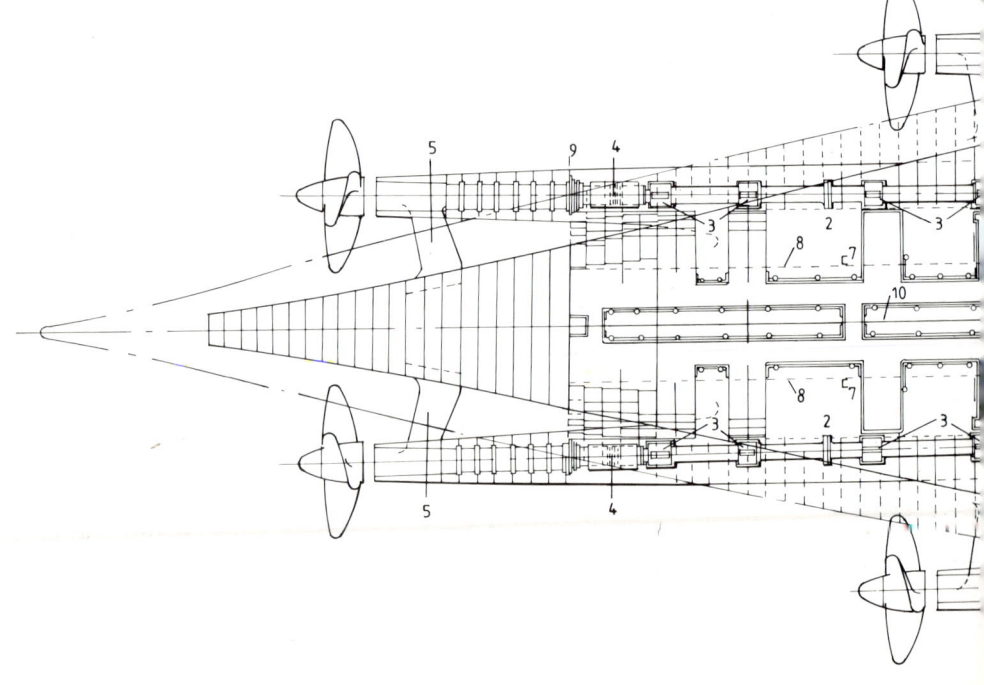

C4 PROPELLER SHAFT ARRANGEMENT, PLAN (1/300 scale)

1. Thrust block
2. Shaft coupling
3. Plummer block
4. Stern tube
5. Shaft bracket
6. Bridge over shaft
7. Pillars
8. Girder (over)
9. Watertight bulkhead
10. Non-watertight bulkhead
11. Horizontally sealed water-tight door
12. Sewage tank
13. Sprinkler pressure tank
14. Brine pump room
15. CO_2 evaporator
16. Turbine set
17. Forced lubrication pumps
18. Main circulation inlet
19. Strong beam (over)
20. Condenser
21. Vertically sealed watertight door

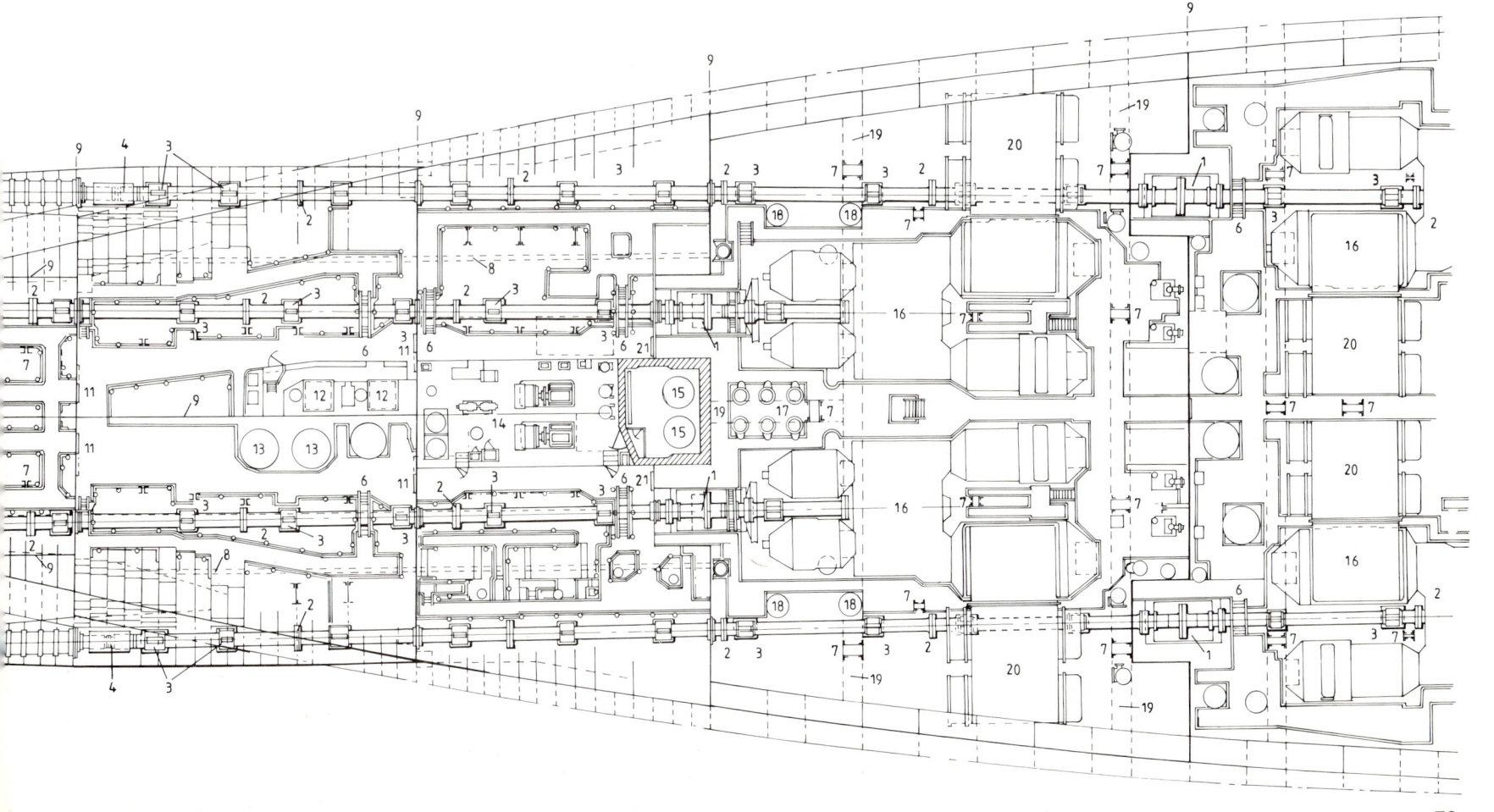

C   Machinery

C5   ELECTRO-HYDRAULIC STEERING GEAR ARRANGEMENT, PLAN
(1/100 scale)

1. Cylinder no 1
2. Cylinder no 2
3. Cylinder no 3
4. Cylinder no 4
5. Rudder post
6. Control valves
7. Electric pumping units
8. Oil tank filling pump units
9. Main hand control pedestal
10. Telemotor charging pump and tank
11. Servo telemotor unit
12. Sperry gyro pilot
13. Servo telemotor hand control pedestal
14. Ladder (down)
15. Electrical switchboard

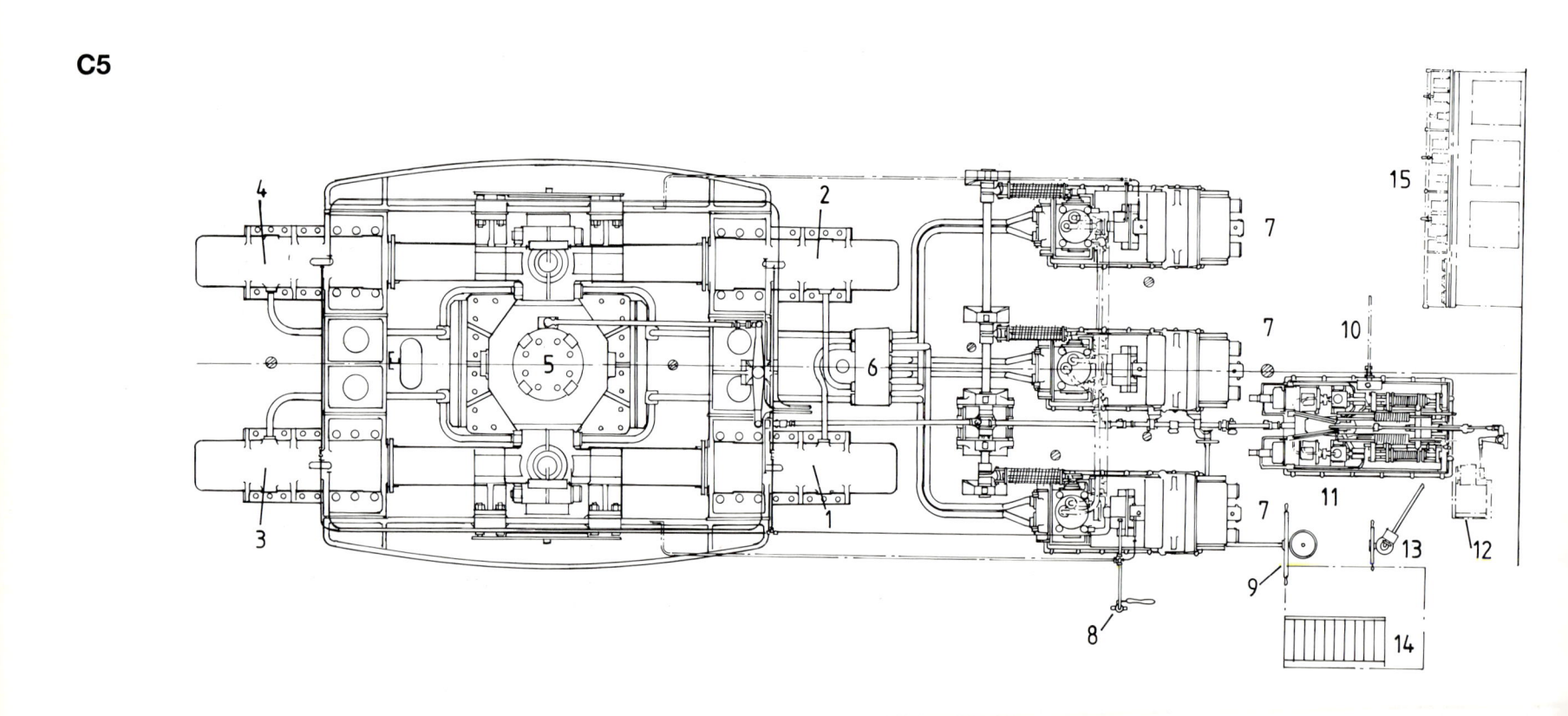

C5

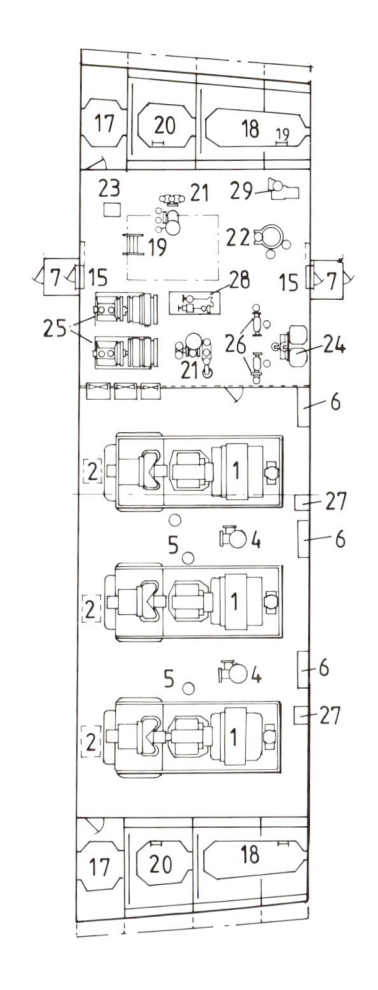

C6/1

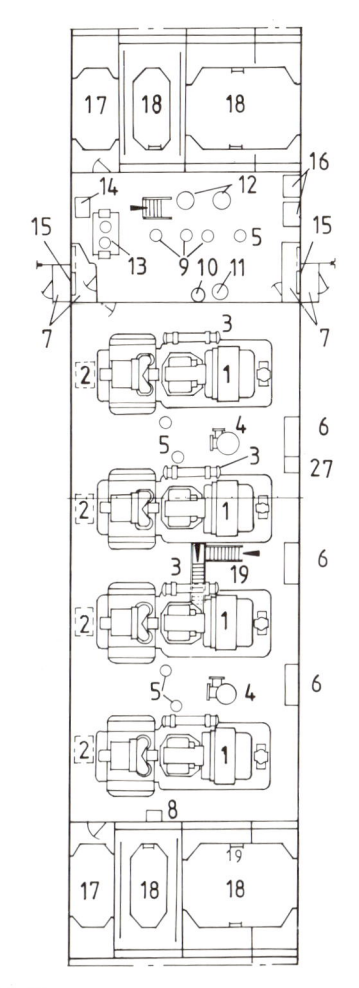

C6/2

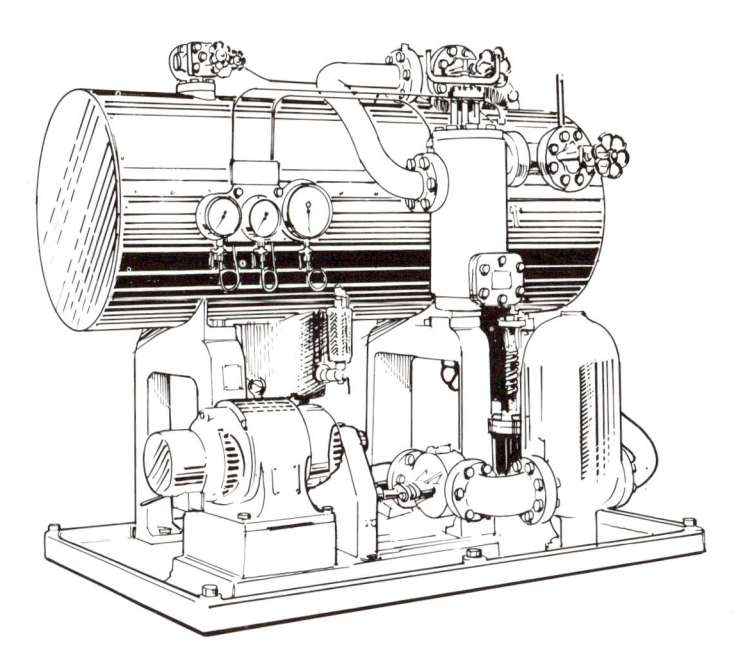

C6	**FORWARD AND AFTER TURBO-GENERATOR ROOM ARRANGEMENTS (1/300 scale)**
C6/1	**Forward turbo-generator room plan**
C6/2	**After turbo-generator room plan**

1. 1,300kw turbo-generator
2. Oil drain tank (under)
3. Turbo-generator oil cooler
4. Circulating pump
5. Extraction pump
6. Air trunk
7. Air lock
8. Sewage expulsion pump starter
9. Spray pumps
10. Condensate pump
11. Air reservoir
12. Domestic water pump
13. Watertight door pump
14. Tank for watertight door pump
15. Horizontally sealed watertight door
16. Starter for domestic water pump
17. Recess for sea valves
18. Oil fuel tank
19. Ladder
20. Overflow tank
21. Ballast trimming pump
22. Auxiliary air pump
23. Ballast trimming pump starter
24. Auxiliary feed filters
25. Air compressors
26. Hotwell pumps
27. Circulating pump starter
28. Auxiliary turbo feed pump
29. Air circulating pump

C7	**WALLSEND-HOWDEN OIL FIRING AND HEATER UNIT**
C8	**WEIR ELECTRICALLY-DRIVEN EXTRACTION PUMP**

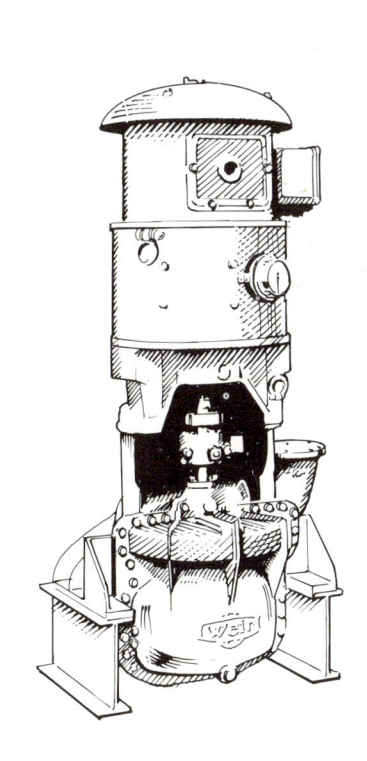

81

C Machinery

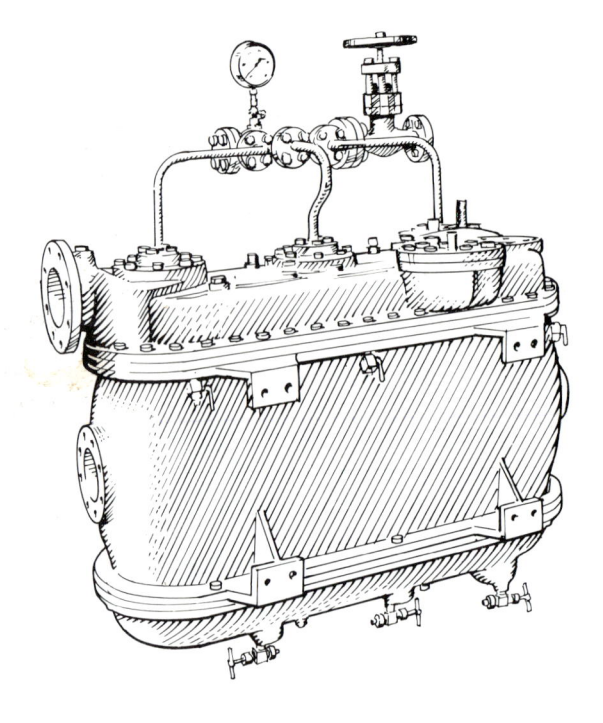

C9   WEIR 3-STAGE AIR EJECTOR

C9

C10   WEIR MULTI-STAGE TURBO FEED PUMP

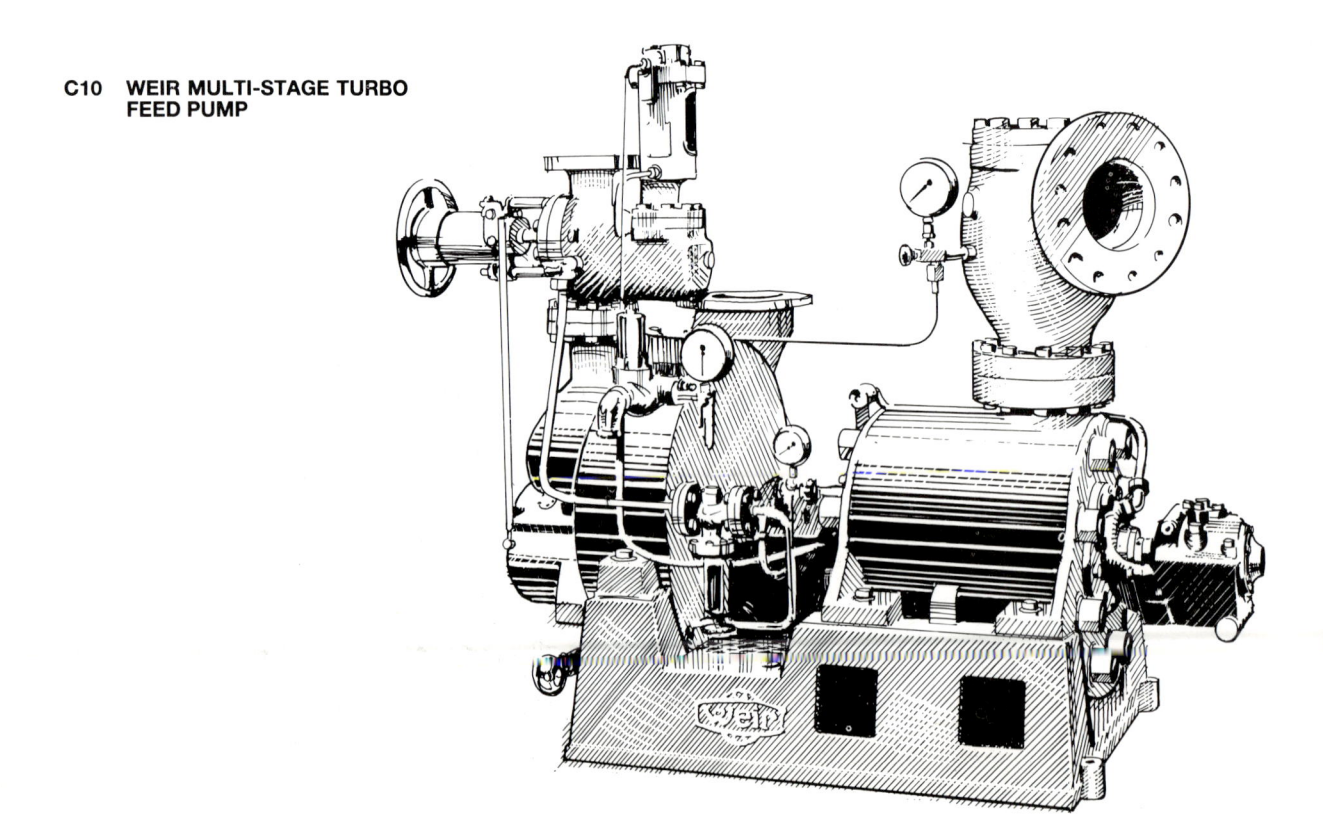

C10

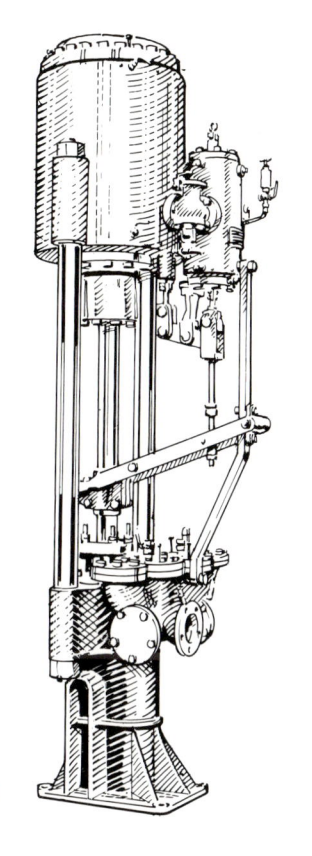

C11 CLARKE-CHAPMAN SINGLE CYLINDER FEED PUMP

C12 MAIN CIRCULATING PUMP

C13 VICKEN 700-GALLON LUBRICATING OIL PURIFIER

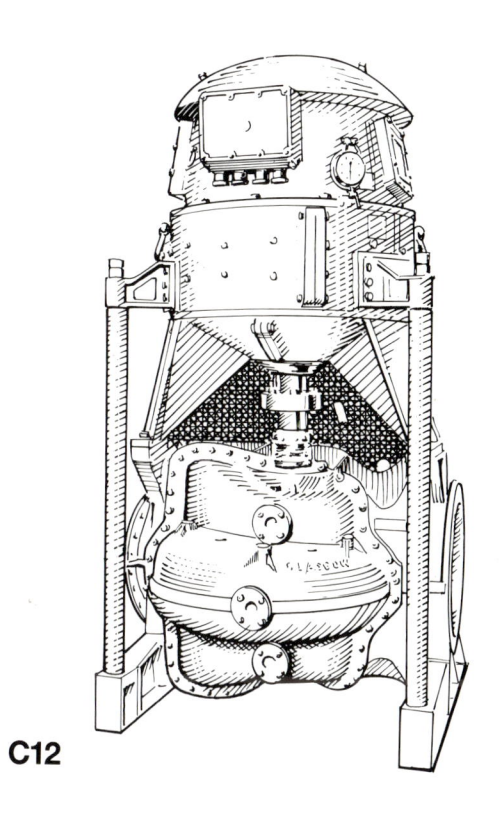

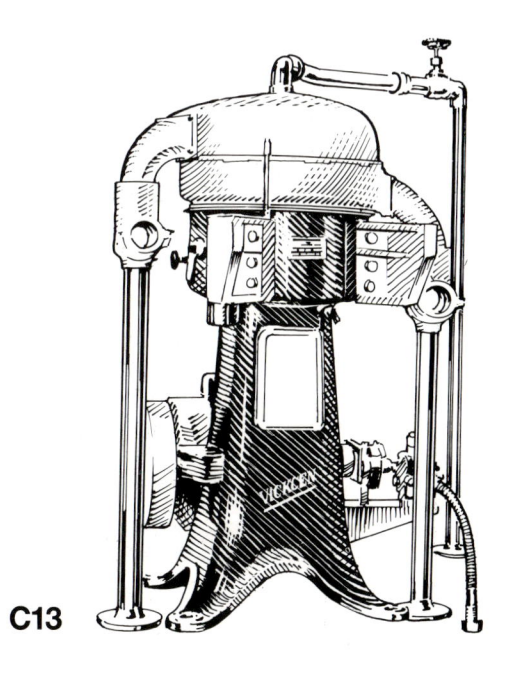

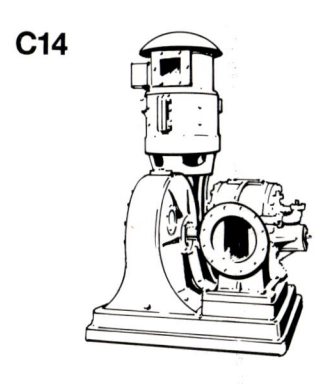

C14 OIL FUEL TRANSFER PUMP

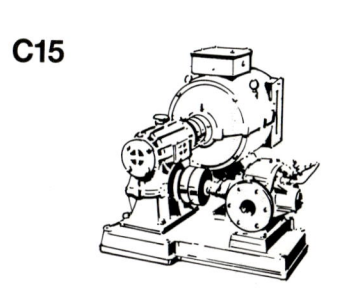

C15 OIL FUEL PRESSURE PUMP

C Machinery

C16 PARSONS 8-CYLINDER KEROSENE ENGINE AND BTH 75kw EMERGENCY DYNAMO (no scale)

C16/1 Side elevation

C16/2 General view

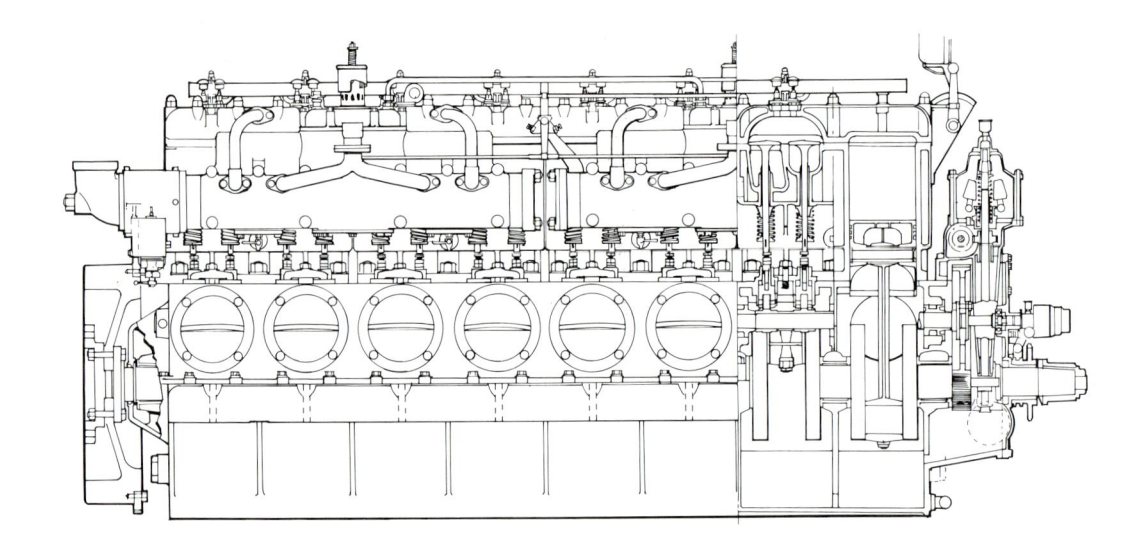

C16/1

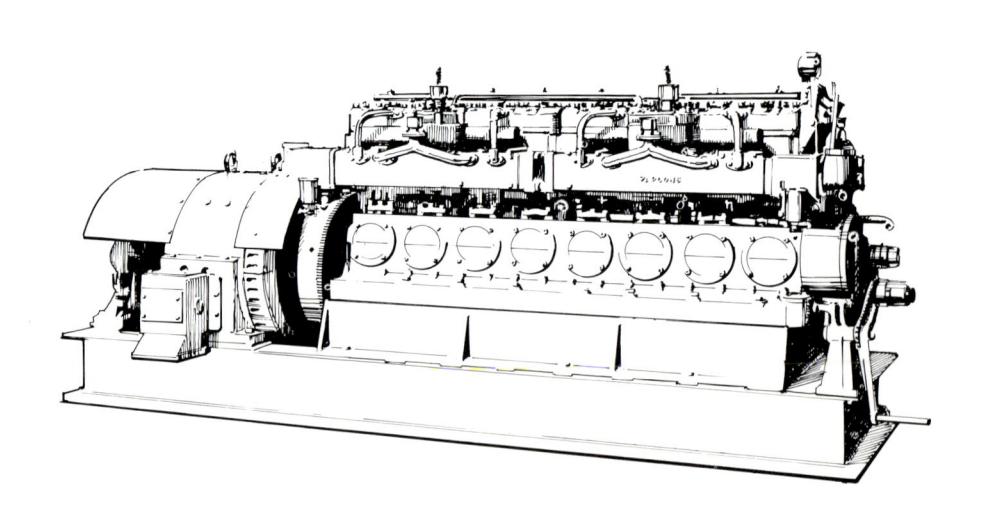

C16/2

C17 WATER-SOFTENING ROOM (1/300 scale)

C17/1 Elevation, looking to port

C17/2 Elevation, looking to starboard

C17/3 Plan of upper flat

C17/4 Plan of lower flat

C17/5 Section, looking aft

C17/6 Section, looking forward

1. Cream-of-lime container
2. Mixing tank
3. Liming tank
4. Sewage plant
5. Salt water calorifier
6. Fresh water tank
7. Calorifier circulating pump
8. Fire and wash-deck pump
9. Water-softening pump
10. Partially softened water tank
11. Oil separator
12. Domestic water pump
13. Fresh water pump
14. Brine tank
15. Domestic water filter
16. Drinking water filter
17. General service pump
18. Drinking water pump
19. Reagent storage bin
20. Salt storage bin
21. Filters
22. Basex softening units
23. Sanitary pump
24. Domestic water tank
25. Cofferdam
26. Starters
27. Pipe passage
27. Fresh water calorifier

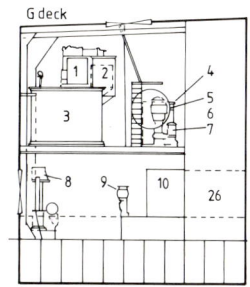

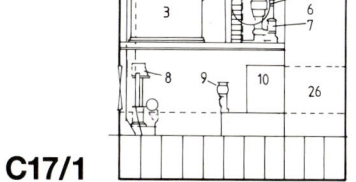

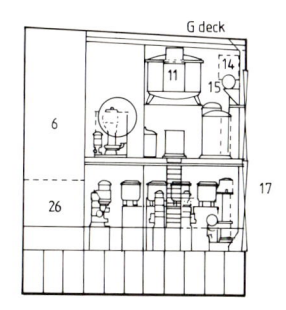

C17/1

C17/2

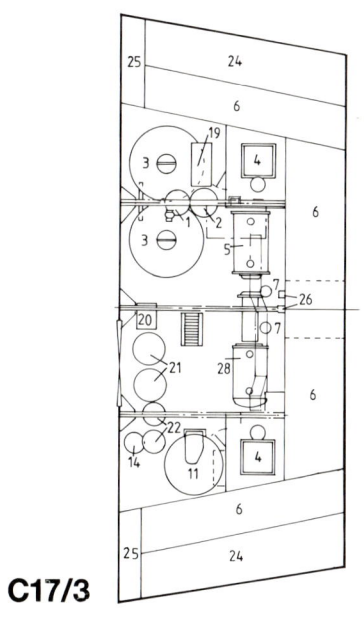

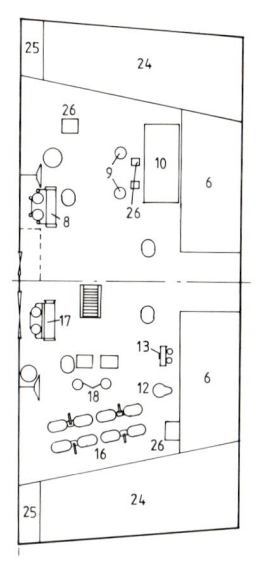

C17/3

C17/4

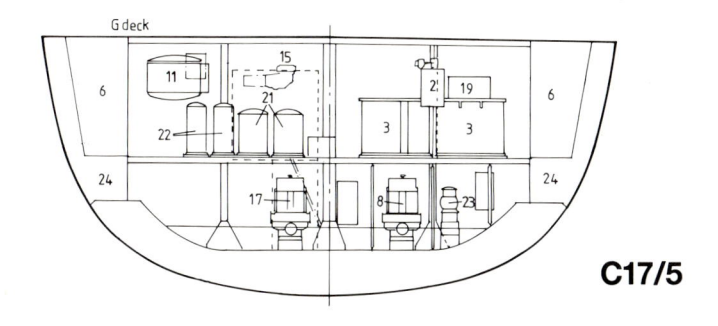

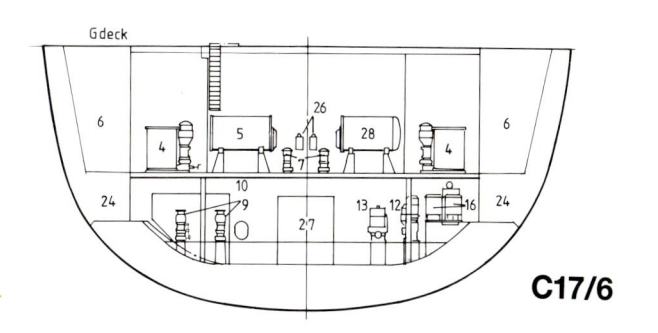

C17/5

C17/6

85

C Machinery

C18 ARRANGEMENT OF STARBOARD STABILISER UNIT IN THE AFTER TURBO-GENERATOR ROOM, 1957 (1/100 scale)

C18/1 Elevation, looking outboard

C18/2 Plan

1. Main power unit starter
2. Main power unit
3. Housing control and stop valve unit
4. Auxiliary power unit
5. Turbo-generator
6. Tilting cylinders
7. Ladder
8. Stabiliser shaft
9. Turbo-generator extraction pump starters
10. Hand-operated hydraulically sealed watertight door
11. Storage tank
12. Valve
13. Auxiliary power unit starter
14. Turbo-generator circulating pump
15. Turbo-generator extraction pump
16. Oil cooler
17. Vent
18. Operating handle for watertight door
19. Finbox
20. Watertight manhole

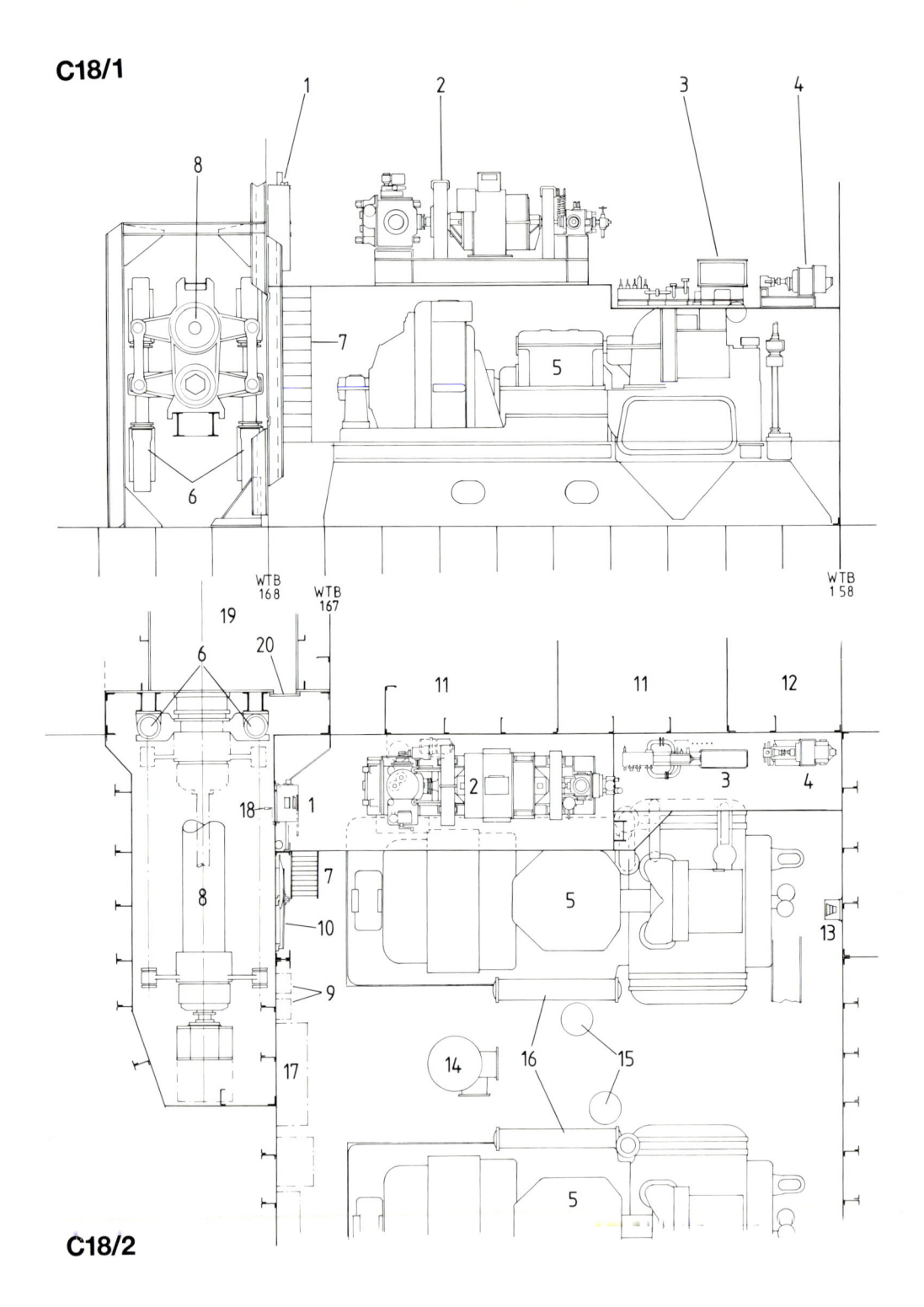

C19 ARRANGEMENT OF DENNY-BROWN STABILISER FIN (1/50 scale)

C19/1 Sectioned elevation of fin socket

C19/2 View of inboard end

C19/3 Plan of main fin

C19/4 Plan of tail flap

C19/5 View of tail flap on inboard end

C19/6 View of tail flap on outboard end

C19/7 Section at 'AA'

C19/8 Section at 'BB'

1. Web
2. Intercostal piece
3. Cotterpin
4. Tailstock boss
5. Torque tube
6. Cover plate
7. Nose plate
8. Maximum movement of tail flap

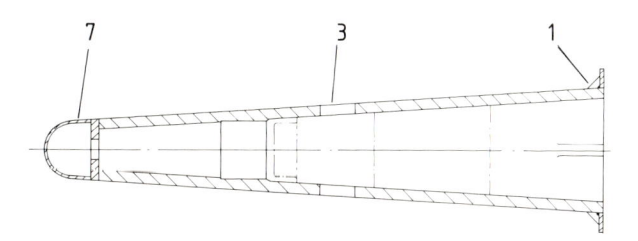

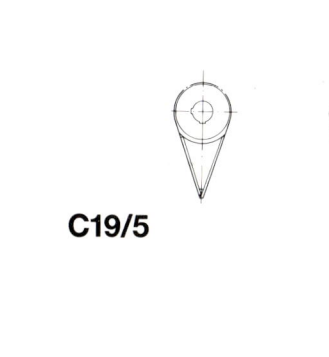

C19/1

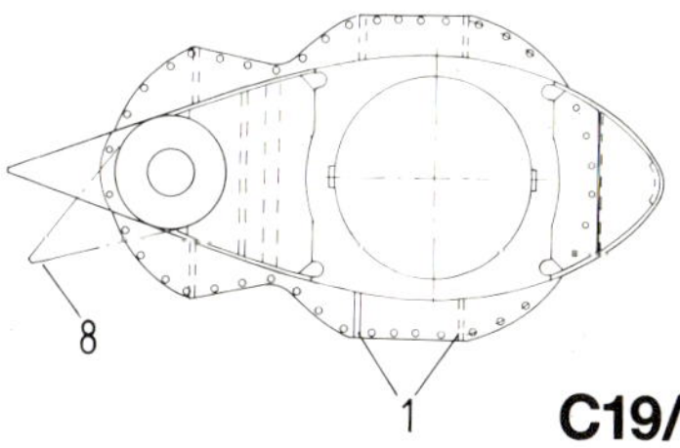

C19/2

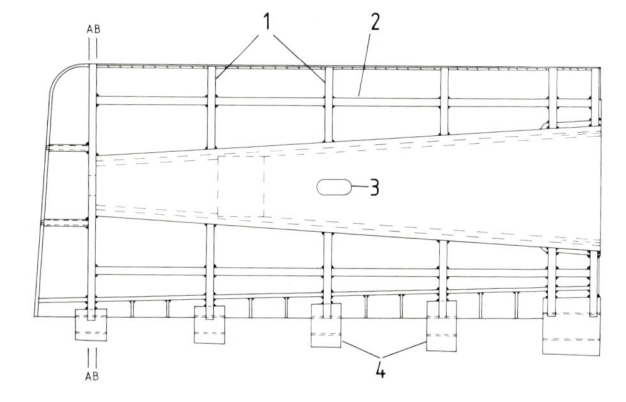

C19/3

C19/4

C19/5

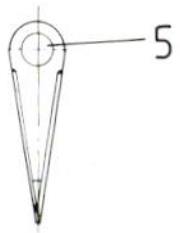

C19/6

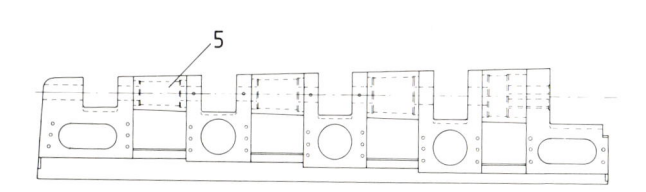

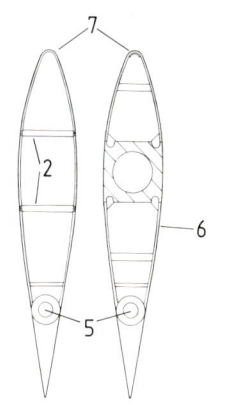

C19/7

C19/8

87

D Accommodation

D1 CABIN CLASS MAIN HALL AND SHOPPING CENTRE (PROMENADE DECK)

D1

D2 CABIN CLASS RESTAURANT (C DECK)

D2

D Accommodation

D3 CABIN CLASS LOUNGE (PROMENADE DECK)

D3

D4 CABIN CLASS LONG GALLERY (PROMENADE DECK

D4

D Accommodation

D5 CABIN CLASS STARBOARD GALLERY (PROMENADE DECK)

D5

D6 CABIN CLASS BALLROOM (PROMENADE DECK)

D6

D Accommodation

**D7   CABIN CLASS SMOKING ROOM
(PROMENADE DECK)**

D7

D8 CABIN CLASS VERANDAH GRILL
(SUN DECK)

D Accommodation

D9 CABIN CLASS STATEROOM

D9

D10 TOURIST CLASS SMOKING ROOM (PROMENADE DECK)

D10

D Accommodation

D11 TOURIST CLASS MAIN LOUNGE (MAIN DECK)

D12 TOURIST CLASS LOUNGE (A DECK)

D12

D Accommodation

D13 TOURIST CLASS DINING SALOON (C DECK)

D14 TOURIST CLASS STATEROOM

D14

D Accommodation

D15 THIRD CLASS GARDEN LOUNGE (MAIN DECK)

**D16 THIRD CLASS SMOKING ROOM
(A DECK)**

D16

D Accommodation

D17 THIRD CLASS LOUNGE AND CINEMA (B DECK)

D17

D18 THIRD CLASS DINING SALOON (C DECK)

D18

D Accommodation

D19 THIRD CLASS STATEROOM (TWO BERTH)

D19

E Superstructure

E1 BRIDGE SUPERSTRUCTURE (AS BUILT)

E1

E Superstructure

E2 SUPERSTRUCTURE, AFTER 1947 (1/500 scale)

E2/1 Profile abaft frame 173

E2/2 Plan

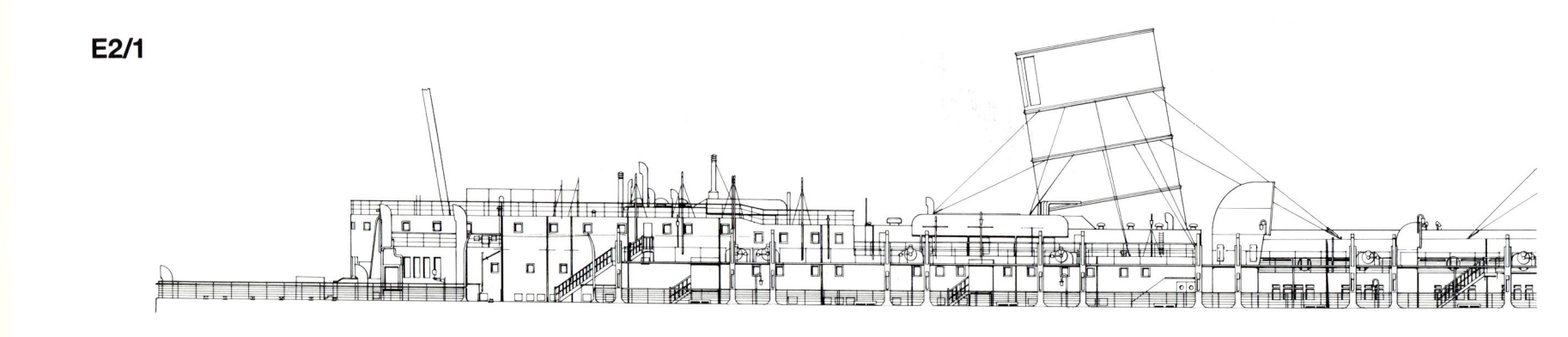

E2/1

E2/2

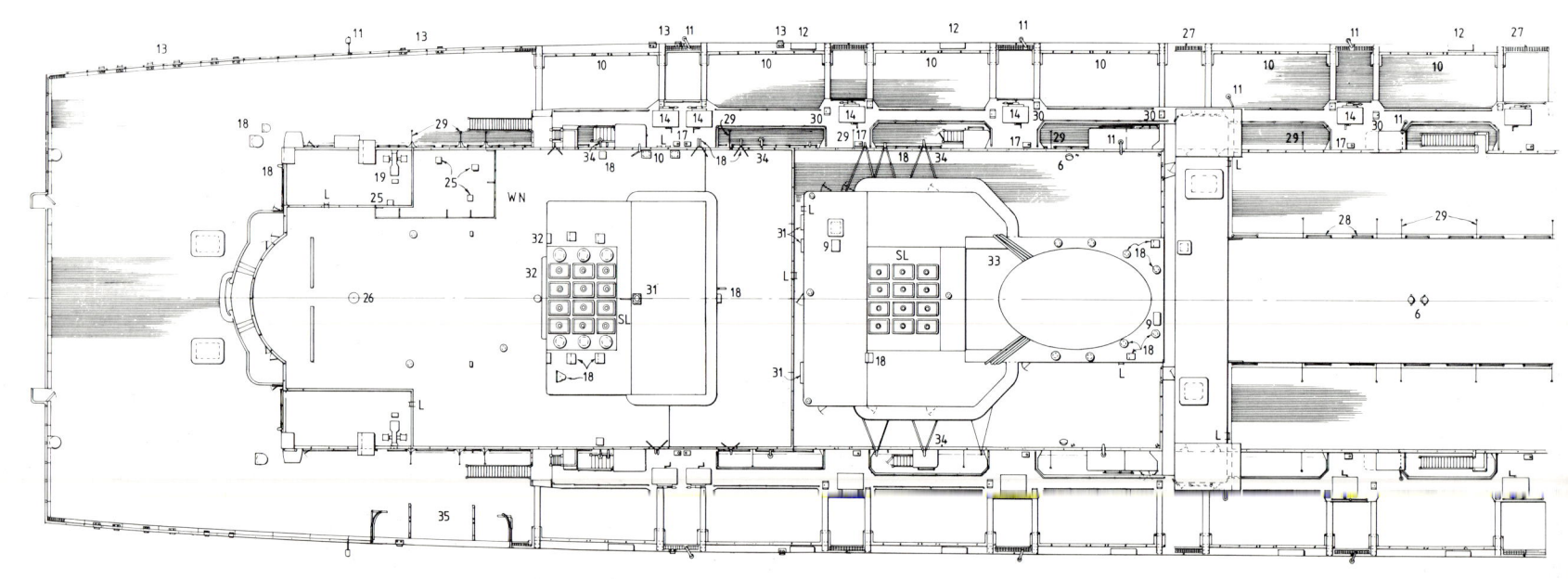

E2/3 Profile forward of frame 173

E2/3

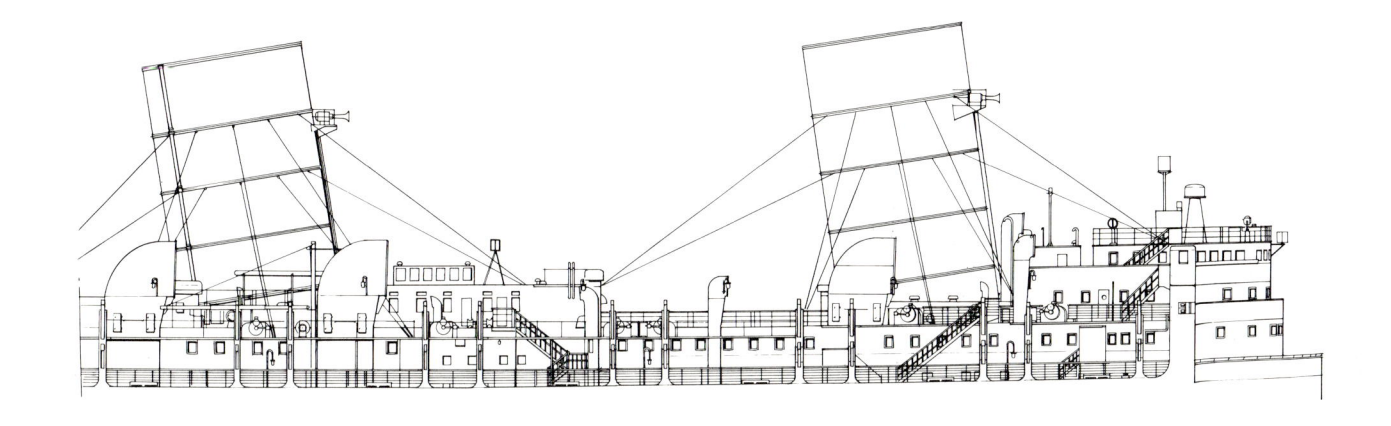

E2/4 Plan

1. Searchlight
2. Compass
3. Wireless direction finder
4. Telegraph repeater
5. Gyro repeater pelorus
6. Floodlight
7. Lifebuoy release gear
8. Navigation radar
9. Hatch
10. Gate
11. Boat lowering light
12. Ship's side ladder
13. Roller fairlead
14. Taylor boat winch
15. Metal screen
16. Funnel shrouds
17. Davit controller
18. Vent
19. 3-ton gangway winch
20. Gangway derrick
21. Gangway stowage
22. Steam pipe
23. New deckhouse
24. Wireless aerial
25. Wireless telegraph lead in
26. After mast
27. Wood grating
28. Handrail
29. Web
30. Sheave
31. Grill funnel
32. Hood over engine exhaust opening
33. Exhaust pipes
34. Standard lamp
35. Extra lifeboat crutches and quadrant davits
L Ladder
SL Skylight
WN Wire netting

E2/4

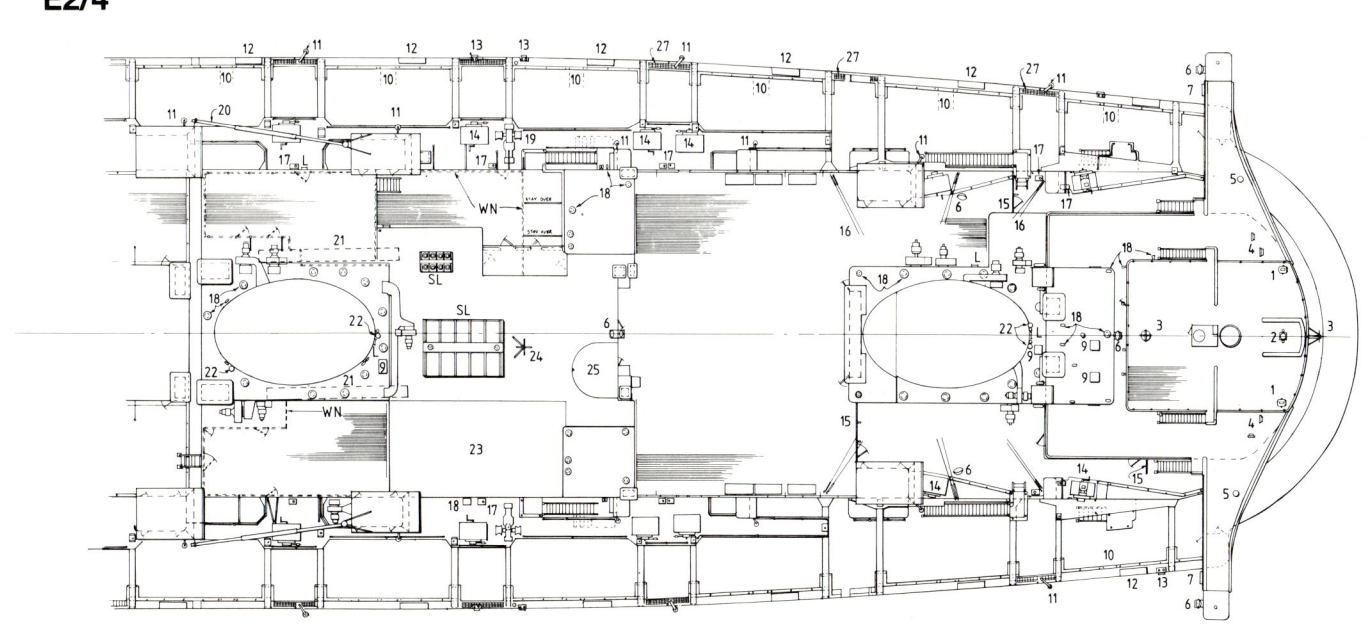

109

E Superstructure

E3 **BRIDGE HOUSE (after 1957)**

E3/1 **Profile**

E3/2 **Plan**
1. Searchlight
2. Compass
3. Wireless direction finder
4. Navigation radar
5. Whip aerial

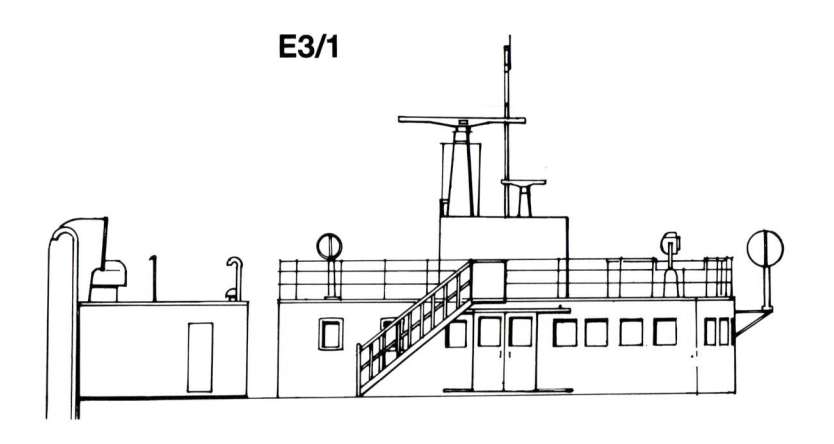

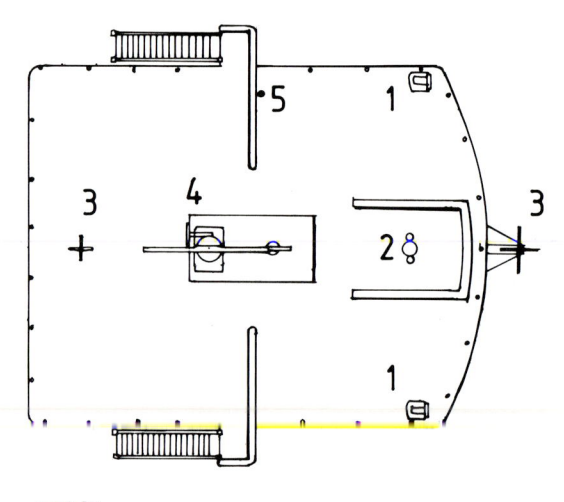

E3/1

E3/2

E4   AFTER FUNNEL (1/150 scale)

E4/1   Elevation

E4/2   Plan at funnel top

E4/3   Plan at funnel base

1. Engine room exhaust
2. Galley exhaust
3. Ladder
4. Wireless aerial bracket
5. Walkway
6. Angle stiffeners
7. Waste steam pipe
8. Inner funnel
9. Riveted joint
10. Bracket

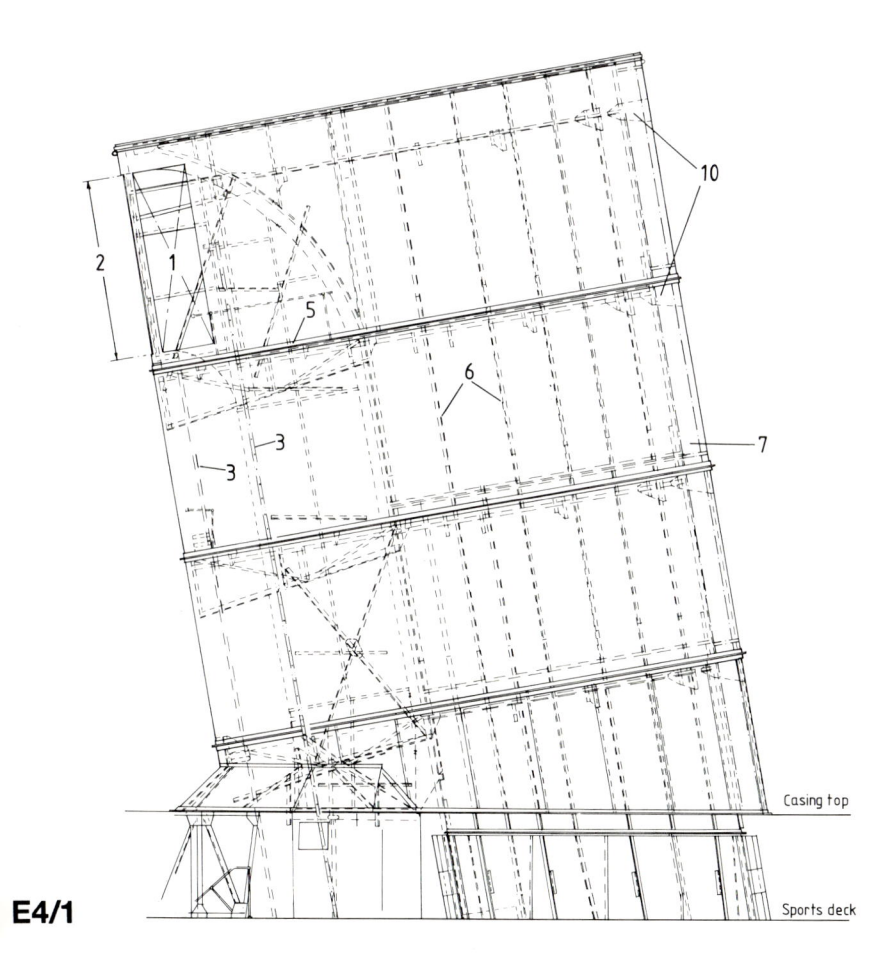

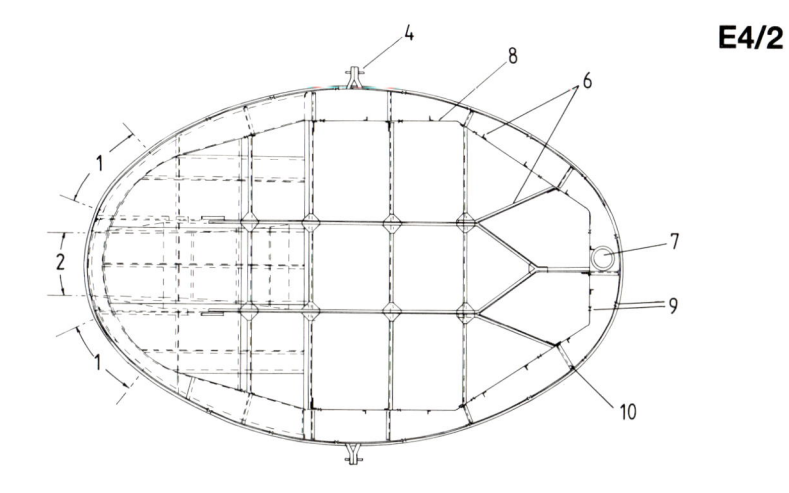

111

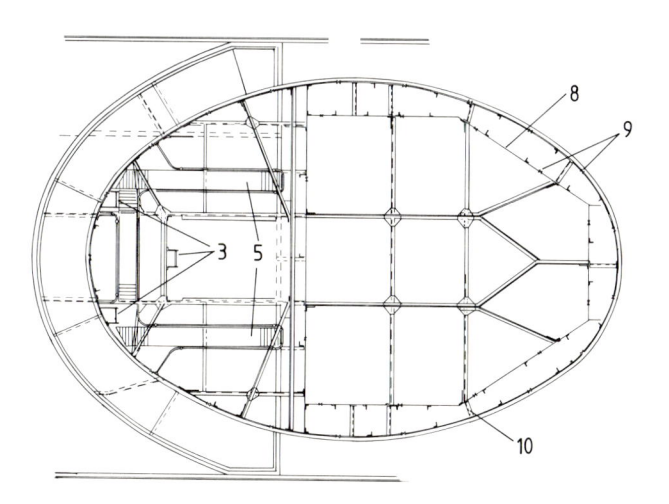

E Superstructure

E4/4 General view

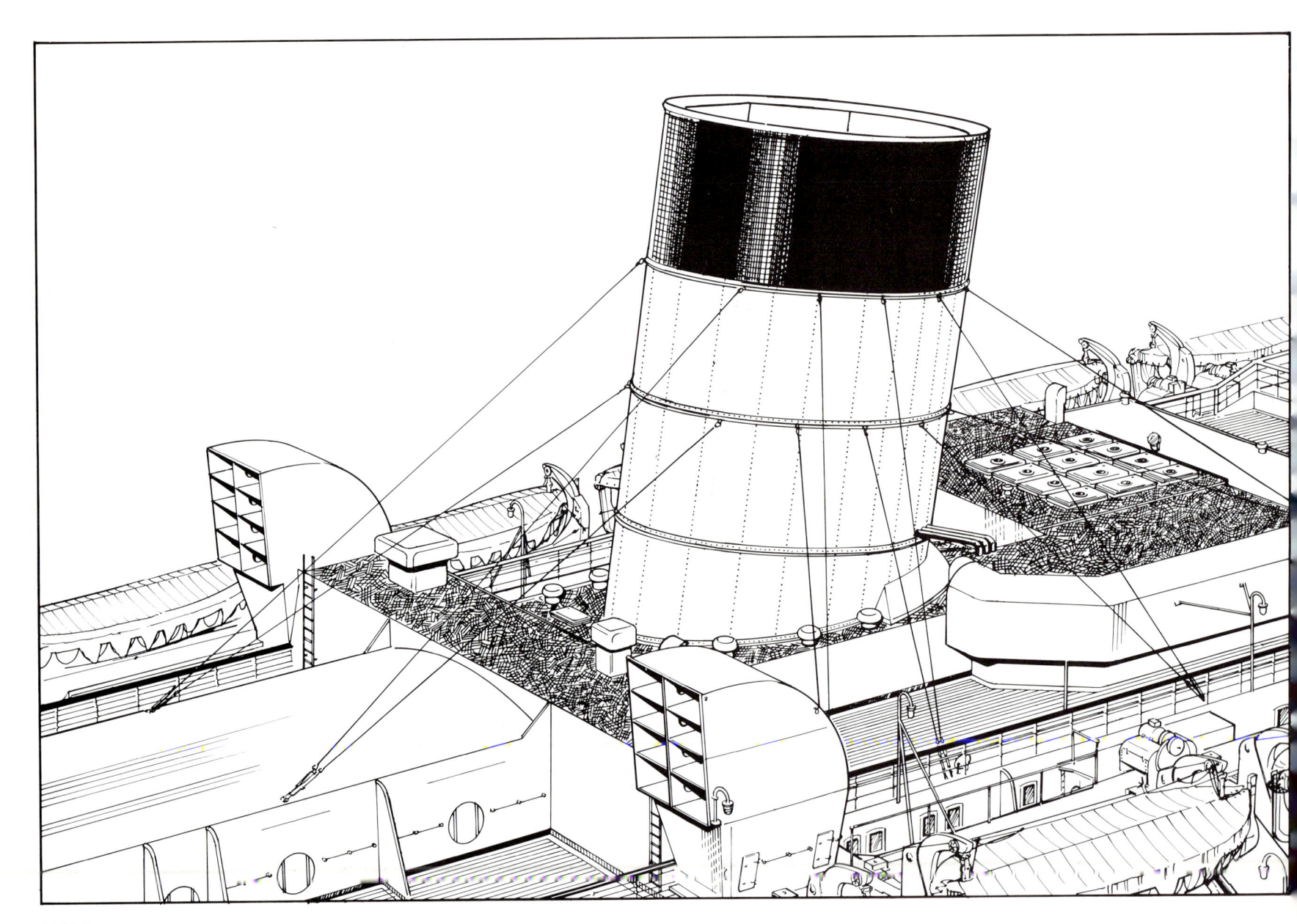

E4/4

E5 FORWARD FUNNEL (1/150 scale)

E5/1 Elevation

E5/2 Plan at funnel top

E5/3 Plan at whistle platform

E5/4 Section through funnel, showing stays

E5/5 Profile and plan of whistle steam pipe fittings

1. Wireless aerial bracket
2. Waste steam pipe
3. Tie bar
4. Stay
5. Angle stiffeners
6. Plate
7. Tyfon navigation whistle
8. Whistle platform
9. Whistle steam
10. Whistle drain
11. Inner funnel
12. Ladder
13. Division plate
14. Wire shrouds

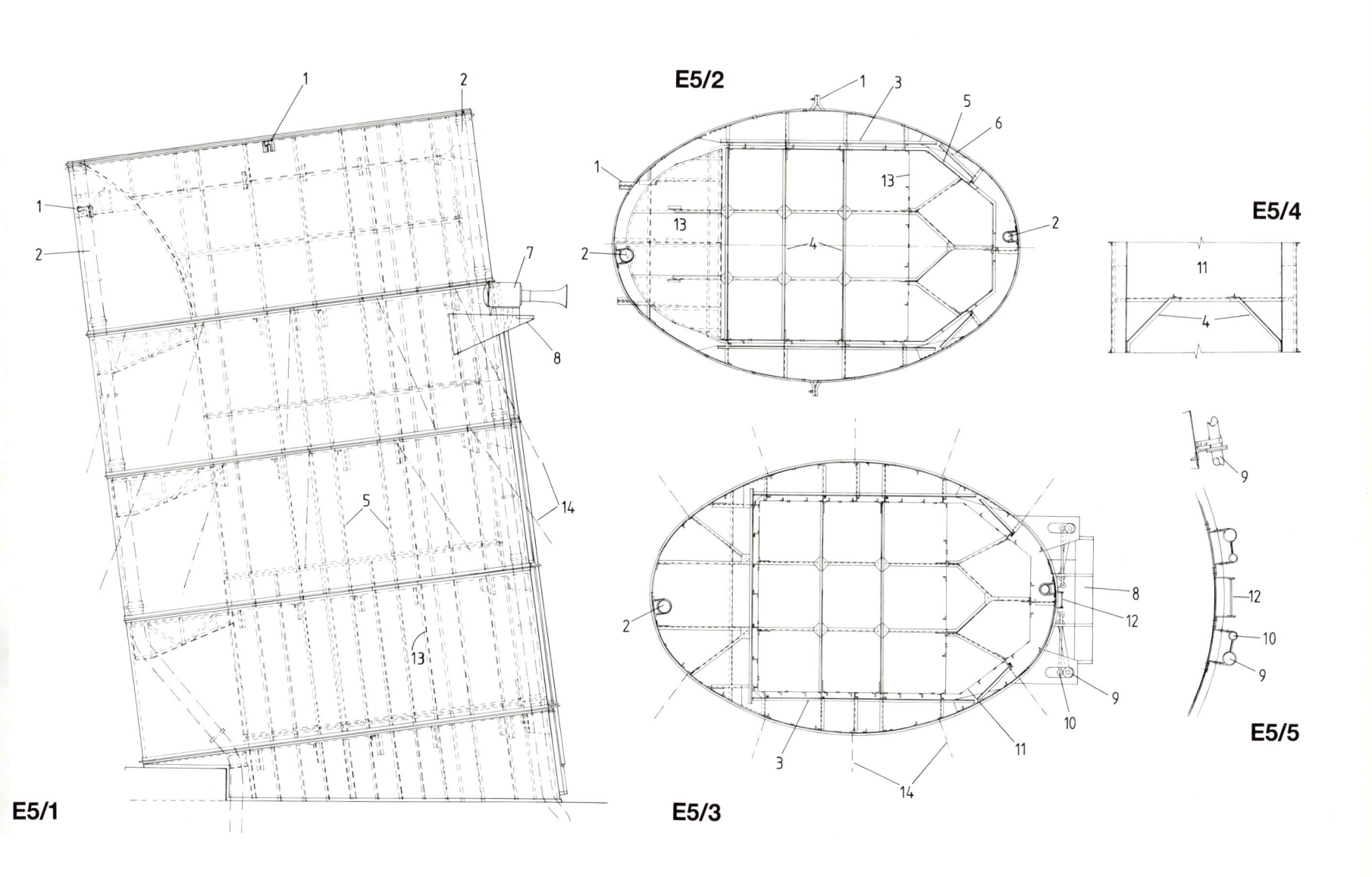

E5/2

E5/4

E5/1

E5/3

E5/5

113

E Superstructure

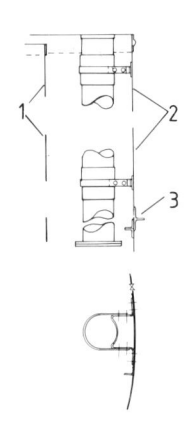

E6/1

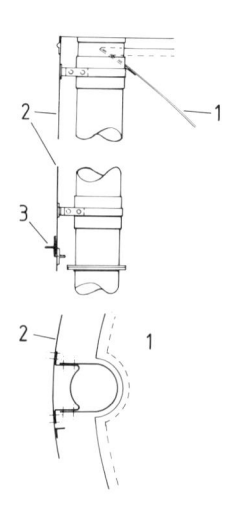

E6/2

E7/1

E7/2

E6 WASTE STEAM PIPES IN FORWARD FUNNEL (1/50 scale)

E6/1 Forward steam pipe

E6/2 After steam pipe

1. Inner funnel
2. Outer funnel
3. Tee bar

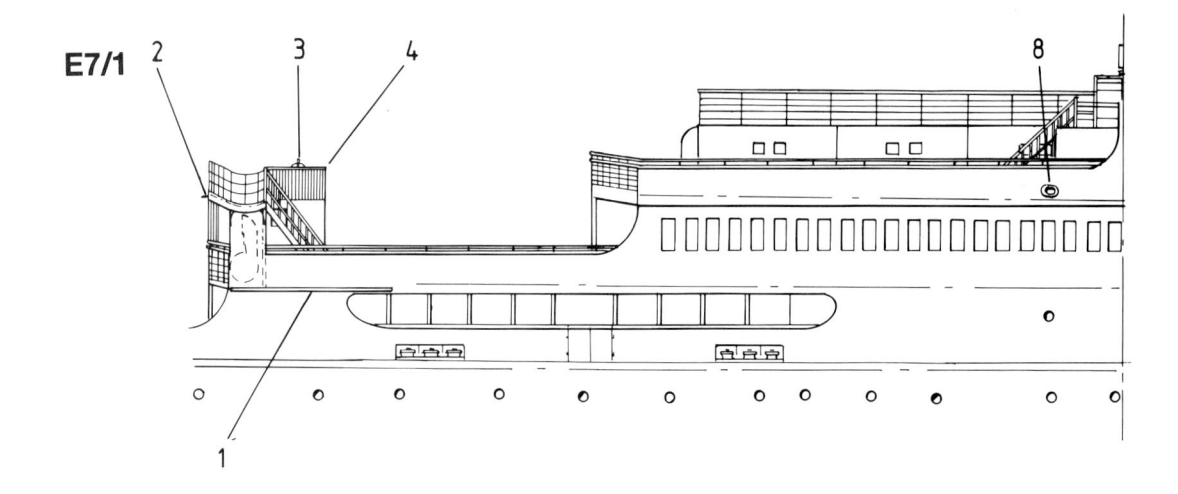

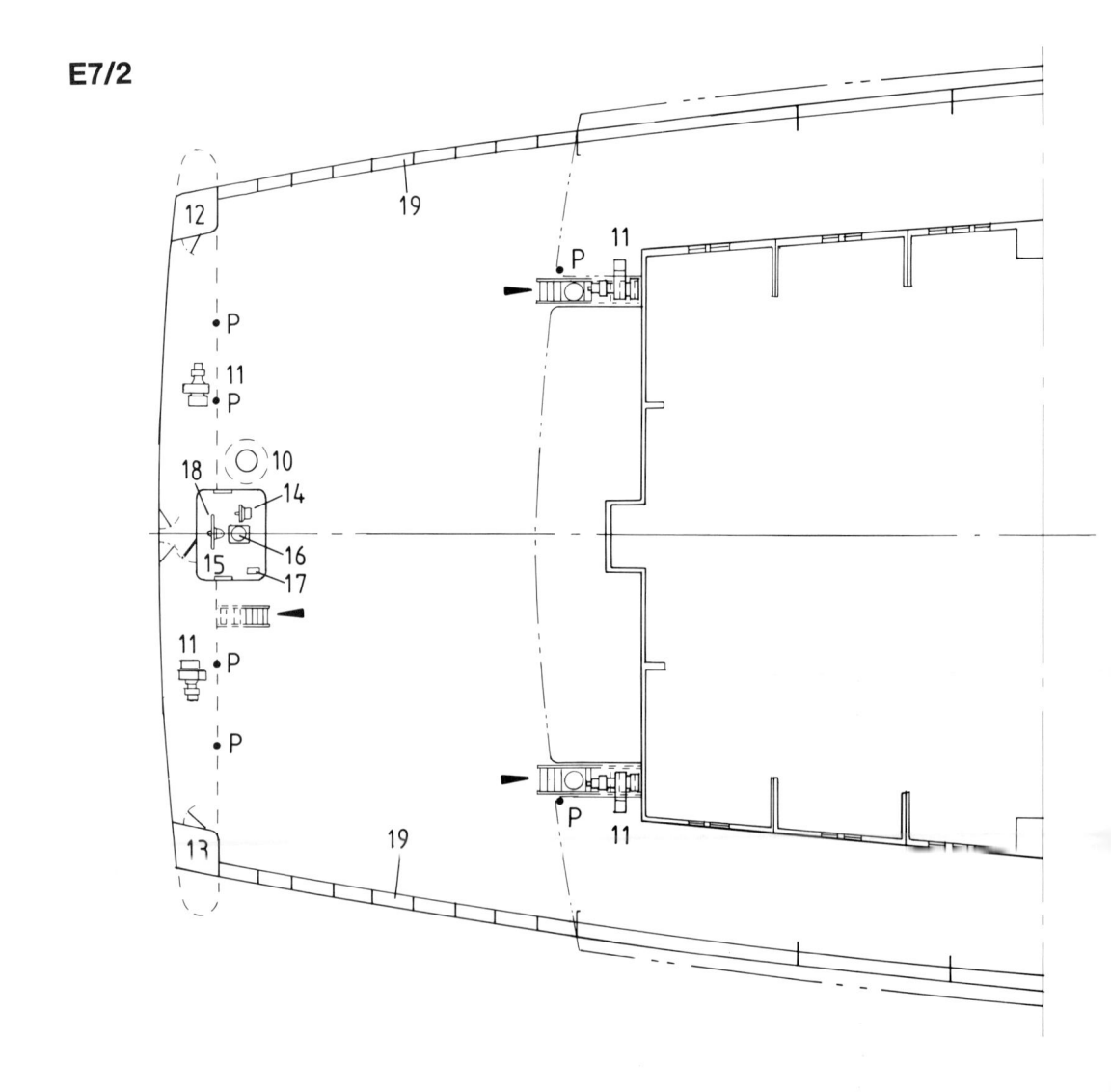

E7	ARRANGEMENT OF AFTER SUPERSTRUCTURE BETWEEN FRAMES 8 AND 51 (1/250 scale)
E7/1	Profile
E7/2	Promenade deck plan
E7/3	Main deck plan
E7/4	General view

1. Sounding boom (stowed position)
2. Stern lamp fitting
3. Docking telegraph
4. Teak screen
5. 3-ton gangway winch
6. Rollers for gangway winch leads
7. Web
8. Mooring pipe
9. Vent
10. Exhaust vent
11. Fan
12. Games locker
13. Quartermaster's locker
14. Steering telegraph
15. Wheelhouse
16. Compass
17. Telephone
18. Wheel
19. Gutterway
20. Docking bridge
P. Pillar

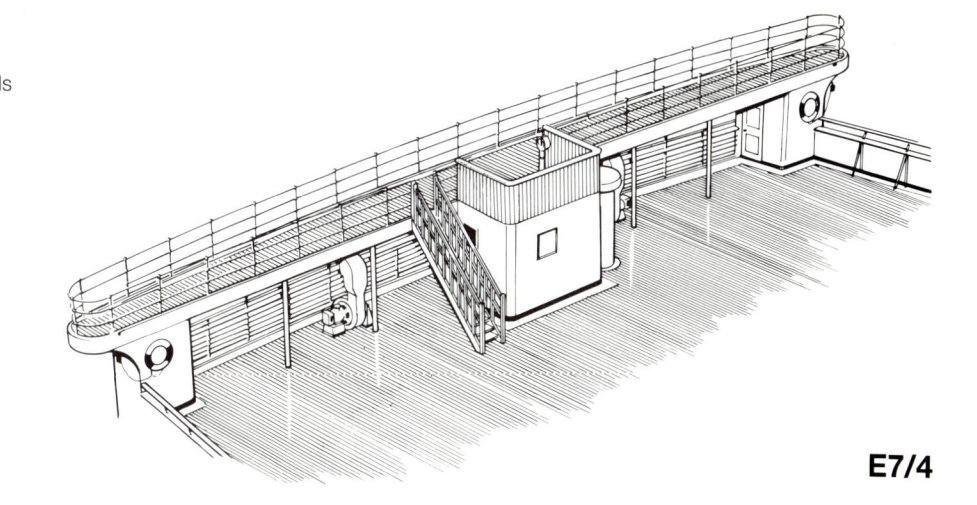

E7/4

E7/3

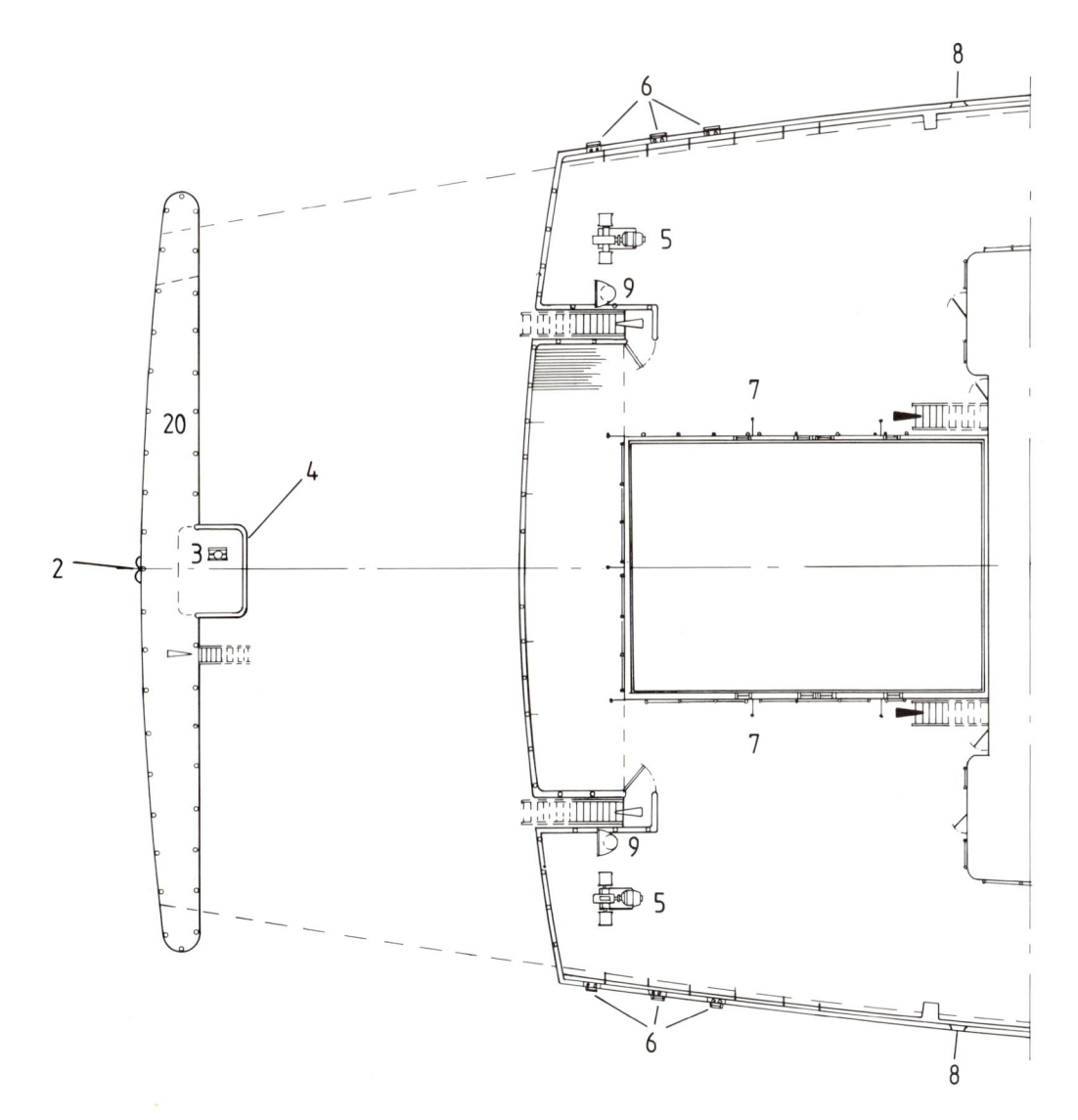

115

F Rig

F1 CARGO DERRICKS AND GEAR (1/250 scale)

F1/1 Plan

F1/2 Starboard elevation

1. 72ft wing derrick (working position)
2. 67ft wing derrick (working position)
3. 52ft centre derrick (working position)
4. 52ft 6in centre derrick (working position)
5. 72ft wing derrick (stowed position)
6. 67ft wing derrick (stowed position)
7. 52ft centre derrick (stowed position)
8. 52ft 6in centre derrick (stowed position)
9. 6-ton electric winch
10. No 1 cargo hatch with watertight hinged cover
11. No 2 cargo hatch with watertight hinged cover
12. Foremast
13. Derrick crutch
14. Manila purchase
15. Single block
16. Double block
17. Derrick guy
18. Pendant
19. Deck cleats
20. Third class promenade deck
21. Treble block
22. Topping lifts
23. Topmast backstay
24. Shrouds
25. Preventer
26. Ratlines
27. 30-ton capstan
28. 36-ton capstan
29. Capstan control pedestal
30. Davit
31. Stores hatch
32. Lead block
33. Crow's nest
34. Link plates
35. Blocks
36. Cargo wire runner
37. Manila whips
38. Tail chains with Cunard cargo hooks
39. Cargo span
40. Anchor lamp
41. Forestay
42. Topmast stay
43. Dressing line
- **B** Bollard
- **JL** Jacob's ladder
- **MV** Mushroom vent
- **V** Vent
- **R** Roller fairlead
- **W** Waterway

F1/1

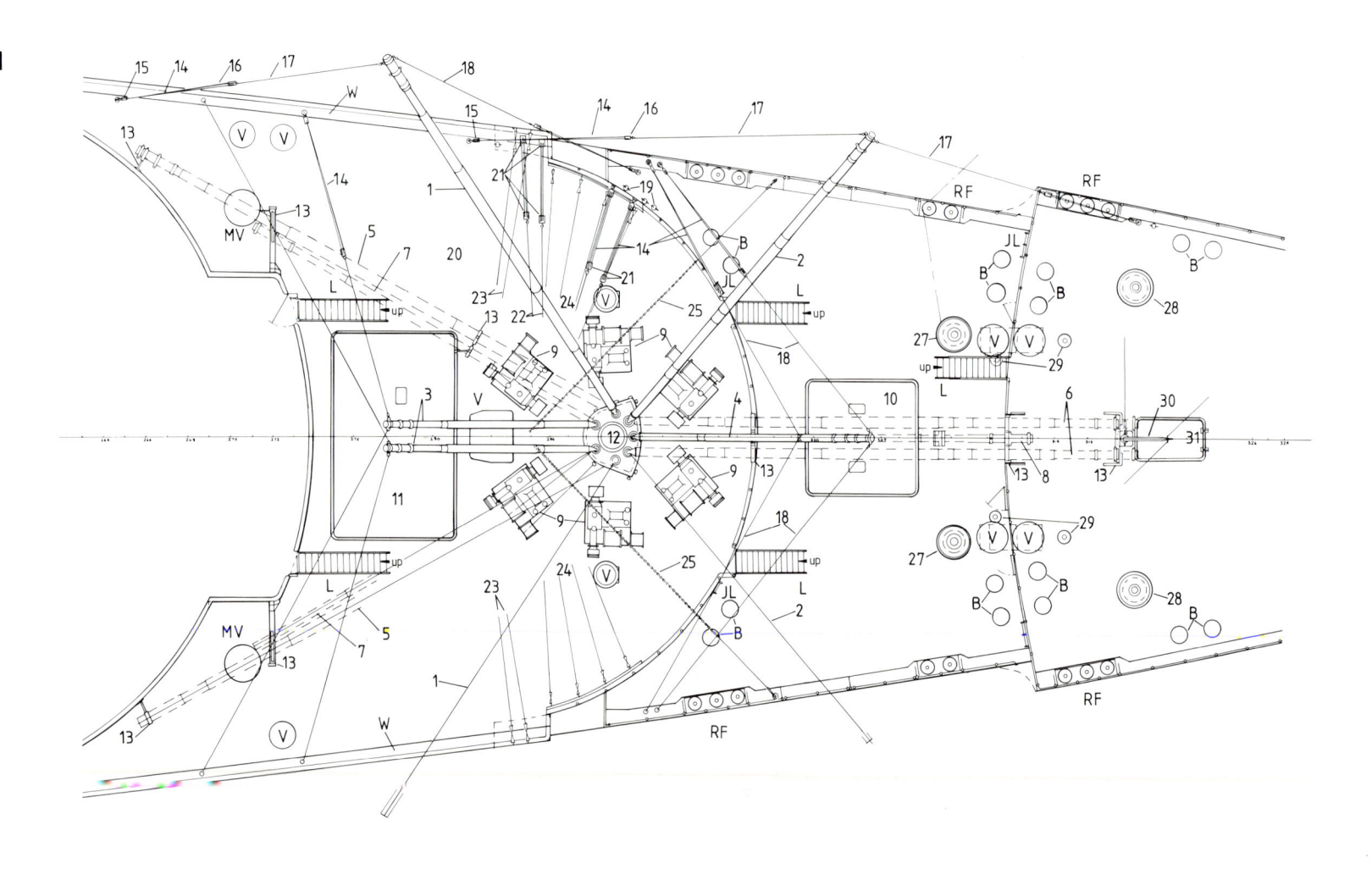

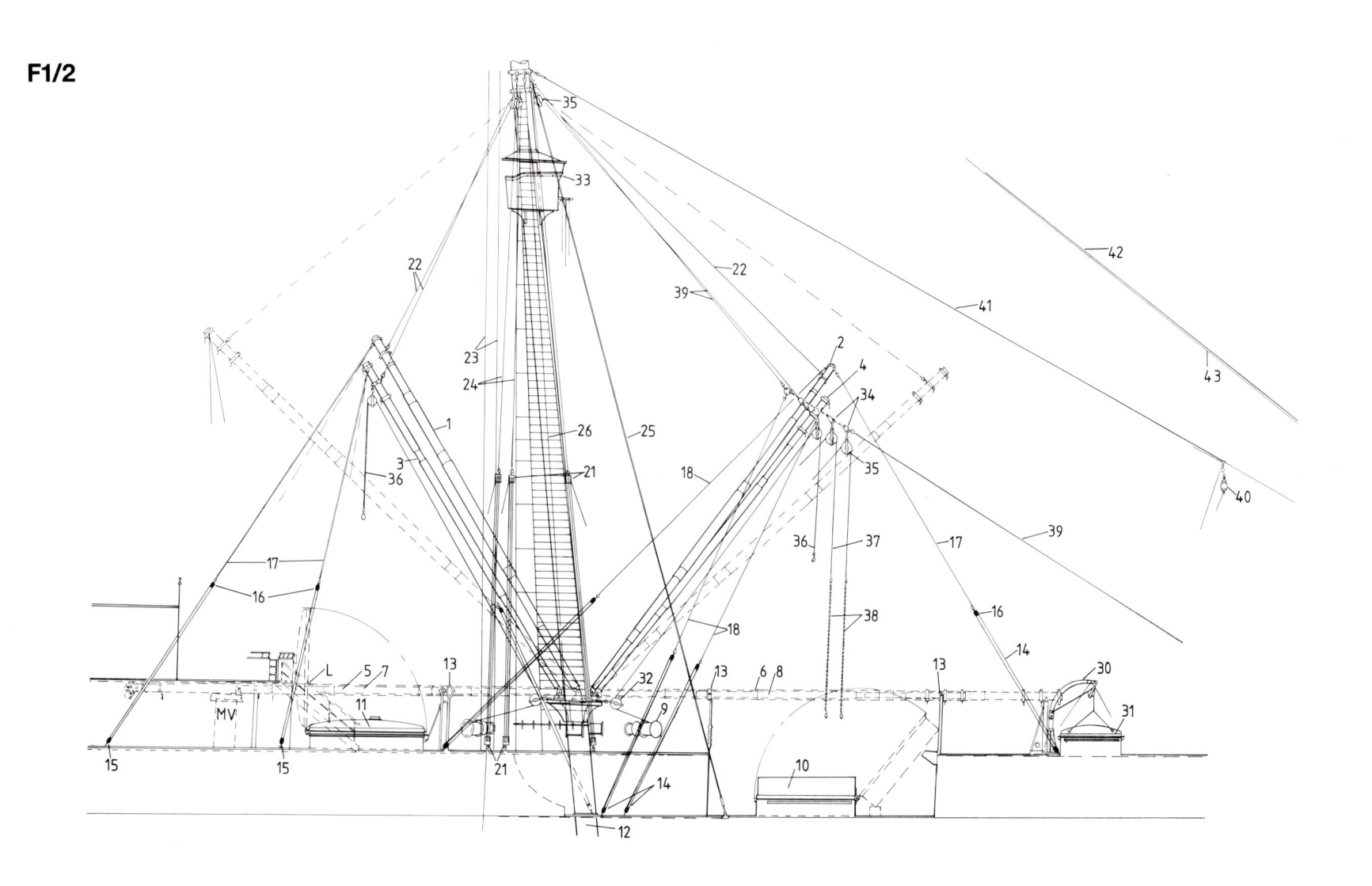

F1/2

117

F Rig

F1/3 General view from forward starboard side

F1/3

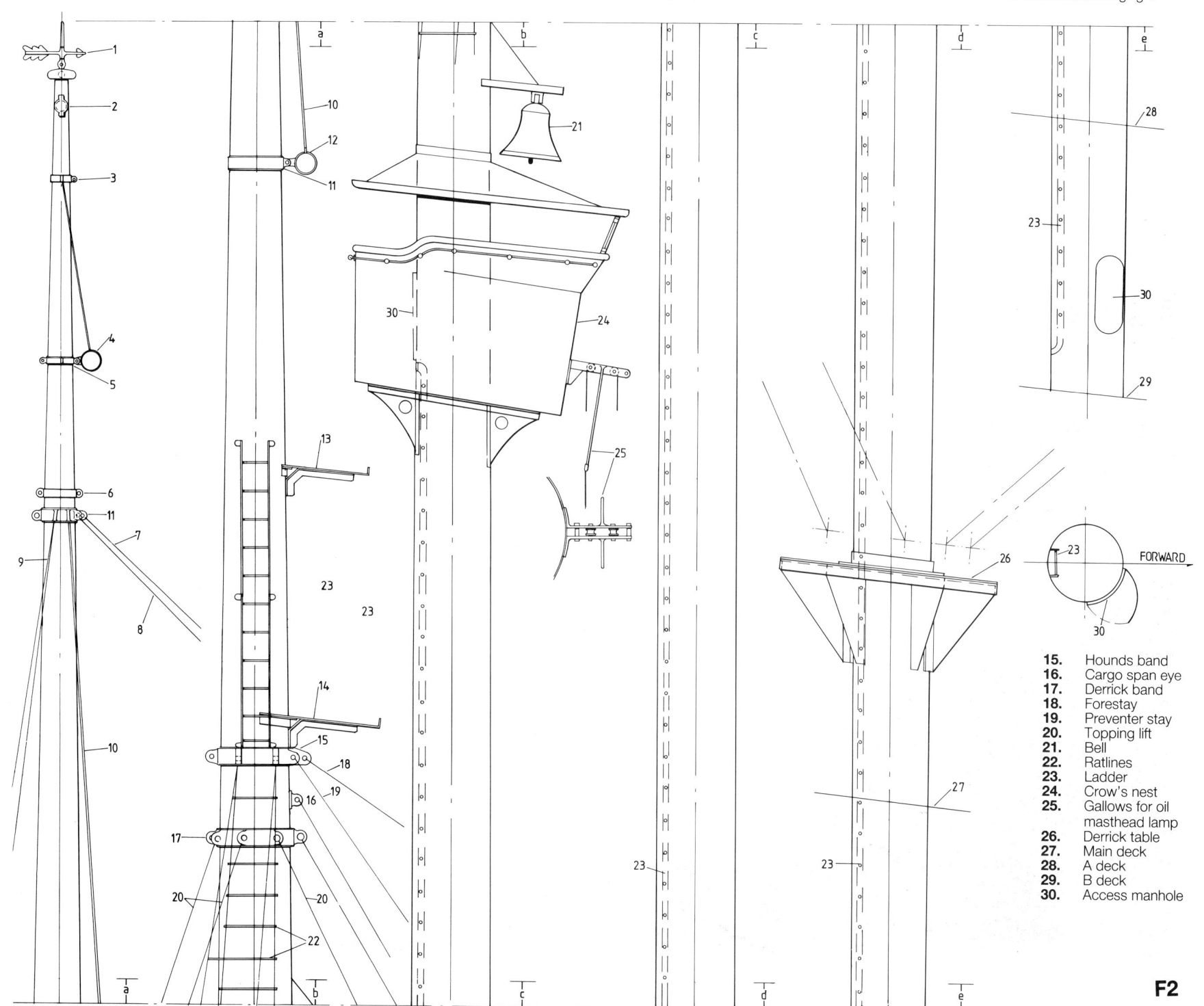

F2 FOREMAST SEGMENTED VIEW, STARBOARD ELEVATION (1/50 scale)

1. Weather vane
2. Gantline sheave
3. Wireless aerial yard band
4. Wireless aerial yardarm (removed 1947)
5. Wireless aerial halyard band
6. Band for dressing line
7. Fore topmast stay
8. Dressing line
9. Fore topmast backstay
10. Signal yard lifts
11. Topmast band
12. Signal yard
13. Platform for electric navigation light (added 1947)
14. Platform for electric steaming light
15. Hounds band
16. Cargo span eye
17. Derrick band
18. Forestay
19. Preventer stay
20. Topping lift
21. Bell
22. Ratlines
23. Ladder
24. Crow's nest
25. Gallows for oil masthead lamp
26. Derrick table
27. Main deck
28. A deck
29. B deck
30. Access manhole

F2

119

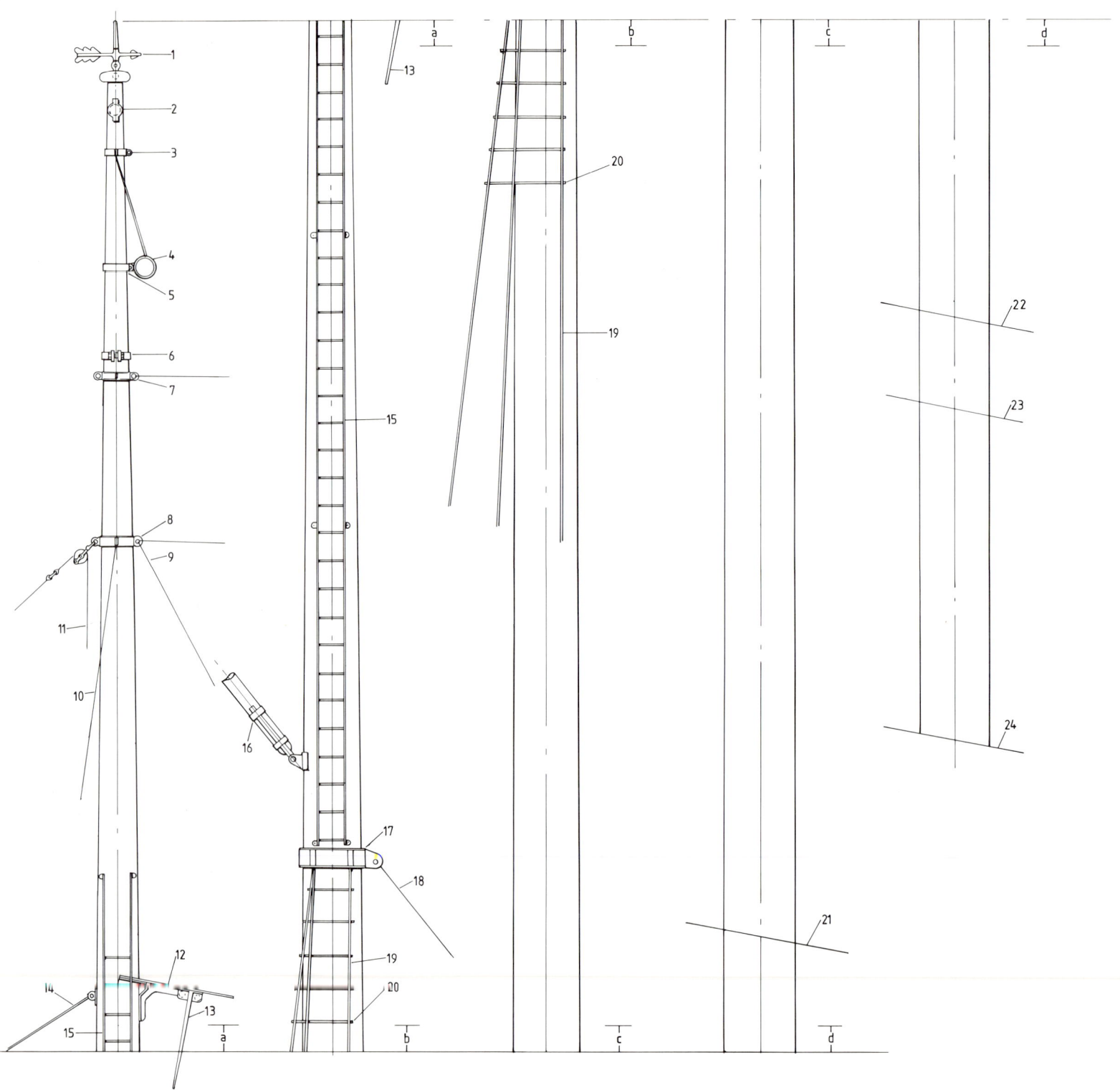

F Rig

F3

F3 MAINMAST SEGMENTED VIEW, STARBOARD ELEVATION (1/50 scale)

1. Weather vane
2. Gantline sheave
3. Wireless aerial yard band
4. Wireless aerial yardarm
5. Wireless aerial band
6. Band for dressing line
7. Wireless aerial band
8. Topmast band
9. Main topmast stay
10. Main topmast backstay
11. Dressing line halyard
12. Platform for after electric steaming light
13. Fork for oil steaming light
14. Gaff topping lift
15. Ladder
16. Gaff
17. Hounds band
18. Mainstay
19. Shrouds
20. Ratlines
21. Sun deck
22. Raised upper promenade deck wooden platform
23. Upper promenade deck
24. Promenade deck

F4 WEATHER VANE AND GANTLINE SHEAVES, FOR BOTH MASTS (1/10 scale)

F4/1 Sectioned side elevation

F4/2 Plan of truck

F4/3 Gantline sheave (end elevation)

F4/4 Gantline sheave (plan)

1. Copper spindle
2. Copper
3. Elm truck
4. Brass sheaves
5. Pin
6. Brass cap
7. Stud

F5 WIRELESS AERIAL BAND ON FOREMAST, MAINMAST SIMILAR (1/20 scale)

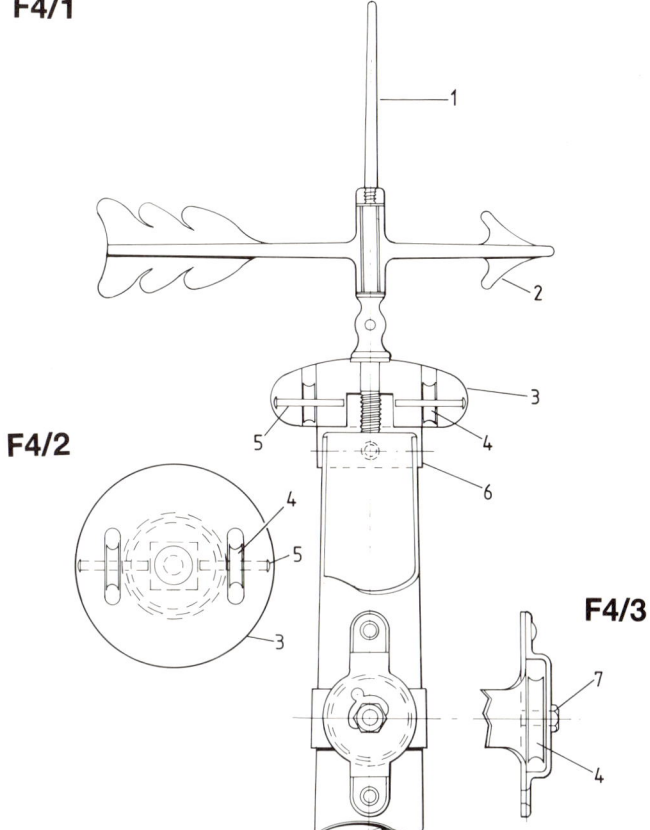

1. Wrot eyes
2. Aerial eye

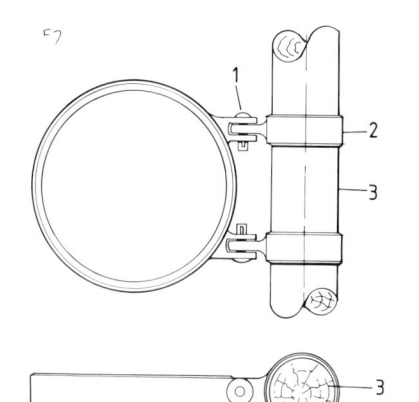

F6 TOPMAST STAY BAND ON FOREMAST (1/20 scale)

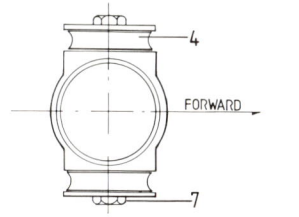

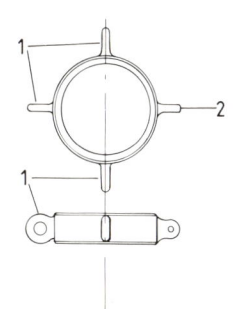

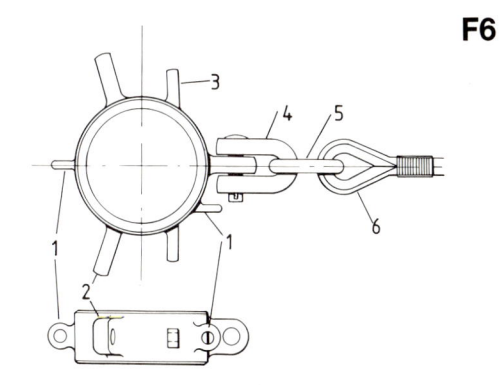

1. Wrot eye for dressing line
2. Eye for 'B' stay
3. Eye for signal yards
4. Shackle
5. Link
6. Fore topmast stay

F7 BAND FOR SIGNAL YARD ON FOREMAST (1/20 scale)

1. Pin with forelock
2. Band
3. Signal yard

F Rig

F8   TOPMAST STAY BAND ON MAINMAST (1/20 scale)

1. Eye for topmast backstay
2. Wrot eye for dressing line
3. Shackle
4. Topmast stay

F9   HOUNDS BAND ON MAINMAST (1/20 scale)

1. Eye for shrouds
2. Shackle
3. Link
4. Double mainstay
5. Double shroud
6. Single shroud

F10   HOUNDS BAND ON FOREMAST (1/20 scale)

1. Eye for jumper stay
2. Eye for preventer stay
3. Double forestay
4. Shackle
5. Link
6. Double shrouds

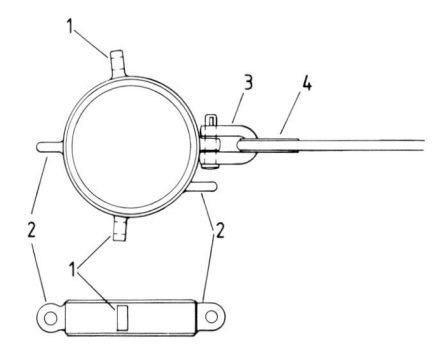

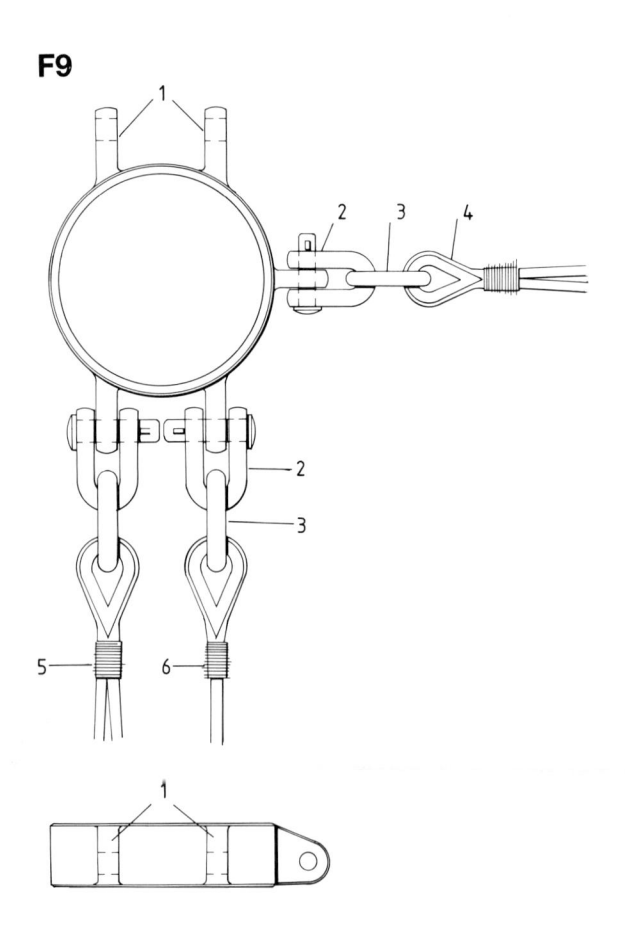

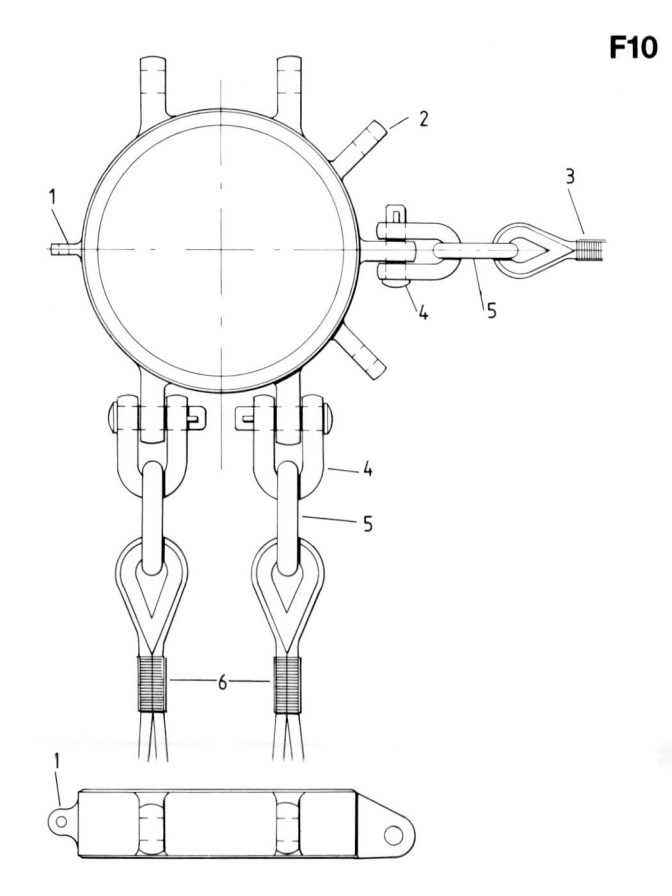

F8

F9

F10

122

F11 MASTHEAD LAMP FITTINGS ON MAINMAST (1/20 scale)

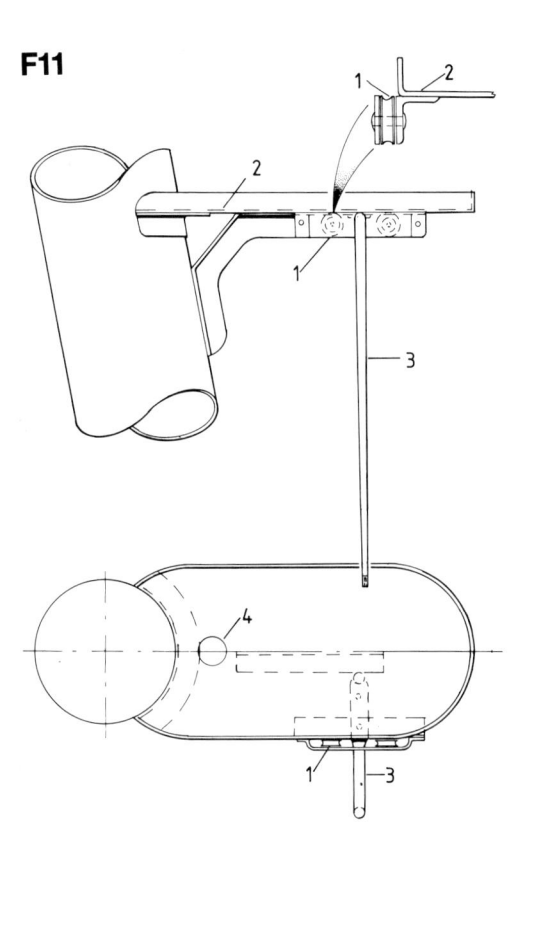

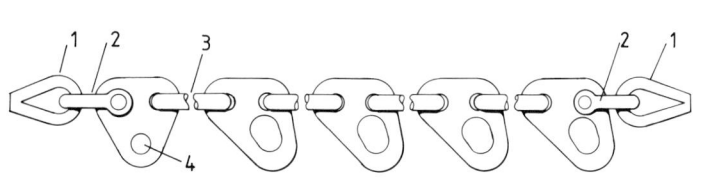

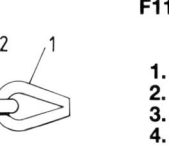

1. Brass sheave
2. Platform
3. Fork for oil lamp
4. Hole for connection

F12 CARGO SPAN GIN PLATES (1/20 scale)

1. Thimble
2. Shackle
3. Chain
4. Eye for steadying guy

F13 BAND FOR DRESSING LINES ON MAINMAST (1/10 scale)

F14 BAND FOR DRESSING LINES ON FOREMAST (1/10 scale)

F15 BAND FOR DERRICK GUYS ON FOREMAST (1/20 scale)

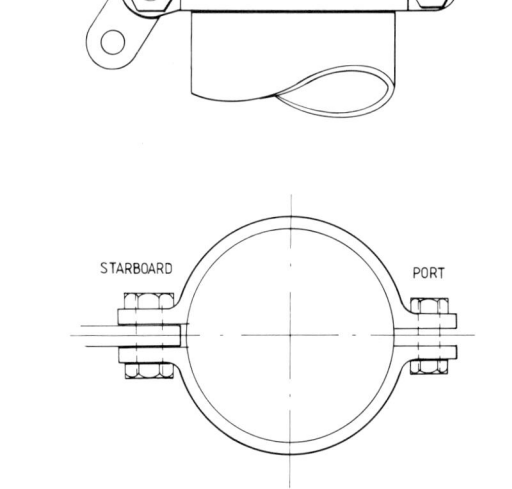

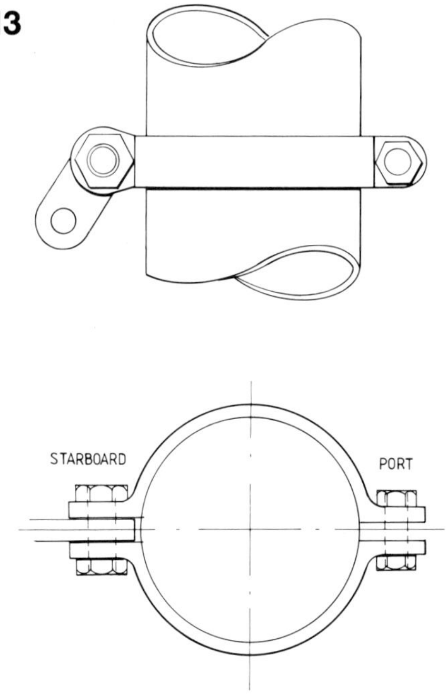

1. Eye for cargo span
2. Links to table topping lifts

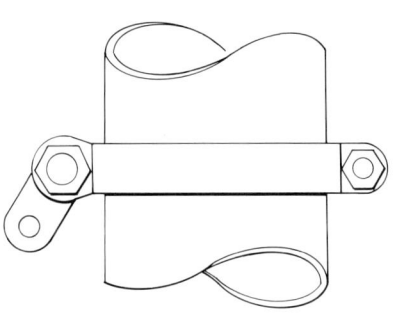

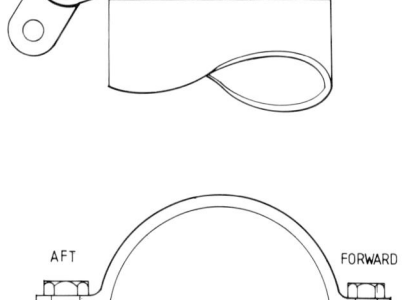

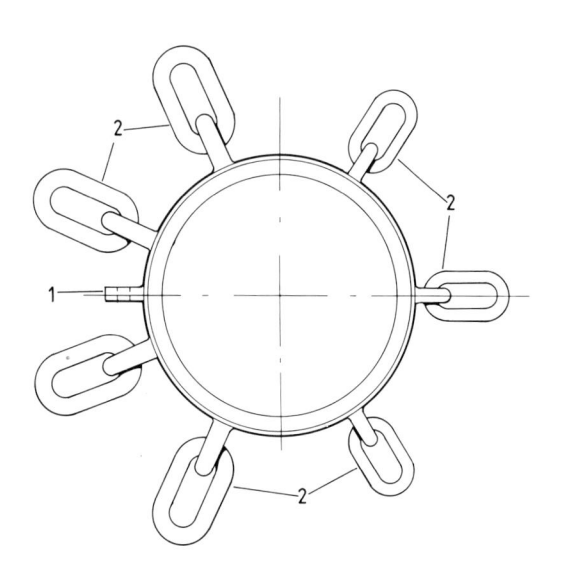

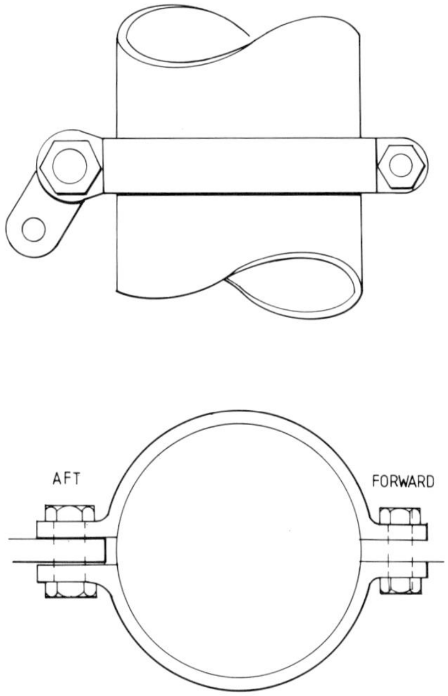

F Rig

F16/1

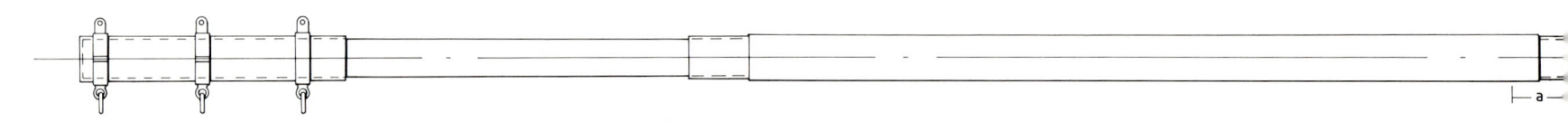

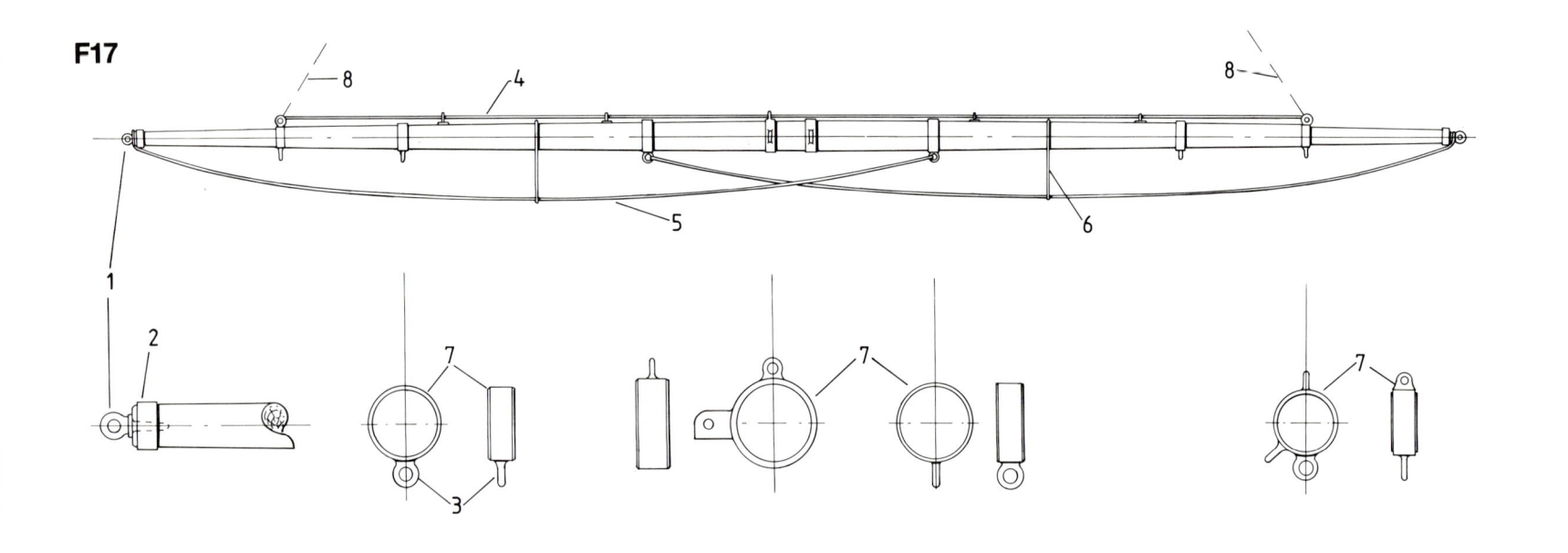

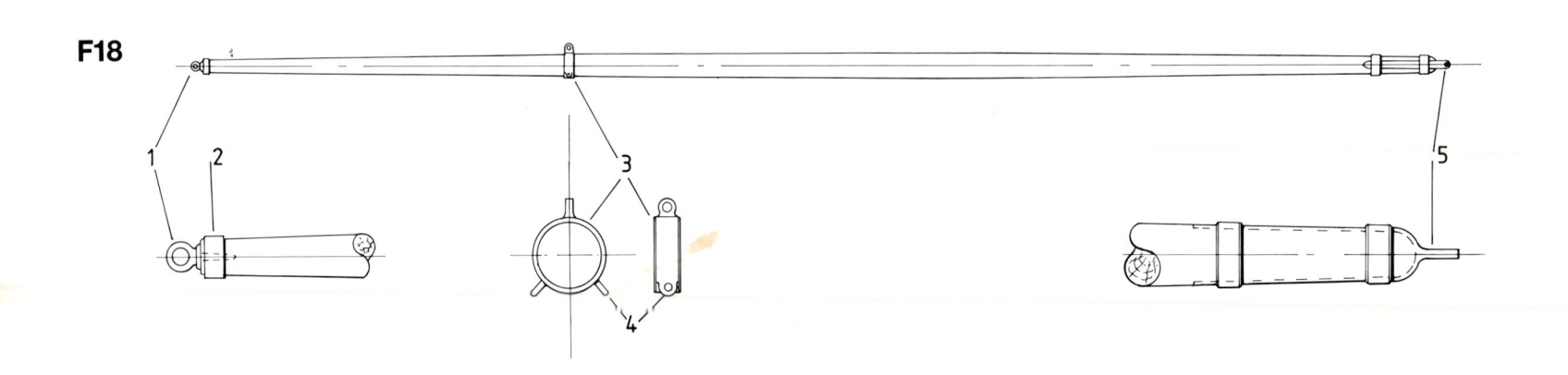

F17

F18

124

F16 CARGO DERRICK (1/50 scale)

F16/1 General view

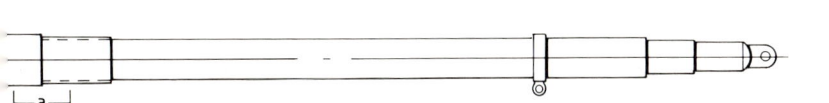

F16/2 CARGO BAND ON DERRICK (1/20 scale)

1. Eyes for guys
2. Link for shackle of gin block
3. Eye for topping lift

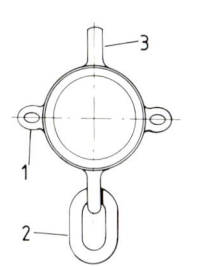

F17 SIGNAL YARD ON FOREMAST (1/50 scale, details 3 × larger)

1. Ragtail eyebolt for signal halyard block
2. Ferrule
3. Wrot eye for signal halyard block
4. Jackstay
5. Footrope
6. Stirrup
7. Parrel bands
8. Yard lift

F18 GAFF ON MAINMAST (1/50 scale, details 3 ø larger)

1. Ragtail eyebolt
2. Ferrule
3. Lift band
4. Eyes for vangs
5. Heel

F19 GOOSENECK FOR 5-TON DERRICK (1/20 scale)

1. Oil well
2. Rivets
3. Hole for pin

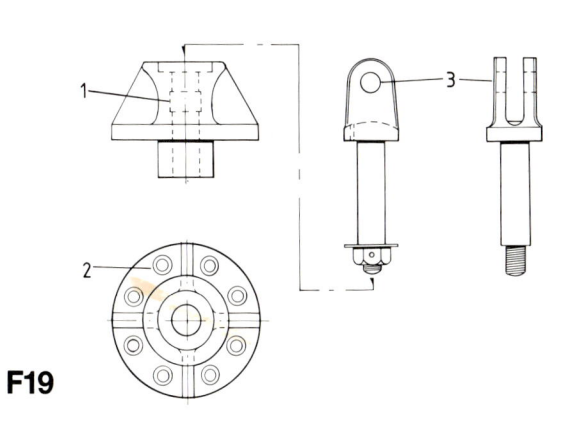

125

F Rig

F20 CROW'S NEST (1/50 scale)

F20/1 Side elevation, sectioned

F20/2 Front view

F20/3 Plan

F20/4 Plan of canopy

1. Canopy
2. Glass panel with wooden frame
3. Entrance
4. Brackets
5. Stiffeners
6. Ladder
7. Line at top of crow's nest
8. Single riveted lap

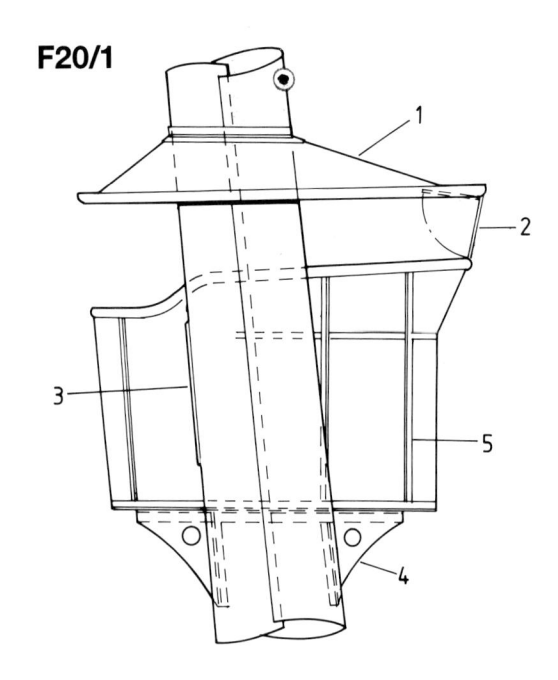

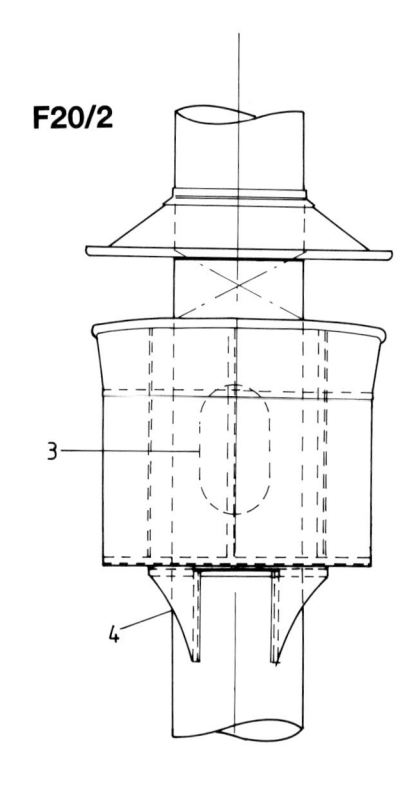

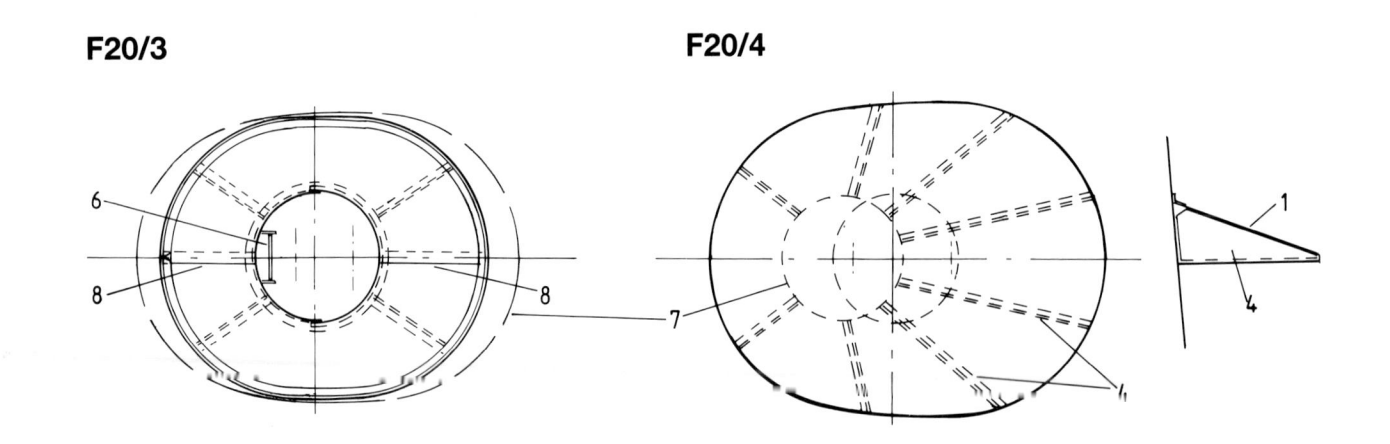

F21

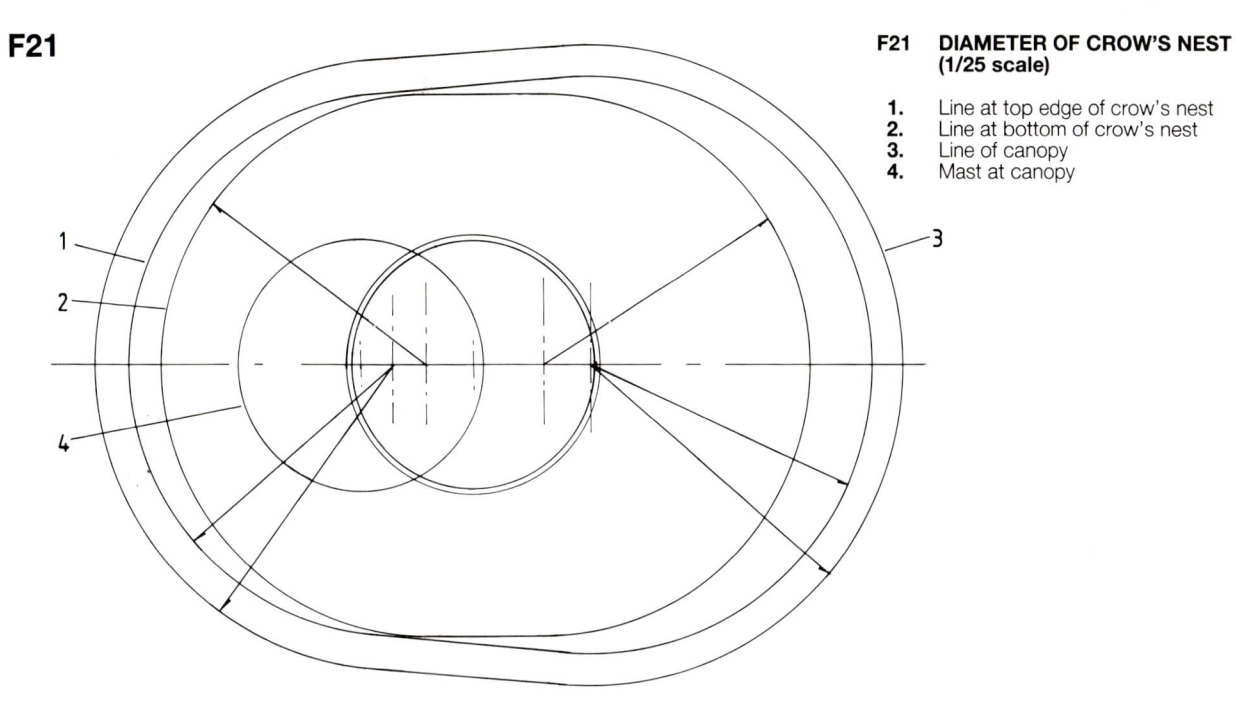

F21 DIAMETER OF CROW'S NEST
(1/25 scale)

1. Line at top edge of crow's nest
2. Line at bottom of crow's nest
3. Line of canopy
4. Mast at canopy

F22

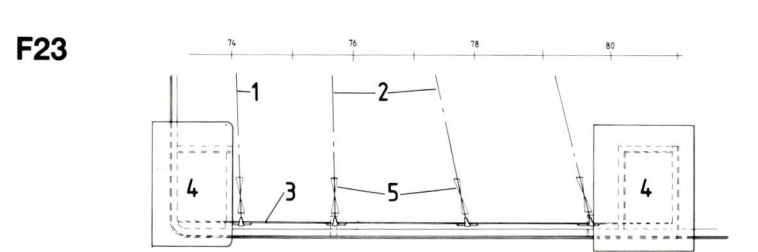

F22 ARRANGEMENT OF FOREMAST SHROUDS ON MAIN DECK PORT SIDE (1/100 scale)

1. Bulb angle
2. Bottle-screw rigging slip
3. Shroud
4. Double riveted seam

F23 ARRANGEMENT OF MAINMAST SHROUDS AT SUN DECK (1/100 scale)

1. Backstay
2. Shroud
3. Bulb angle
4. Thermotank vent exhaust
5. Bottle-screw rigging slip

F24 MAINMAST STAY CONNECTIONS ON FAN HOUSE TOP (1/100 scale)

1. Mainstay
2. Bottle-screw rigging slip
3. Main topmast stay
4. Bulb angle
5. Girder
6. Eyeplate
7. Bulb angle beams
8. Stiffening at centre of ship
9. Double deck connections

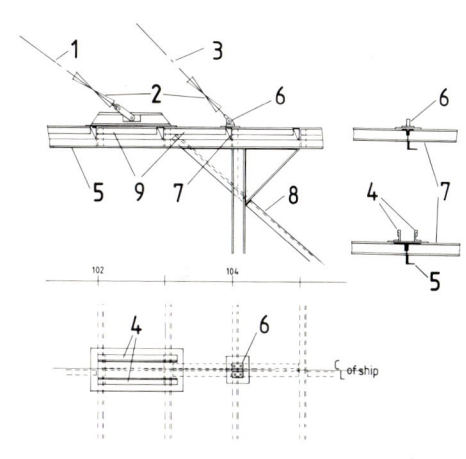

F23

F24

F Rig

F25/1

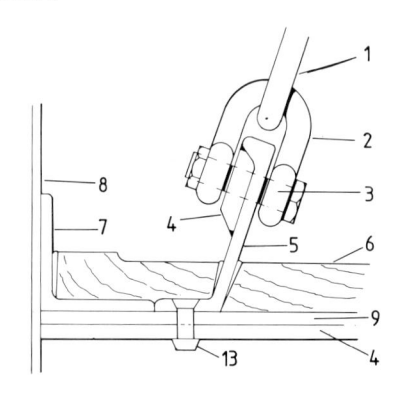

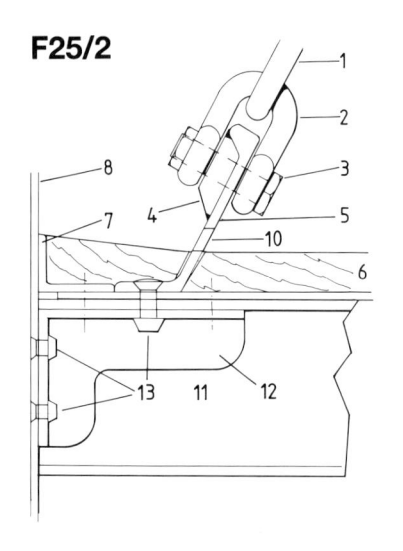

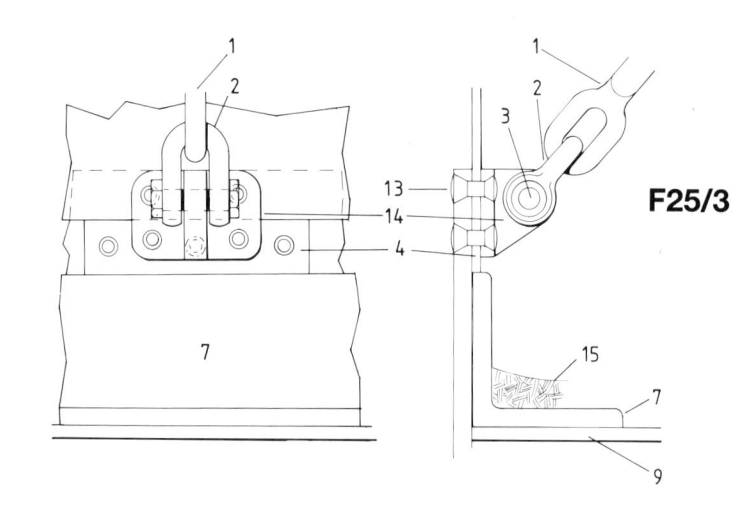

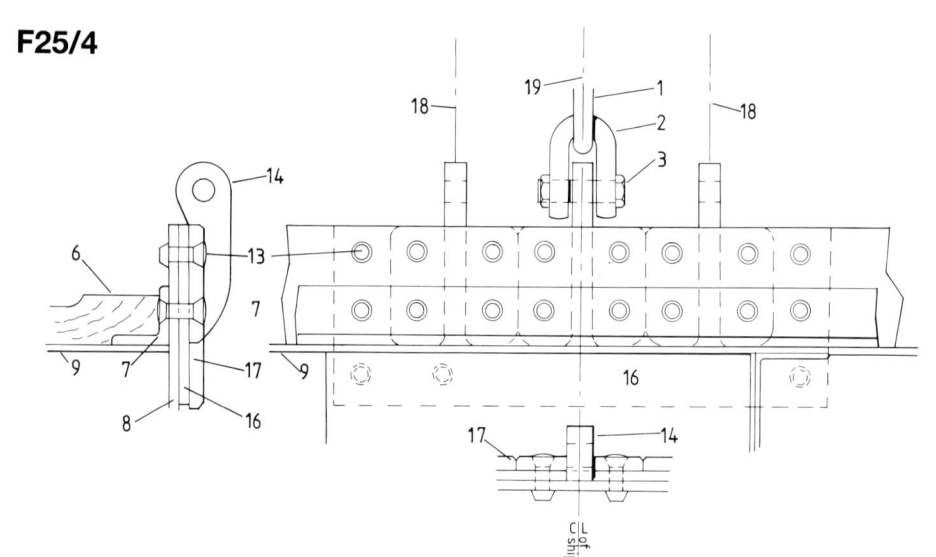

F25/2

F25/3

F25/4

F25/5

F25	MAST RIGGING MOUNTINGS (1/10 scale, except as noted)
F25/1	Section in way of bulb angle to take foremast shrouds
F25/2	Section in way of bulb angle to take mainmast shrouds and backstay
F25/3	Eyeplates to take foremast backstays (side elevation and end elevation)
F25/4	Eyeplates to take main topmast stay and mainstay (elevations and plan)
F25/5	Eyeplates to take fore and topmast stays and forestay (elevation and plan)

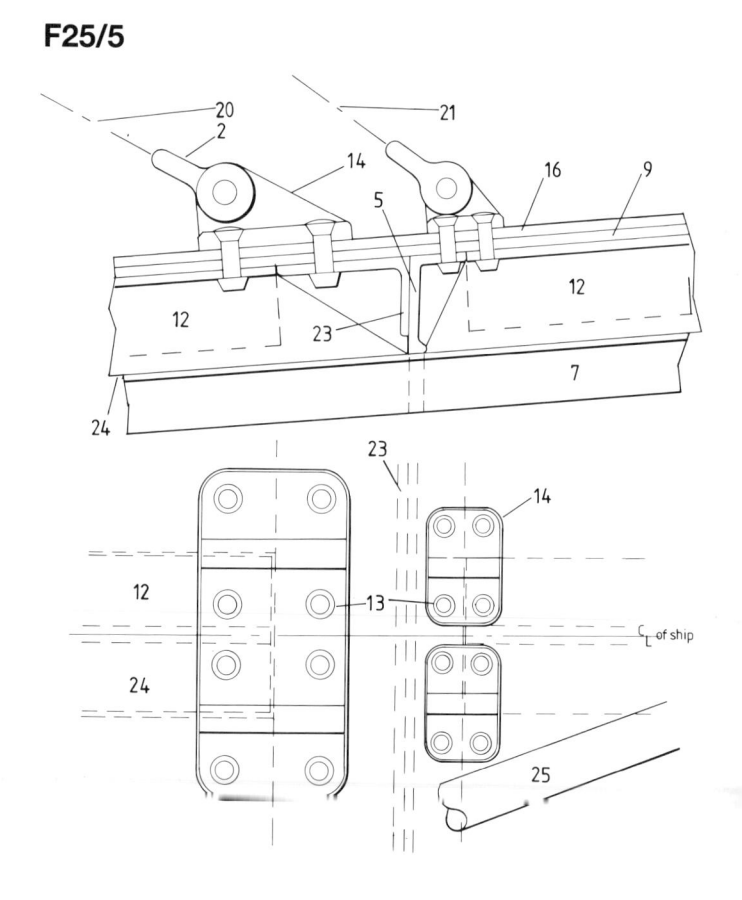

F25/6

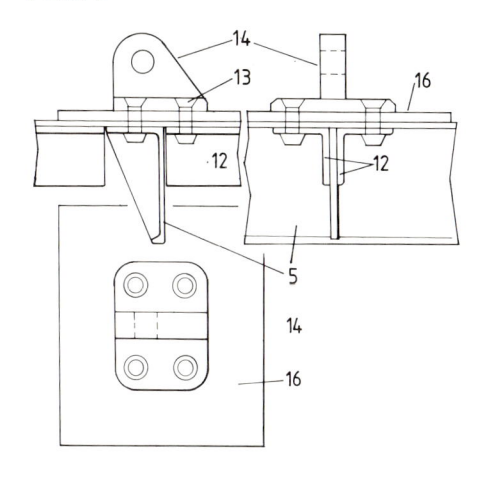

F25/7

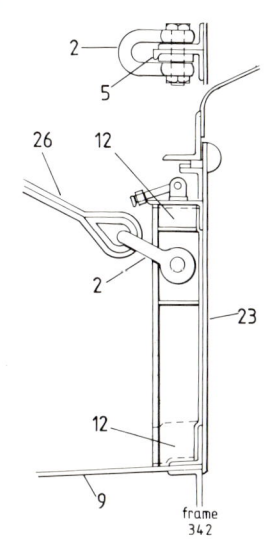

F25/8

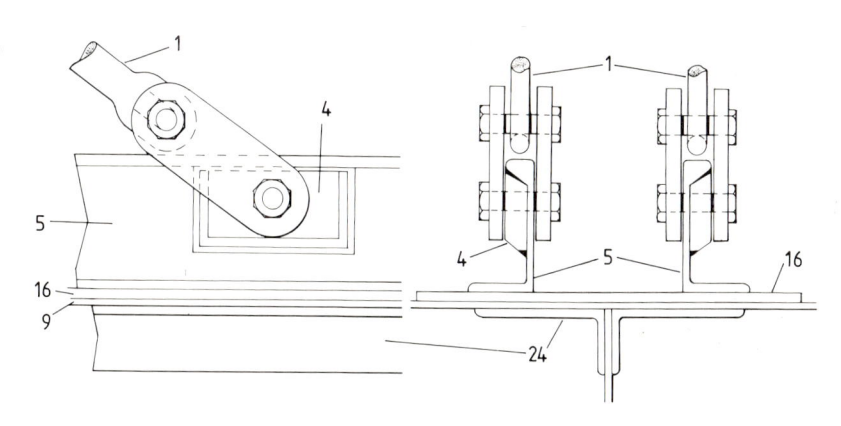

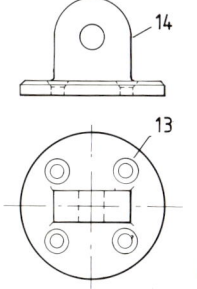

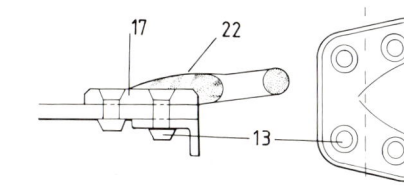

F25/9

F25/10

F25/6	Eyeplate to take main topmast forestay (elevation, end elevation and plan)
F25/7	Cargo span connection to forepeak stores hatch (1/20 scale)
F25/8	Bulb angle to take mainstays (side elevation, end elevation)
F25/9	Eyeplate to take foremast preventer stay (side elevation and plan)
F25/10	Eyeplate on derrick table (sectioned elevation and plan)

1. Bottle-screw rigging slip
2. Shackle
3. Pin
4. Filling piece
5. Bulb angle
6. Wooden deck
7. Stringer angle
8. Side plating
9. Deck plating
10. Drainage hole
11. Channel beam
12. Lug
13. Rivet
14. Eyeplate
15. Cement
16. Doubling plate
17. Palm
18. Mainstay
19. Main topmast stay
20. Forestay
21. Fore topmast stay
22. Fillet
23. Backpiece
25. Hinged jackstaff
26. Cargo span

F Rig

F26 DERRICK CRUTCH DETAILS
(1/20 scale, except as noted)

F26/1 Crutch at side of house (1/10 scale)

F26/2 Crutch at frame 282 port and starboard on main deck

F26/3 Detail of stay

F26/4 Detail of eyeplate

F26/5 Detail of crutch head (1/10 scale)

F26/6 Detail of socket (1/10 scale)

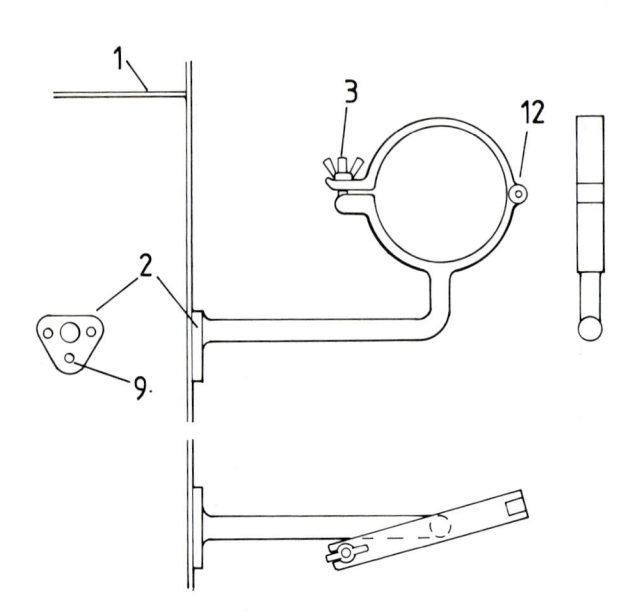

F26/1

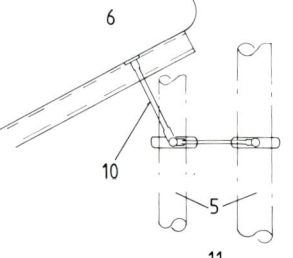

F26/2

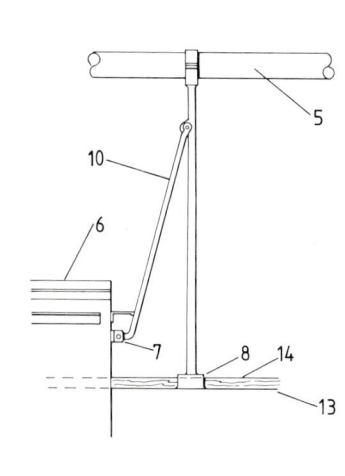

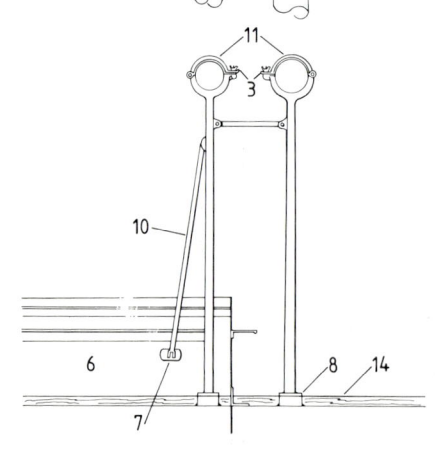

F26/3

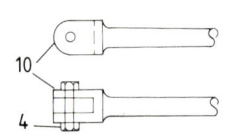

F26/4

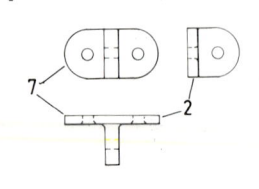

F26/5

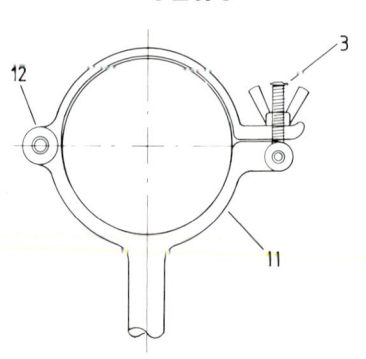

F26/6

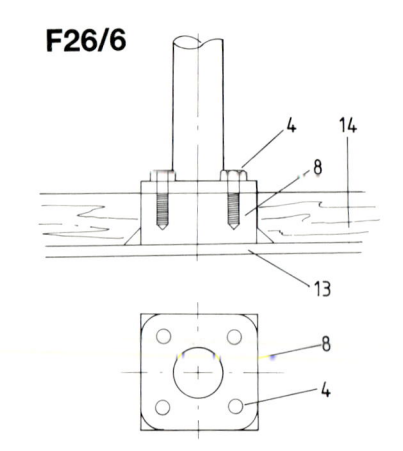

130

F26/7

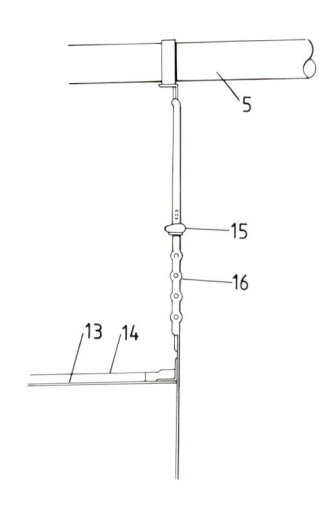

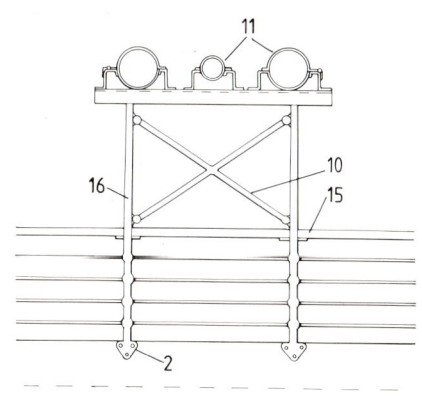

F27 JACKSTAFF (1/50 scale, details 1/8 scale)

F27/1 Side elevation

F27/2 Detail of head

F27/3 Detail of cleat

F27/4 Detail of heel

1. Brass truck
2. Brass sheave
3. Pin
4. Bolt
5. Tube

F26/7 Crutch at fore end of main deck (1/20 scale)
1. Promenade deck
2. Palm
3. Screw fastening
4. Bolt
5. Derrick
6. No 2 cargo hatch
7. Eyeplate
8. Steel pad
9. Rivets
10. Stay
11. Crutch head
12. Hinge
13. Main deck
14. Wooden deck
15. Teak rail
16. Stanchion

F27/1

F27/2

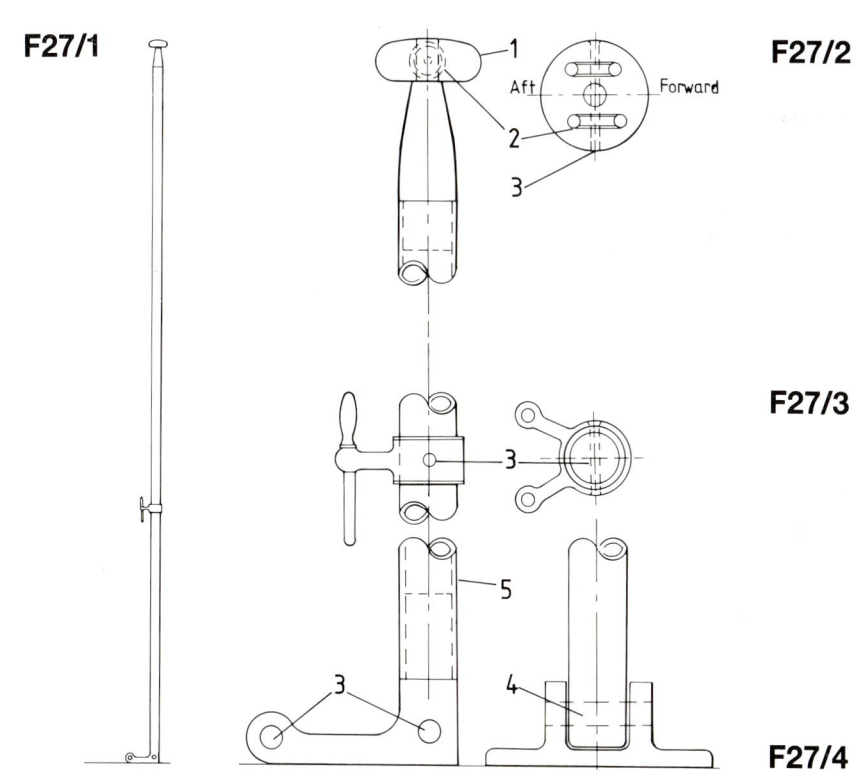

F27/3

F27/4

F Rig

F28   ENSIGN STAFF (1/8 scale)

F28/1   Detail of head

F28/2   Plan at rail

F28/3   Plan of deck fitting

F28/4   Side elevation

1. Brass truck
2. Brass sheave
3. Wood staff
4. Teak rail
5. Chafer
6. Bolt
7. Cleat
8. Plate stays
9. Wood deck

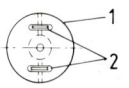

F28/1

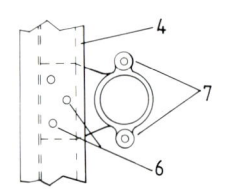

F28/2

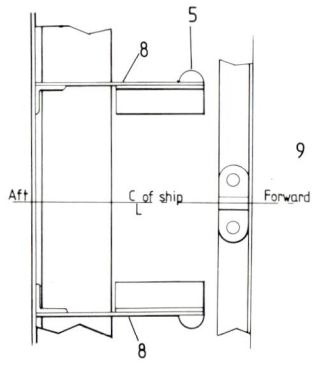

F28/3

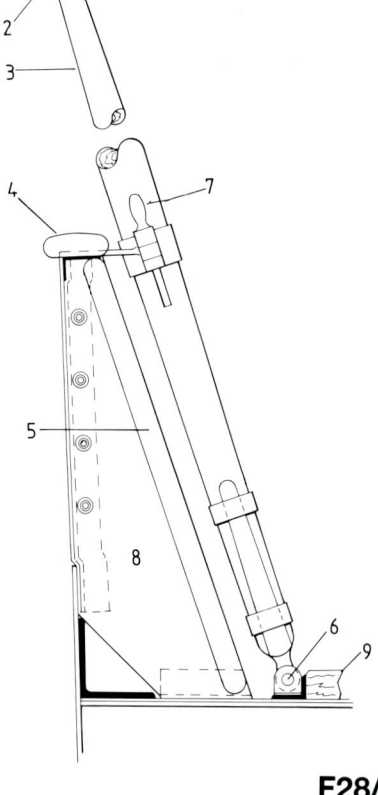

F28/4

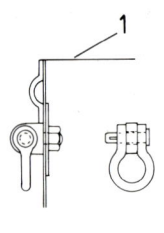

F29/1

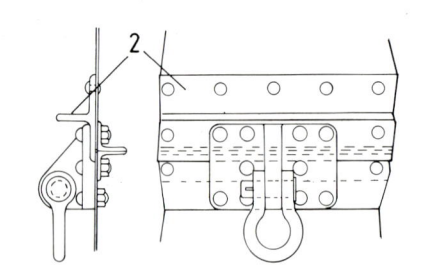

F29/2

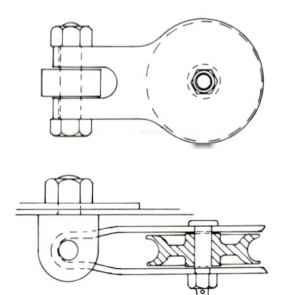

F29/3

F29   FUNNEL FITTINGS (1/8 scale)

F29/1   Eyebolt and shackle for gantling

F29/2   Palm and shackle for shrouds

F29/3   Gantling block

1. Top of funnel
2. Tee bar banding

G Fittings

G1 **SPERRY SEARCHLIGHTS**

G2 **SPERRY GYRO REPEATER PELORUS**

G3 **TYFON NAVIGATIONAL SIREN**

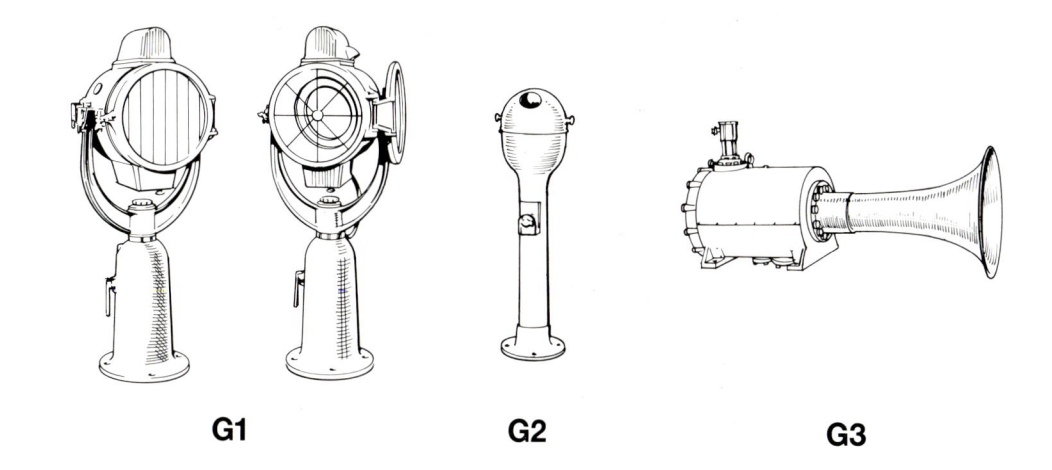

G1

G2

G3

G4/1

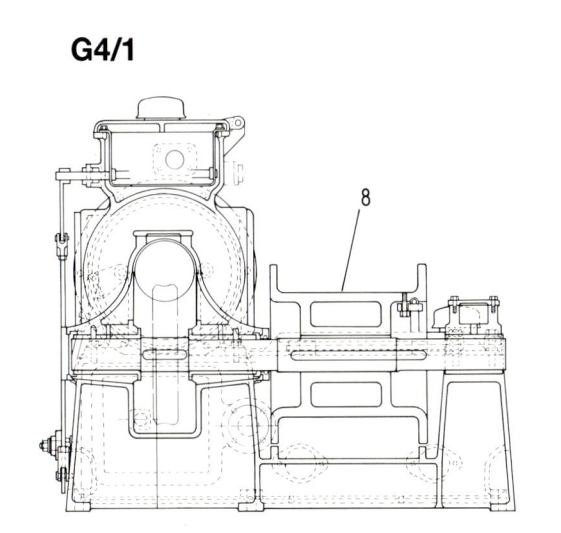

G4/2

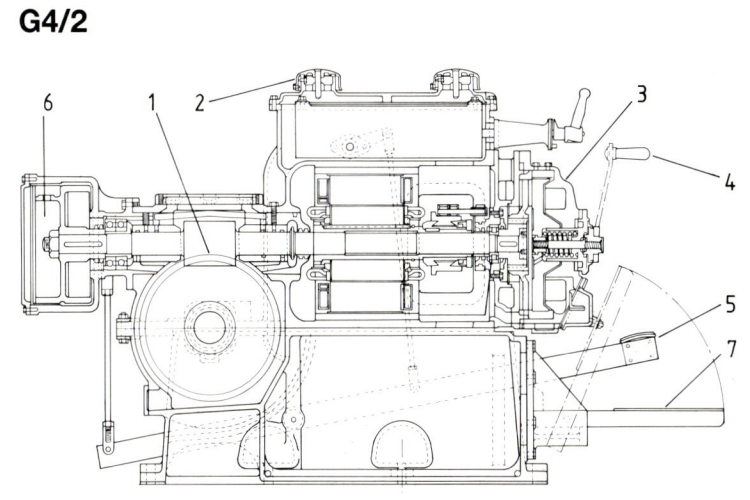

G4 **ARRANGEMENT OF 1-TON MAIL AND BAGGAGE ELECTRIC WINCH, RIGHT HAND PATTERN (1/25 scale)**

G4/1 Sectioned end elevation

G4/2 Sectioned elevation

G4/3 Plan

G4/4 General view

1. Worm gear
2. Cowl ventilators
3. Magnetic brake
4. Hand release
5. Foot brake
6. Centrifugal brake
7. Footplate
8. Warping drum

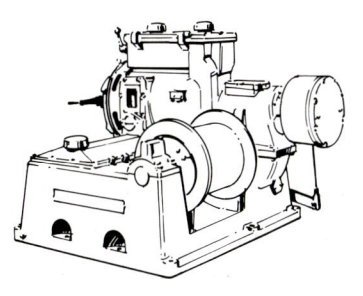

G4/4

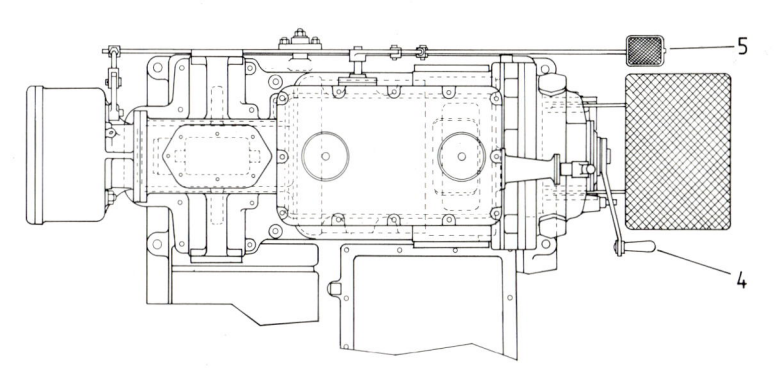

G4/3

133

G Fittings

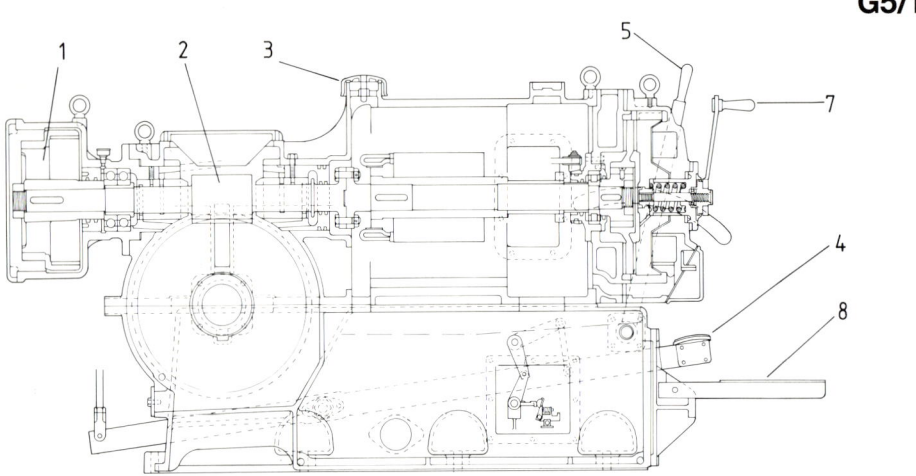

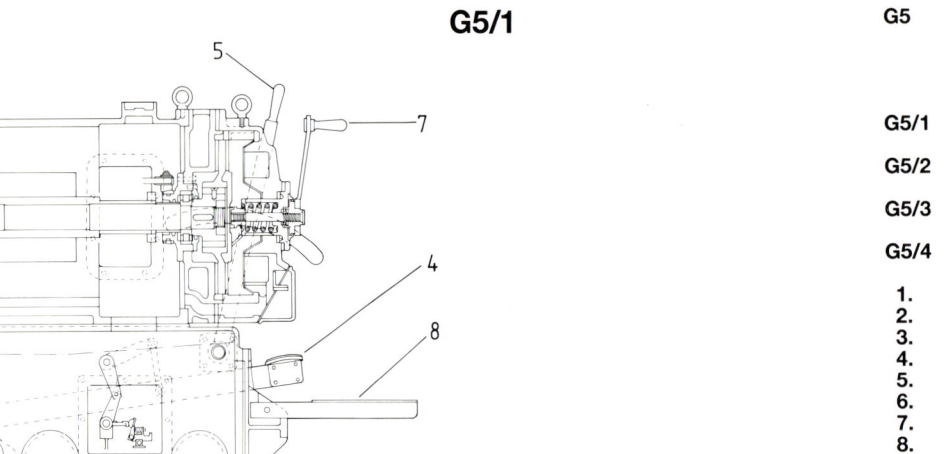

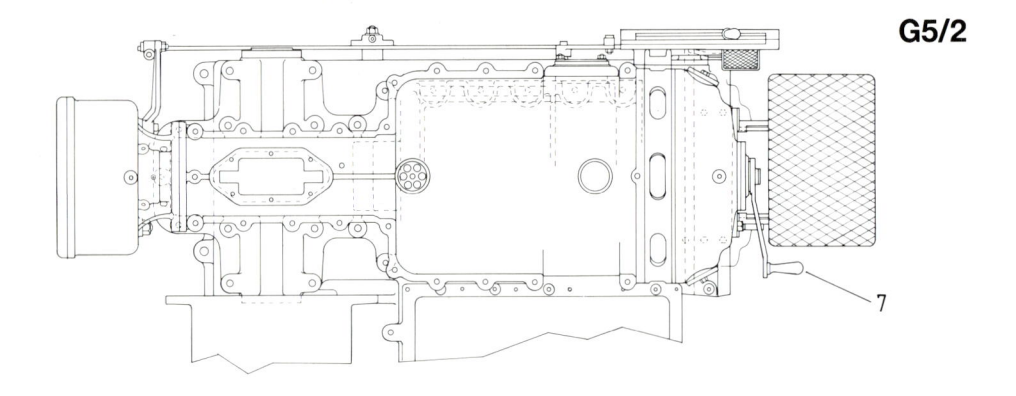

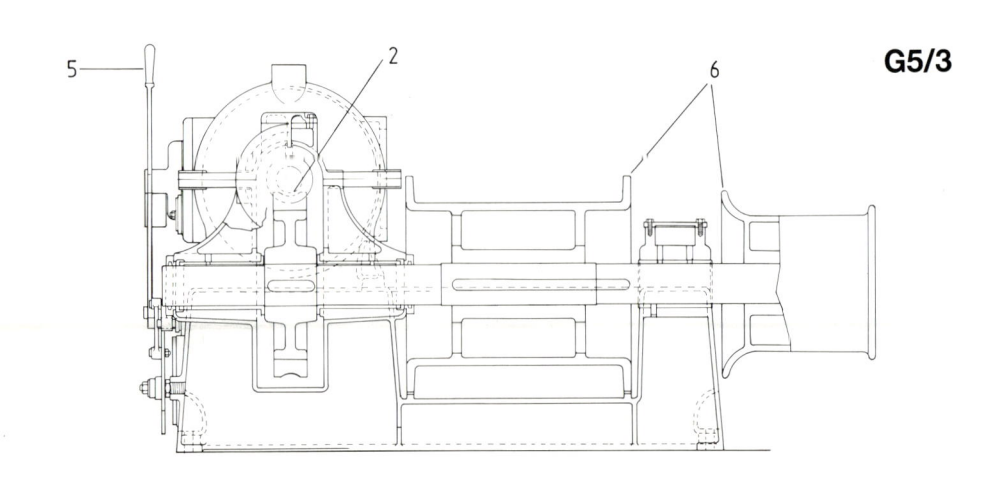

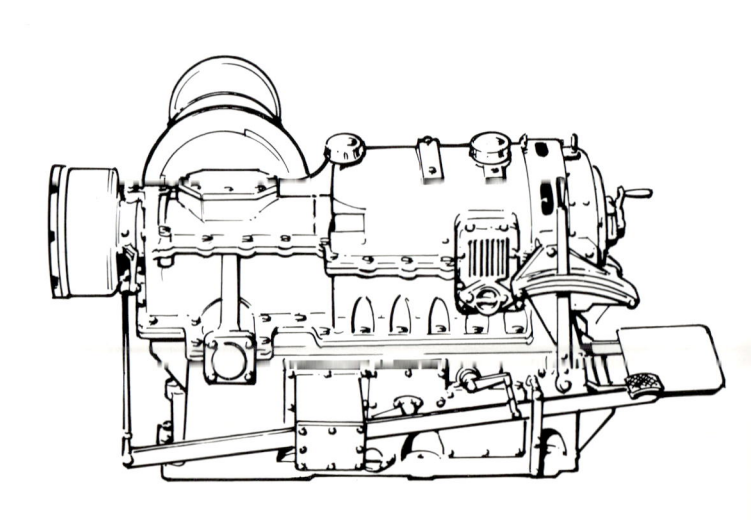

G5/1

G5 ARRANGEMENT OF 6-TON CARGO ELECTRIC WINCH, RIGHT HAND PATTERN (1/25 scale)

G5/1 Sectioned elevation
G5/2 Plan
G5/3 Sectioned end elevation
G5/4 General view (left hand pattern)

1. Centrifugal brake
2. Worm gear
3. Cowl ventilators
4. Pedal brake
5. Gear lever
6. Warping drum
7. Hand release
8. Footplate

G5/2

G5/3

G5/4

134

G6 ARRANGEMENT OF 3-TON GANGWAY ELECTRIC WINCH (1/25 scale)

G6/1 Sectioned elevation

G6/2 End elevation

G6/3 End view of base frame

G6/4 End view of base frame

1. Worm gear
2. Magnetic brake
3. Electric motor
4. Two way push-button switch
5. Isolating switch
6. Warping drum
7. Cable inlet

G6/1

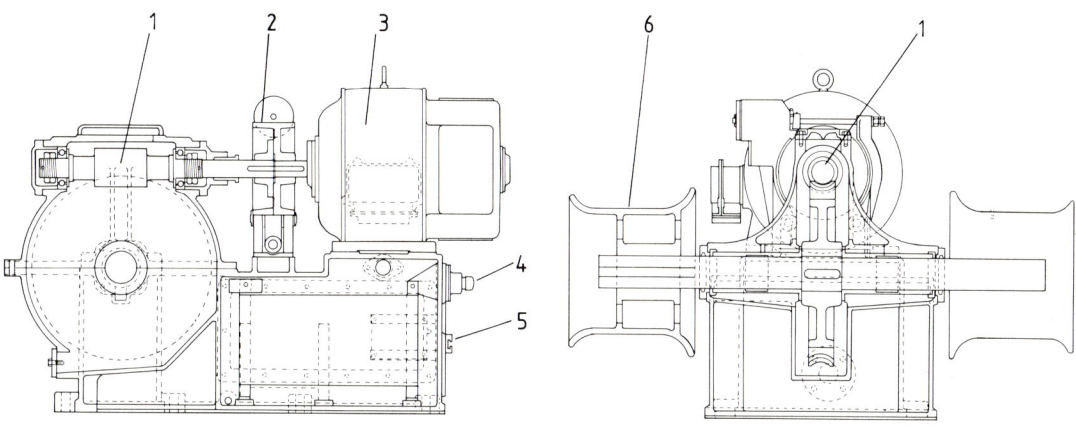

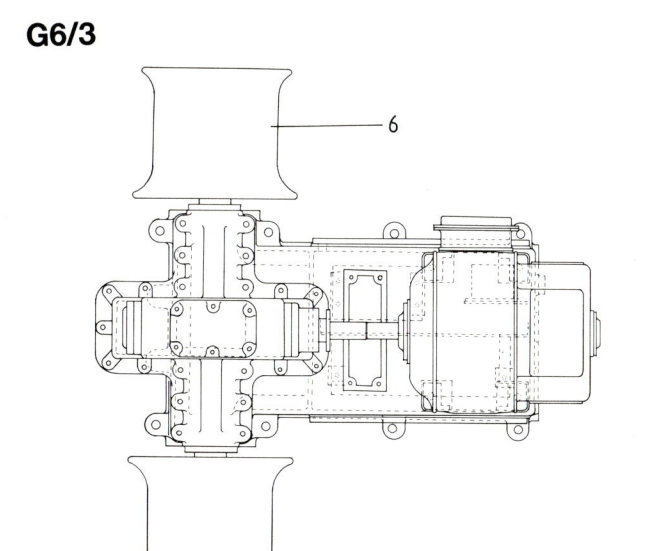

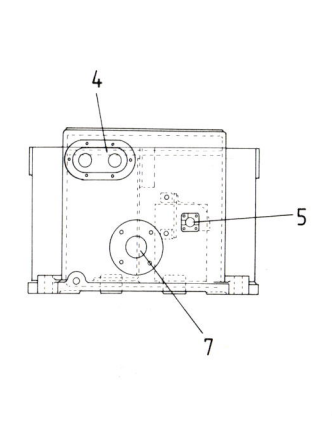

G6/2

G6/3

G6/4

G Fittings

G7 ARRANGEMENT OF 10-TON ELECTRIC CAPSTAN (1/25 scale)

G7/1 Sectioned end elevation
G7/2 Sectioned elevation
G7/3 Plan
G7/4 Plan of bedplate

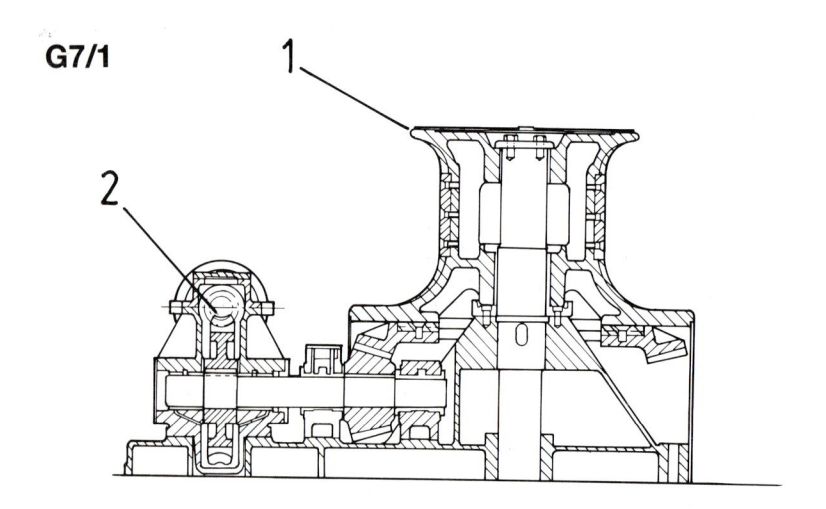

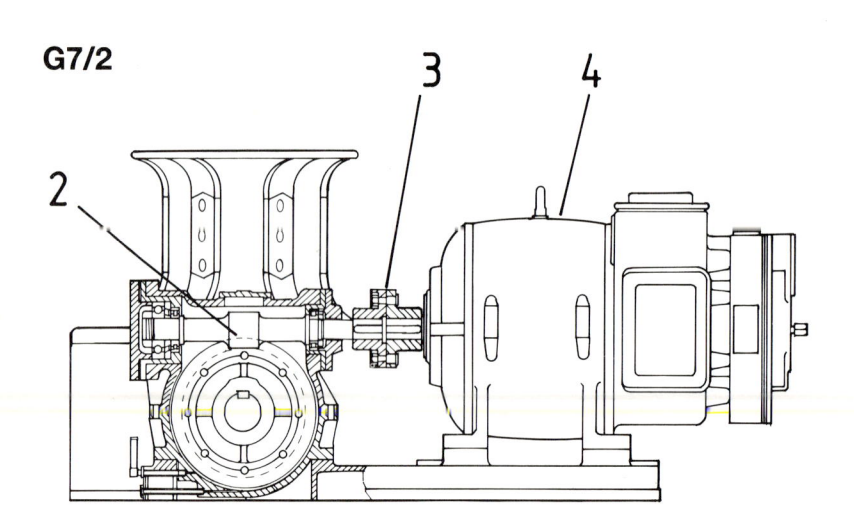

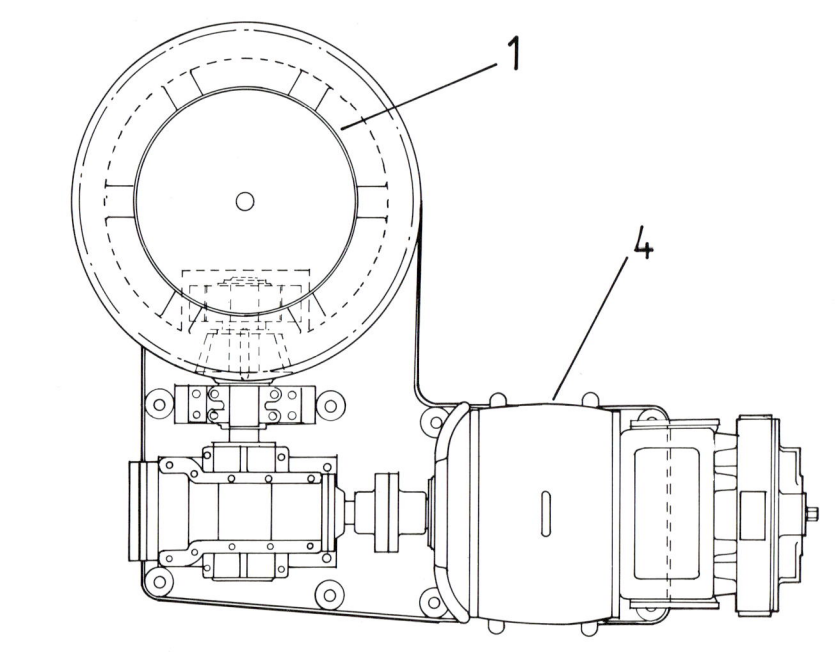

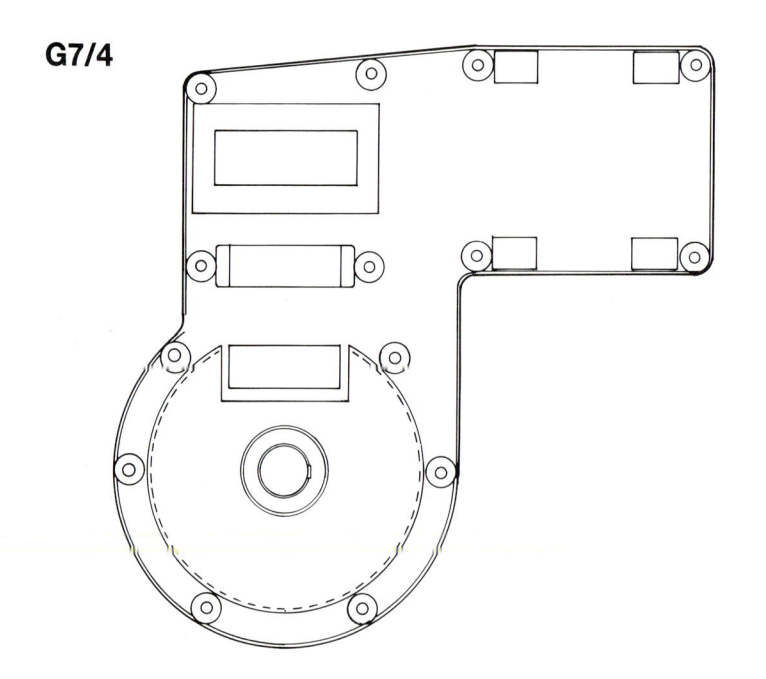

1. Warping drum
2. Worm gear
3. Flexible coupling
4. Electric motor

G7/1

G7/2

G7/3

G7/4

G8   **ARRANGEMENT OF 36-TON ELECTRIC WARPING WINCH**
(1/100 scale)

G8/1   **Plan**

G8/2   **Sectioned elevation**

1. Warping drum
2. Electric motor
3. Controller
4. Flexible coupling
5. Gearing

G8/1

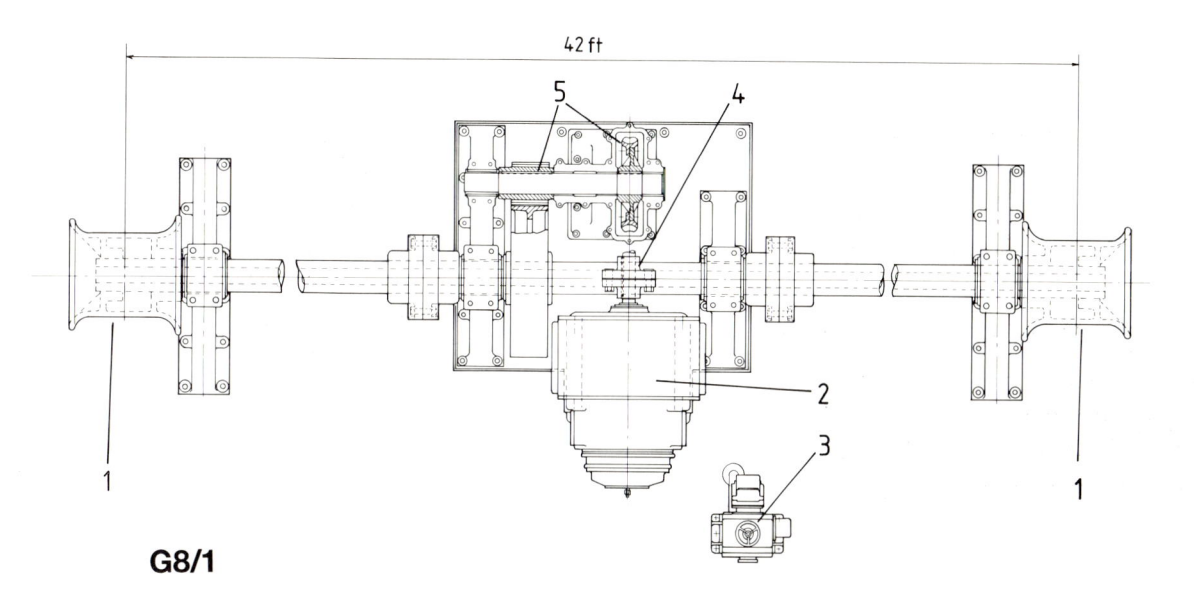

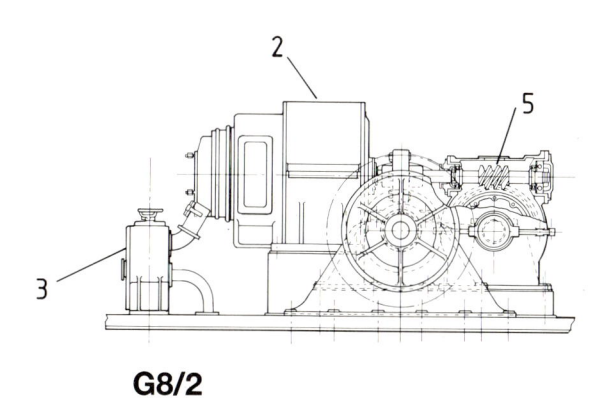

G8/2

G Fittings

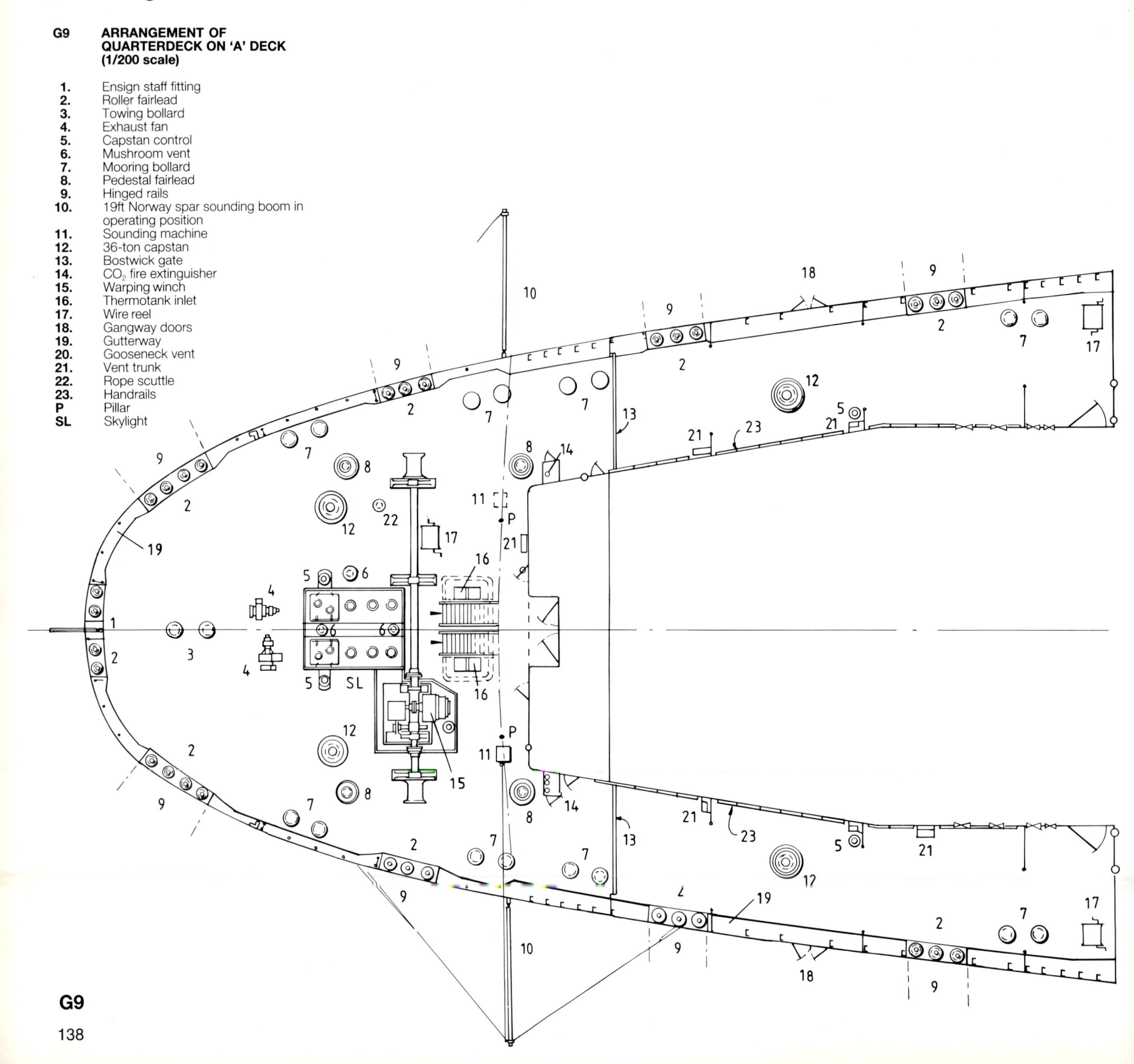

G9 ARRANGEMENT OF QUARTERDECK ON 'A' DECK
(1/200 scale)

1. Ensign staff fitting
2. Roller fairlead
3. Towing bollard
4. Exhaust fan
5. Capstan control
6. Mushroom vent
7. Mooring bollard
8. Pedestal fairlead
9. Hinged rails
10. 19ft Norway spar sounding boom in operating position
11. Sounding machine
12. 36-ton capstan
13. Bostwick gate
14. CO_2 fire extinguisher
15. Warping winch
16. Thermotank inlet
17. Wire reel
18. Gangway doors
19. Gutterway
20. Gooseneck vent
21. Vent trunk
22. Rope scuttle
23. Handrails
P   Pillar
SL Skylight

G10 ARRANGEMENT OF CARGO GANGWAY DECK ON 'A' DECK, BETWEEN FRAMES 289 AND 313 (1/200 scale)

1. Roller fairlead
2. Mooring bollard
3. Vent
4. Jacob's ladder
5. Steel domed cover to No 1 cargo hatch
6. 30-ton capstan
7. Capstan control
8. Gutterway
9. Handrail

G10

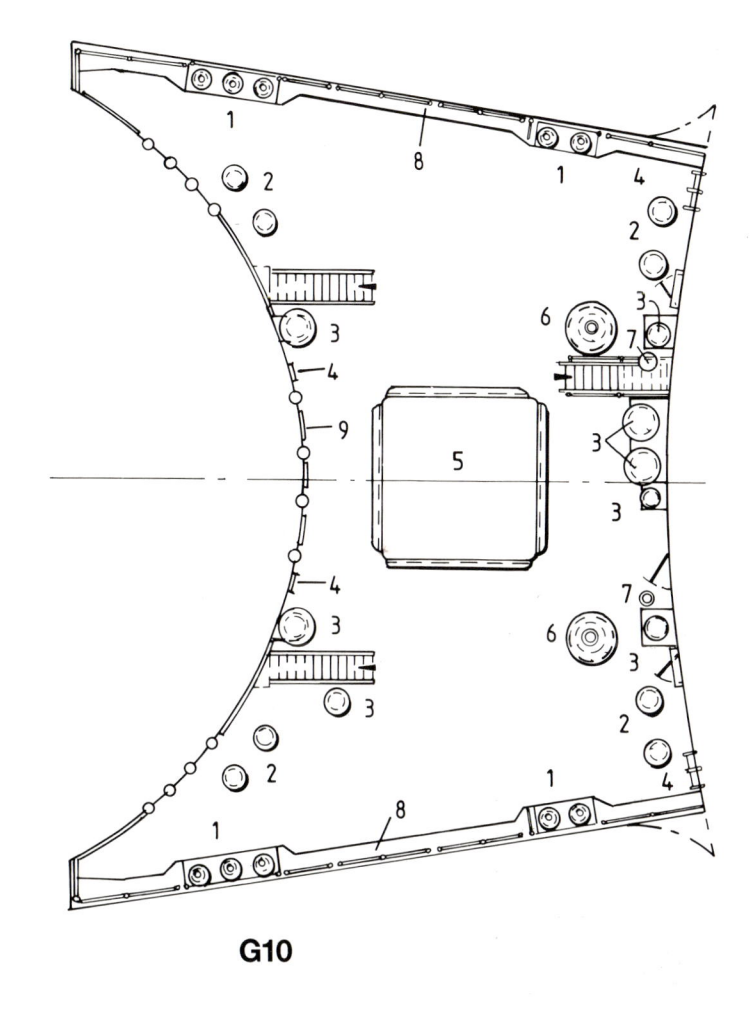

G11 KELVITE SOUNDING MACHINE, GENERAL VIEW (no scale)

G11

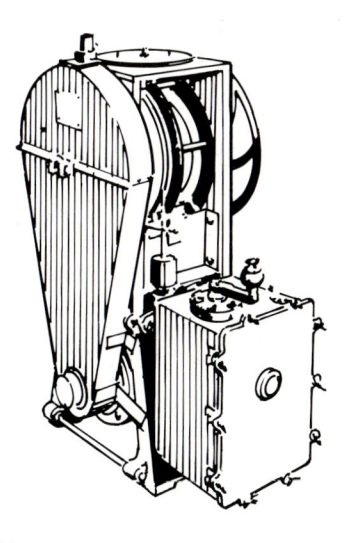

139

H Ground tackle

H1 ARRANGEMENT OF CABLE DECK (1/200 scale)

1. Jacob's ladder
2. Bollard
3. Roller fairlead
4. Hinged rails
5. 36-ton capstan
6. Capstan control pedestal
7. Derrick crutch
8. Davit for working stores
9. Stores hatch
10. Vent
11. Brake
12. Control pedestal for cable lifter
13. Cable lifter
14. Cable pipe
15. Gutterway
16. Hawsepipe
17. Mooring pipe
18. Store
19. Deck clench
20. Bottle-screw for slip

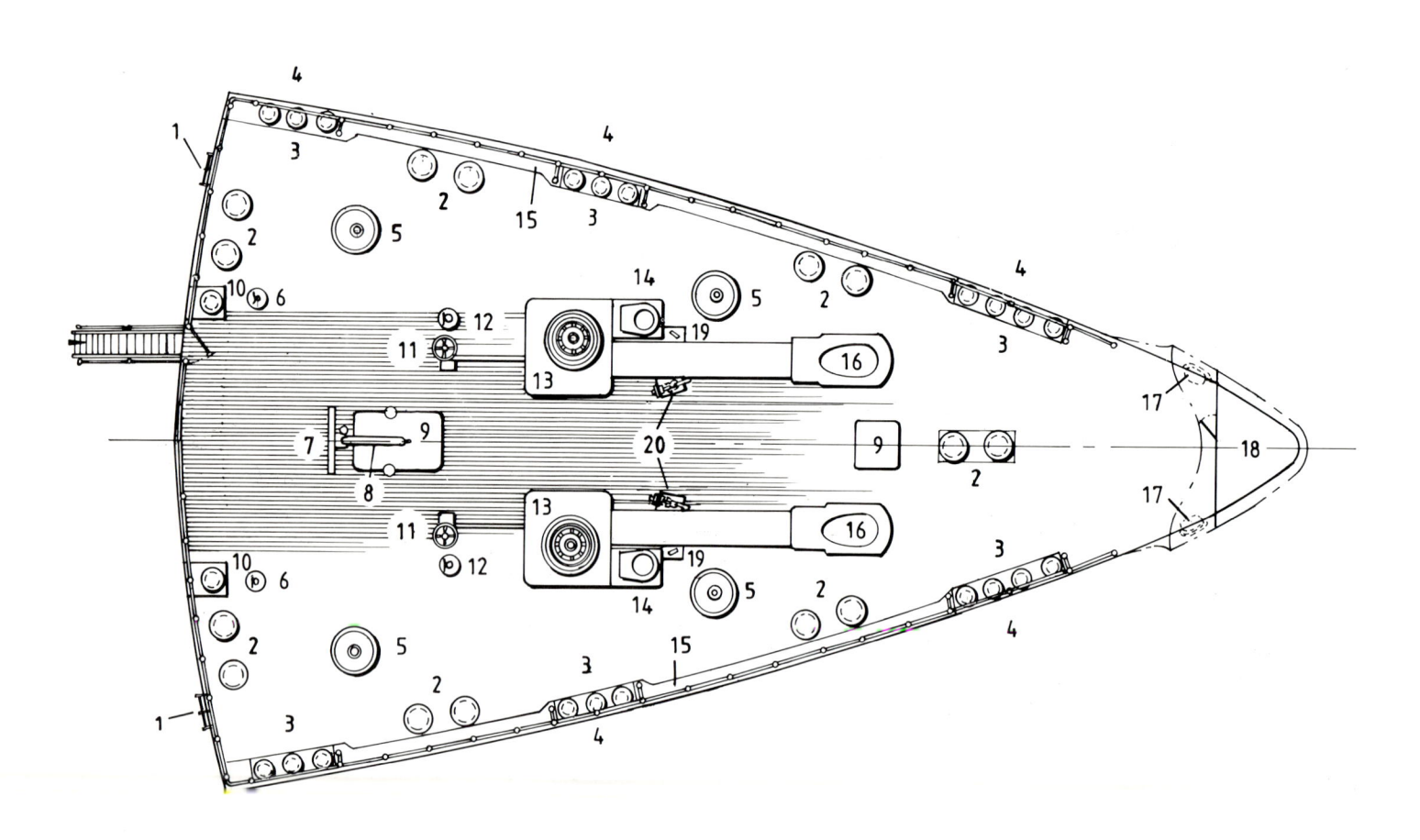

H1

H2	16-TON DREADNOUGHT STOCKLESS ANCHOR (1/100 scale)
H2/1	Front elevation
H2/2	Side elevation
H2/3	End elevation

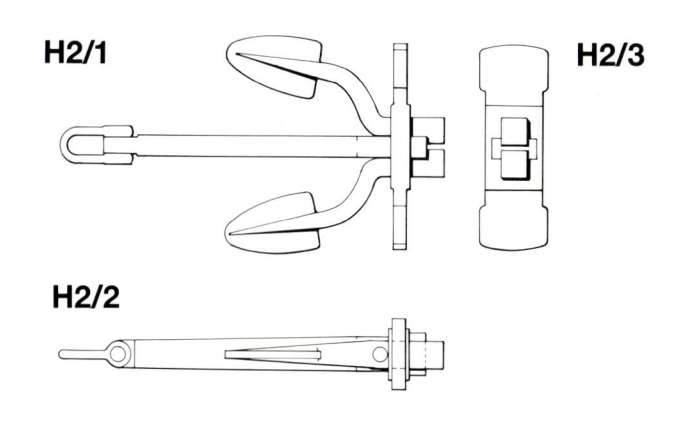

H3 ARRANGEMENT OF ANCHOR LIFT AND CAPSTAN MACHINERY ON 'A' DECK (1/200 scale)

1. Switchboard
2. Rope store
3. Lobby
4. Shelf
5. Wire reel
6. Relay controller
7. 36-ton capstan machinery
8. Capstan motor generator
9. Anchor gear motor generator
10. Anchor lifting and capstan machinery
11. Cable pipe
12. Hose
13. Vice bench
14. Hawsepipe
15. Stores hatch
16. Hatch
17. Master controller
18. Vent trunk
P   Pillar

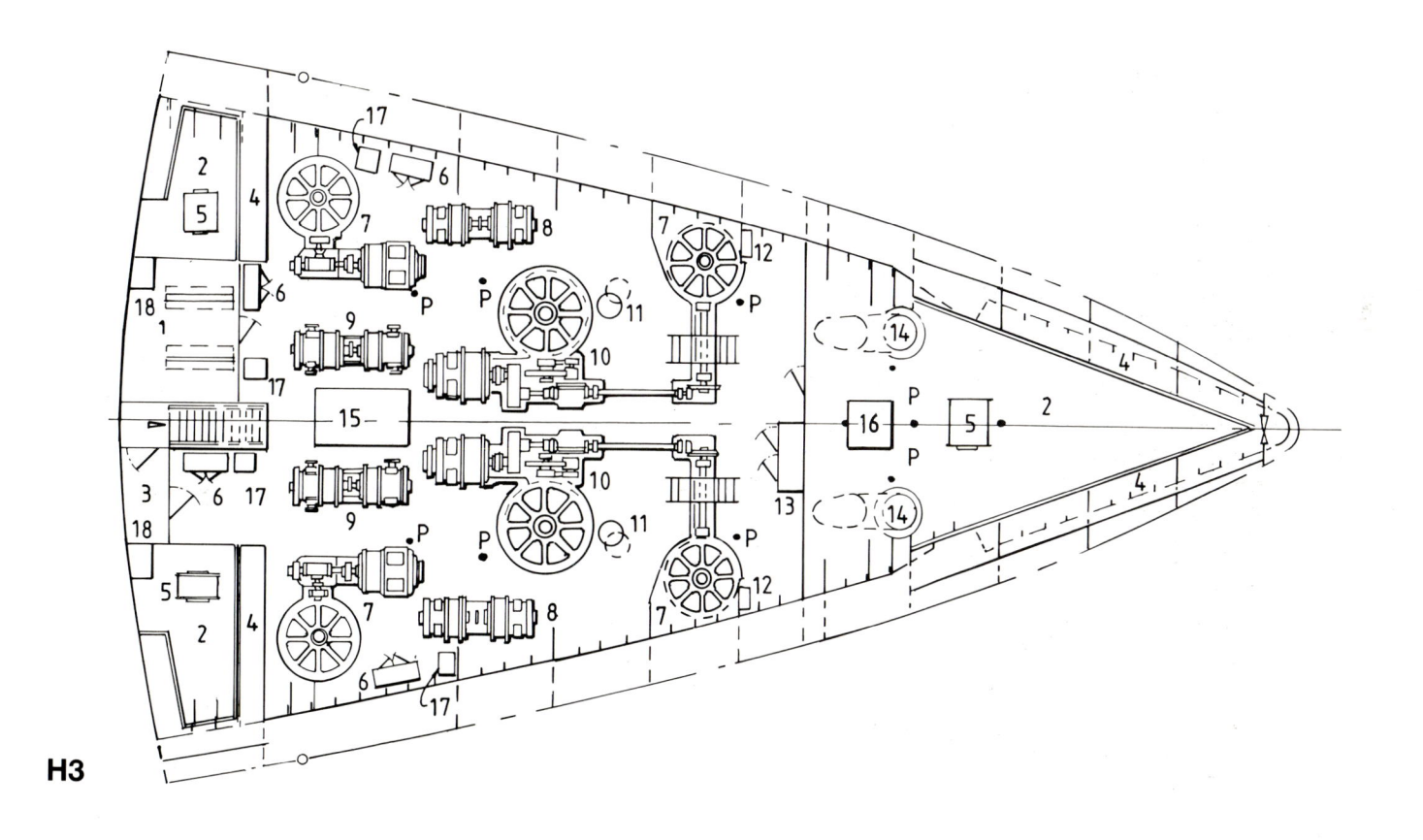

141

I Boats

I1 ARRANGEMENT OF 36FT AND 30FT LIFEBOAT TAYLOR GRAVITY DAVITS (1/100 scale)

I1/1 30ft lifeboat (section, looking aft)

I1/2 Detail of 30ft lifeboat inboard trackway (1/50 scale)

I1/3 36ft lifeboat (section, looking aft)

I1/2

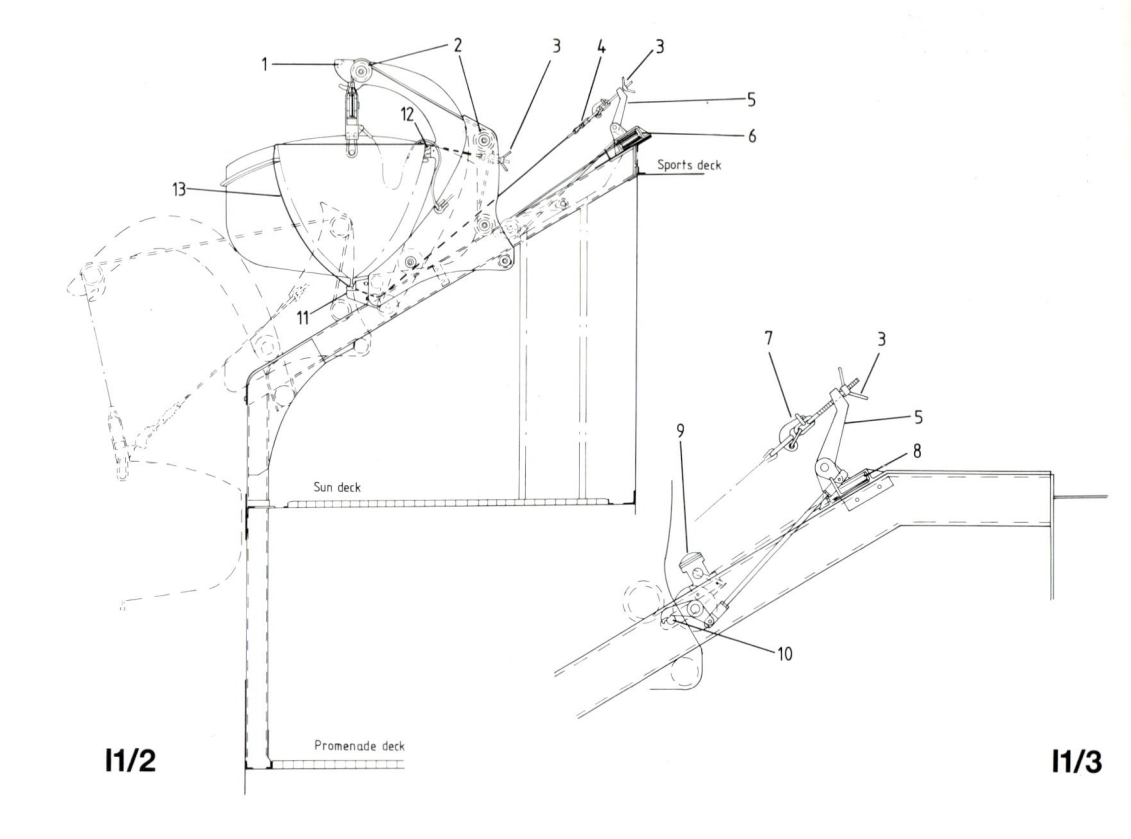

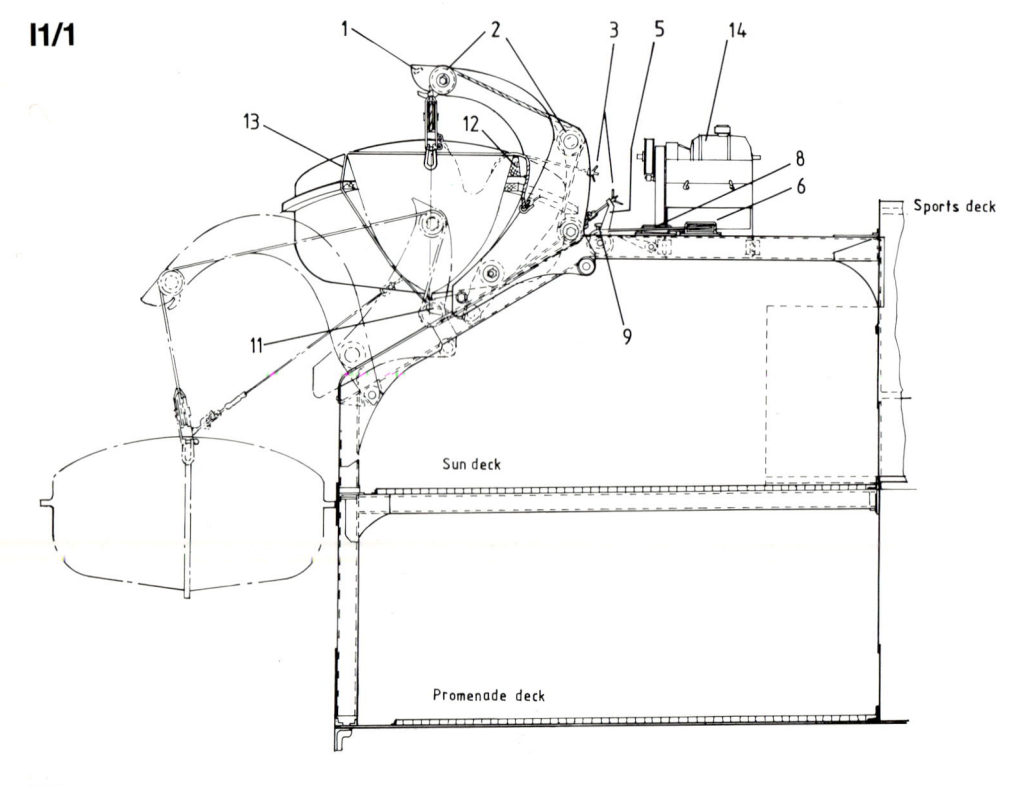

I1/3

I1/1

1. Eyebolt for lifeline span
2. Rope sheave
3. Adjusting screw
4. Lanyard lashing
5. Release lever
6. Double sheave
7. Slip
8. Single lead sheave
9. Limit switch
10. Striker bar
11. Keel chock
12. Wood chock
13. Gripe
14. Electric boat winch

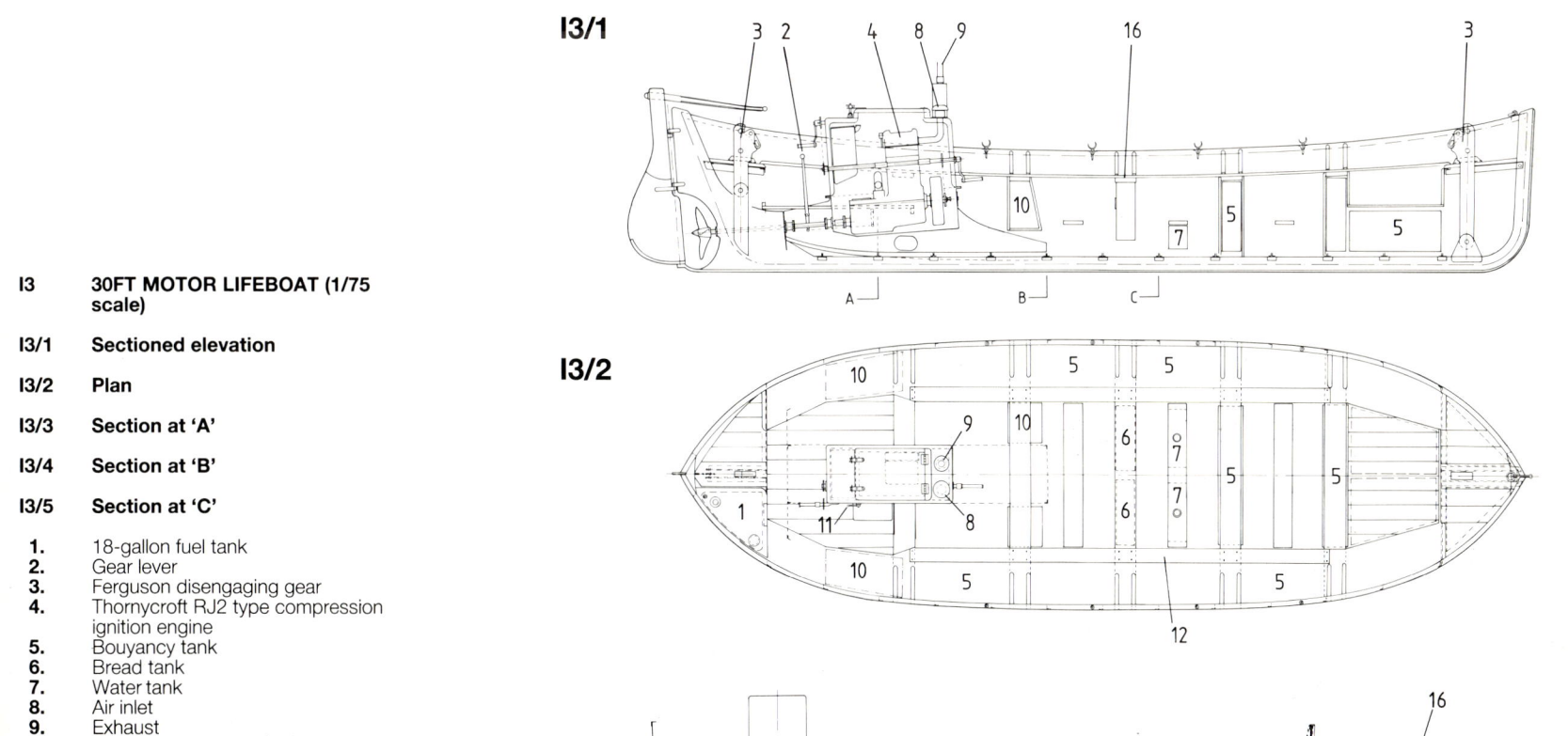

I2 TAYLOR ELECTRIC BOAT WINCH, SECTIONED ELEVATION (1/25 scale)

1. Watertight DC motor
2. Flexible coupling
3. Speed control brake
4. Main lowering brake
5. Wire drum

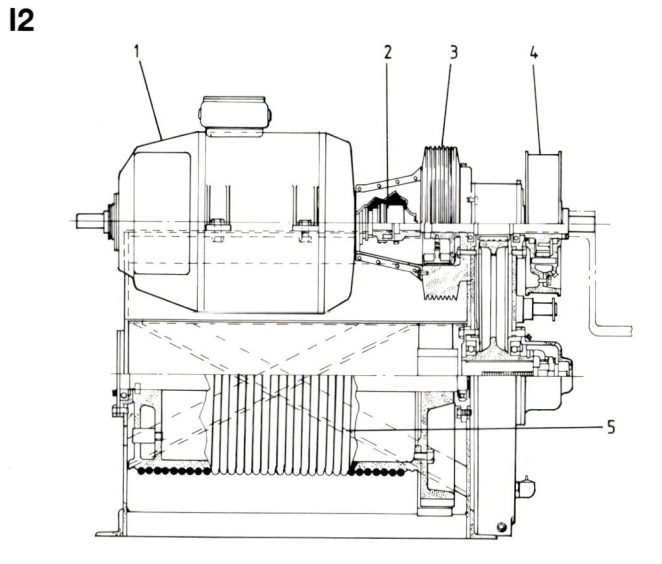

I3 30FT MOTOR LIFEBOAT (1/75 scale)

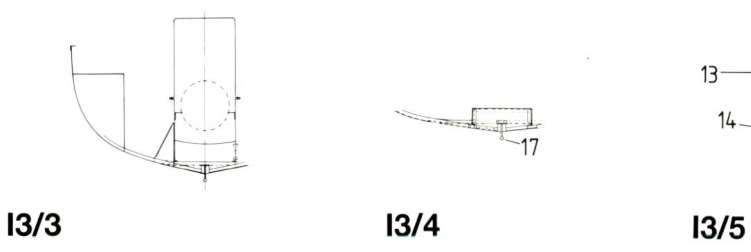

I3/1 Sectioned elevation

I3/2 Plan

I3/3 Section at 'A'

I3/4 Section at 'B'

I3/5 Section at 'C'

1. 18-gallon fuel tank
2. Gear lever
3. Ferguson disengaging gear
4. Thornycroft RJ2 type compression ignition engine
5. Bouyancy tank
6. Bread tank
7. Water tank
8. Air inlet
9. Exhaust
10. Equipment locker
11. Engine speed control
12. Hatch for removing tanks
13. Fender
14. Vertical fender
15. Bilge rail
16. Teak thwarts
17. Bulb plate keel

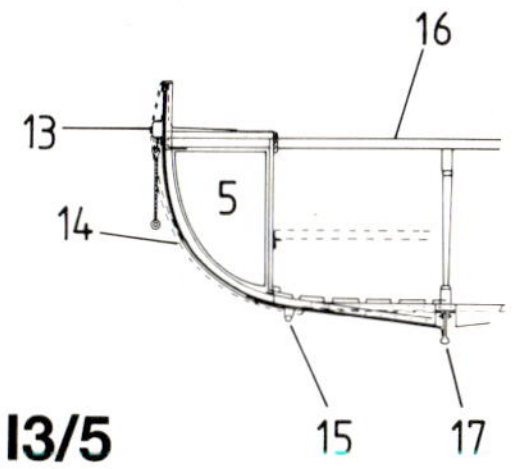

I Boats

I4   36FT MOTOR LIFEBOAT (1/75 scale)

I4/1   Sectioned elevation
I4/2   Plan
I4/3   Section at 'A'
I4/4   Section at 'B'
I4/5   Detail of locking bar (1/37.5 scale)

1. 21-gallon fuel tank
2. Gear lever
3. Ferguson disengaging gear
4. Thornycroft RJ2 type compression ignition engine
5. Bouyancy tank
6. Portable casing
7. Bread tank
8. Water tank
9. Condensed milk tank
10. Air inlet
11. Exhaust
12. Fire extinguisher, 1 gallon, foam
13. Engine speed control
14. 16-gallon circulating water tank
15. Equipment locker
16. Ferguson releasing gear lead
17. Seats
18. Locking bars
19. Fender
20. Vertical fender
21. Bilge pump
22. Bilge rail

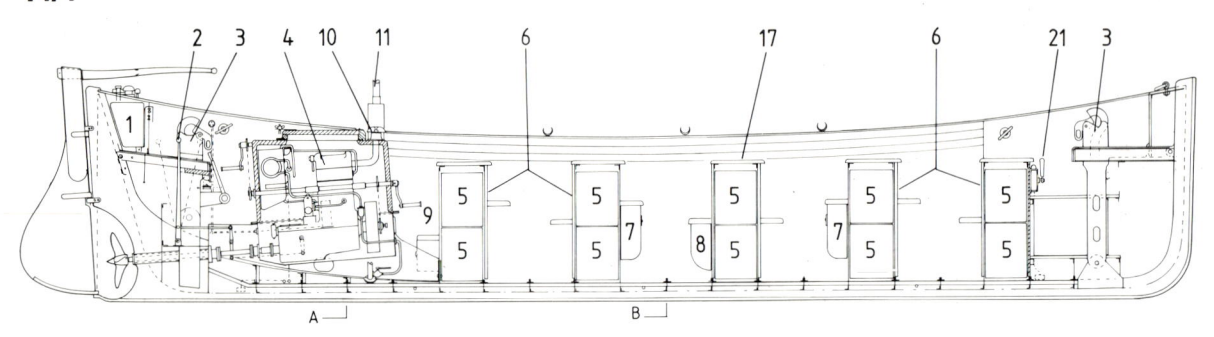

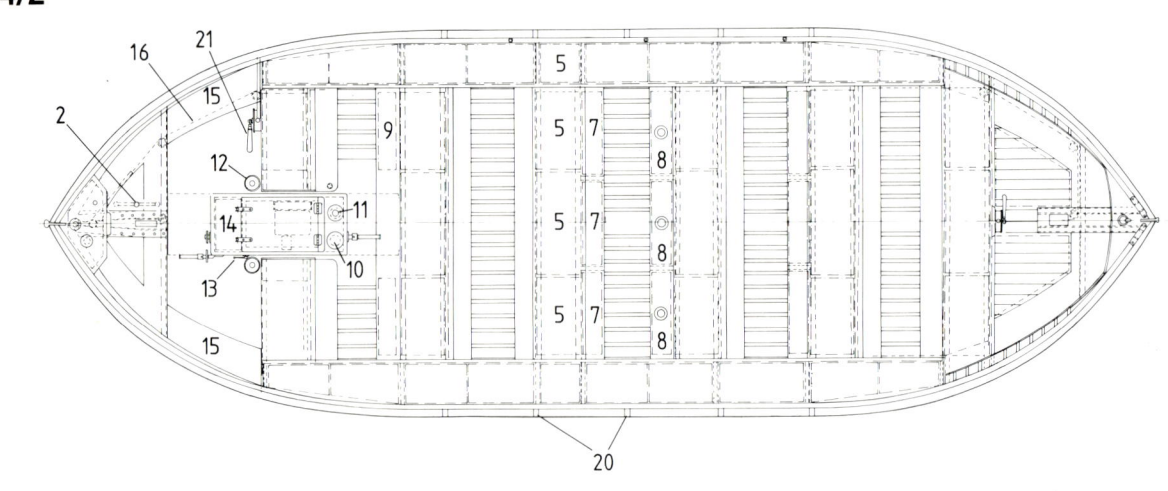

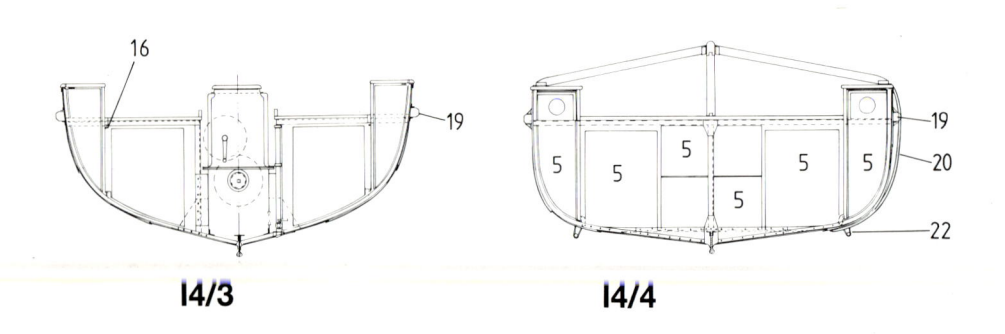

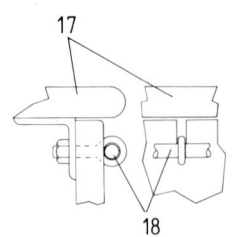